HERO
OF THE
HEARTLAND

HERO
OF THE
HEARTLAND

*Billy Sunday and the
Transformation of American Society,
1862–1935*

ROBERT F. MARTIN

INDIANA **INDIANA**
University Press
BLOOMINGTON AND INDIANAPOLIS

This book is a publication of

Indiana University Press
601 North Morton Street
Bloomington, Indiana 47404-3797 USA

http://iupress.indiana.edu

Telephone orders 800-842-6796
Fax orders 812-855-7931
Orders by e-mail iuporder@indiana.edu

The paper used in this publication meets the minimum
requirements of American National Standard for Information
Sciences—Permanence of Paper for Printed Library
Materials, ANSI Z39.48-1984.

Manufactured in the United States of America

Library of Congress Cataloging-in-Publication Data

Martin, Robert Francis.
Hero of the heartland : Billy Sunday and the transformation of
American society, 1862–1935 / Robert F. Martin.
p. cm.
Includes bibliographical references and index.
ISBN 0-253-34129-9 (alk. paper)
1. Sunday, Billy, 1862–1935. I. Title.
BV3785.S8 M27 2002
269'.2'092—dc21   2001008698

1 2 3 4 5 07 06 05 04 03 02

For Kate and Andrew

CONTENTS

ACKNOWLEDGMENTS

The generosity and insights of many people have helped bring this project to fruition. Among them are my colleagues and friends at the University of Northern Iowa (UNI). The UNI Graduate College facilitated my work by awarding me a Summer Fellowship in 1992, a Professional Development Leave in the Spring of 1996, and a Project Grant in 2001. Deans Aaron Podolefsky, James Chadney, and Julia Wallace of the College of Social and Behavioral Sciences provided funds to defray some research costs. The staff of the Rod Library patiently and efficiently secured voluminous amounts of material through interlibrary loan. Colleagues Wallace Hettle, John Johnson, Donald Shepardson, and David Walker in the Department of History read all or parts of the manuscript in a valiant effort to broaden my horizons and minimize my mistakes. Departmental secretaries Judith Dohlman and Vickie Hanson generously shared their knowledge of the more arcane features of word processing and assisted with the formatting and printing of the manuscript. Over the years, a number of UNI graduate and undergraduate students contributed in various ways to this endeavor. Although space does not permit the individual recognition which all of them are due, Sarah Steil, who worked with me throughout her entire undergraduate career at UNI, deserves a special word of thanks. So, too, do Sarah Stubbe and her mother, Cecilia A. Stubbe, who, though not directly involved in the project, provided me with some valuable material regarding one of Sunday's early revivals in Perry, Iowa.

A number of other individuals have made this book better than it might otherwise have been. Gaines Foster of Louisiana State University read the manuscript and, as he always has when I have called upon him in the past, suggested ways in which it could be significantly improved. My lifelong friend Karen Seay brought a perceptive non-academic reader's perspective to portions of the manuscript dealing with Sunday's early years. Staff members at the Iowa Historical Society, Iowa Genealogical Society, Ames Public Library, and the Story and Boone County courthouses helped as I labored to sort out the details of Sunday's childhood in Iowa and gathered photographs to document the evangelist's life and work. Local historian Farwell T. Brown shared his insights into the Sunday and Cory families in Ames and introduced me to the photographic archive he has been assembling for the Ames Public Library. Janet Klaas, curator of the Farwell T. Brown Archive, graciously took time to help me locate and reproduce relevant pictures for the book. Robert Neymeyer, independent scholar and publisher, and Tim Wiles, director of research at the National Baseball Hall of Fame and Museum, provided valuable information about the history of baseball in general and Sunday's athletic career in particular. Attorney Harold Strever helped me to better grasp the meaning of the handful of legal documents that hold clues to the complexities of Sunday's childhood. Carole Shelley Yates carefully edited the manuscript in an effort to eliminate as many of my errors of grammar and style as possible.

William Darr and the staff of the Morgan Library at Grace College and Theological Seminary in Winona Lake, Indiana, granted permission to use materials in the Billy Sunday Archives and provided prints of several photographs included among the illustrations in the following pages. Bill Firstenberger, curator of the Billy Sunday Historic Site Museum at Winona Lake, took time from a busy schedule to talk with me about the collection of Sunday memorabilia there and shared one of the pictures in his collection for this book. Material adapted from my article "Billy Sunday and the Mystique of the Middle West" (*The Annals of Iowa* 55 [1996]: 345–360, Copyright 1996 State Historical Society of Iowa) appears in Chapter 7 with the permission of the publisher. Sections of my article "Billy Sunday and Christian Manliness" (*The Historian* 58, no. 4 [1996]: 811–823) appear in Chapter 5 with the permission of the journal.

Robert Sloan, senior sponsoring editor at Indiana University Press (IUP), shepherded the manuscript through the review process, always responded promptly to an anxious author's inquiries, and patiently waited while I struggled to arrive at a title. Those who reviewed the work for IUP responded with constructive criticism that helped me to reorganize and expand upon certain portions of it. Kate Babbitt, copyeditor with the press, carefully and thoughtfully read the manuscript, called both stylistic and substantive problems to my attention, and caught several mistakes that had eluded everyone else. Jane Lyle, managing editor at IUP, graciously and knowledgeably responded whenever I contacted her with questions regarding the production of the book.

My wife, Kate Martin, employed her skills as a librarian to assist in the search for relevant resources, endured my periodic musings aloud about Sunday's life and work, offered much-needed encouragement, read the completed manuscript, and made many constructive suggestions. Andrew, our son, grew from childhood into early adolescence watching his dad struggle with a seemingly interminable research project and spending more time than any boy his age would like entertaining himself in cars, libraries, courthouses, and cemeteries while his parents attended to the necessary details of scholarship. Finally, a very special word of appreciation goes to Gayle E. Lundgren, without whose patience and good humor as researcher, clerical assistant, editor, typist, and friend my work on Sunday would have been a much more daunting and much less enjoyable task. To all of those who have done so much to make this book possible, I can do no more at present than to say an inadequate but sincere thank-you.

Robert F. Martin
November 19, 2001

INTRODUCTION

Few religious figures have had a greater impact on American popular culture than did William Ashley "Billy" Sunday. The colorful Iowa-born evangelist was the best-known and most influential revivalist in the United States during the first half of the twentieth century. Between 1896 and 1935, he toured first his native Midwest and then the nation, preaching in tent and tabernacle, espousing a simplistic but, for many, satisfying interpretation of Christianity. By the 1910s, his name had become a household word. Millions of his contemporaries quoted "Sundayisms." The religious and secular press routinely gave extensive coverage to his exploits in and out of the pulpit. Politicians and businessmen courted him. References to him appeared in the poetry of Carl Sandburg and Ogden Nash and even in one popular song of the day.[1]

Fame, of course, is not necessarily synonymous with admiration, and opinion of Sunday was as sharply divided as the dichotomy between good and evil that he so theatrically portrayed in his sermons. Secular critics scorned or ridiculed the methods and message of the revivalist, while those of a liberal religious bent criticized what they regarded as the exclusivity and provincialism of his ministry. Proponents of liberal Protestantism also frequently condemned his message as outmoded and considered Sunday either a reactionary or a charlatan. Even some conservative Evangelicals had reservations about his unorthodox methods, but a substantial segment of the population believed him to be God's admittedly unconventional messenger to a sinful and unrepentant nation. Associates and admirers have contended that during his career Sunday preached to between 80 and 100 million people and was responsible for the salvation of a million souls. Although such claims are probably extravagant, they accurately suggest the scope of the evangelist's enormous appeal.[2]

Sunday's fame and success stemmed, in part, from the theatrical quality of his evangelism. He was an exceptionally gifted showman with an extraordinary ability to capture the attention of audiences and to evoke, in quick succession, emotions running the gamut from grief and remorse to joy and hope. Those who attended his meetings expected to be entertained and were rarely disappointed. Applause and laughter, hardly commonplace in the middle- and upper-class white Protestant churches of the day, were routine occurrences in his services. In the small towns of the Midwest and even in the nation's larger cities, he was sometimes the best show in town.

His flare for the dramatic became the trademark of Sunday's evangelism and that for which he is most often remembered, but his theatricality was not primarily responsible for his rise to national prominence. Neither was the conservative theology that provided the religious underpinning of his message. While both style and, to a degree, doctrine were crucial to his success, ultimately what enabled the revivalist to reach millions of Americans was the congruence between his life and work and the hopes and fears of people struggling to cope with the myriad of uncertainties inherent in the transition from a rural, agricultural nation to an urban, industrial one. For many such Americans, he became a kind of heroic figure.

In 1941, only a few years after Sunday's death, historian Dixon Wecter wrote of the hero in American history,

> He is an index to the collective mind and heart. His deeds and qualities are those which millions endorse. He speaks words that multitudes want said; he stands for things that they are often willing to spill their blood for. The hero is he whom every American should wish to be. His legend is the mirror of the folk soul.[3]

The notion of a "folk soul" in a nation as diverse as the United States is, of course, problematic; heterogeneity is often antithetical to consensus. Nevertheless, Sunday was a hero for millions who were struggling to reconcile the present with the past. His message spoke to their desire for continuity while his life and ministry represented a link with tradition and demonstrated the possibilities inherent in change.

Although anchored in the quest to save souls, successful mass evangelism is very much about coping with the challenges of the present world. Billy Sunday's revivalism was no exception. Contemporary and subsequent generations of critics have argued that his ministry was more a matter of escapism or obstructionism than an honest confrontation of the issues of his day. They contend that he was popular with the establishment and the masses because he upheld the status quo, offering solace and hope by reaffirming traditional conservative religious and social values. There is truth in these allegations, but a careful examination of his life and work in its entirety reveals a more complex picture.

To be sure, a great many people found Sunday's interpretation of the gospel both comforting and familiar. There was nothing new in either the theological or social content of his message. Aside from a few basic tenets of fundamentalist dogma, the intricacies of theology actually mattered little to the evangelist. He viewed reality through the prism of his deeply personal redemption experience. He believed and preached only enough doctrine to make sense of his own conversion and that which he hoped to engender in others.

The majority of Sunday's sermons were exhortations to live like a Christian rather than expositions of the theological foundations upon which Christianity rested. In an era when the cultural mystique of the Midwest was beginning to represent, for at least some, the quintessence of Americanism, he took for granted the mainstream social and economic orthodoxy of his native region and equated the evangelical moral code of rural and small-town mid- and late-nineteenth-century Iowa with Christian conduct. His version of the gospel contained little subtlety or recognition that personal and social problems often sprang from complex circumstances and could not always be resolved through faith and will alone. Unrealistic though it may have been, there was about his analysis of the human condition a kind of comprehensible and empowering commonsense simplicity, a sense that things were as they appeared to be, which lent credibility to his case. Furthermore, he asserted his views with such sincerity and conviction that those predisposed to believe found it easy to do so, and even skeptics were sometimes persuaded.

Sunday reaffirmed traditional values not only through his religious and social message but also because the story of his life seemed to exemplify the national myth of success. He was born and reared in relative poverty, never knew his father, lived for a time in an orphanage, and earned his own way by his mid-teens. He nevertheless achieved fame and fortune in the service of his God and fellow man. Though firmly anchored in and committed to the verities of an idealized past, he was also a product of the modern world. He had the good fortune to play professional baseball just as that sport was emerging as the national pastime. Thus, he was admired as an athlete in an increasingly leisure-oriented, sports-minded nation. In an age that venerated the man of business, there was about his ministry an air of professionalism and entrepreneurial acumen that millions of people appreciated and to which they aspired. At a time when concerns about the deterioration of American masculinity were rife in certain middle- and upper-class circles, the story of his triumph over adversity and his athleticism complemented his aggressive public persona to create about him a much-admired aura of manliness. In an age absorbed with progressive change, his devotees believed the revivalist's championing of Prohibition and other moral causes placed their hero in the first ranks of American reform.

An athlete, businessman, clergyman, reformer, and son of the heartland who personified manliness and exemplified the American myth of success, Sunday bridged the gap between tradition and modernity in a way that millions of his contemporaries found gratifying and inspiring. Venerated by many, vilified by some, he was neither saint nor sinner but a complex and fascinating constellation of the remarkable and the regrettable. In both his strengths and weaknesses, however, he resonated with diverse facets of the changing times in which he lived, and that resonance was a major source of his appeal.

HERO
OF THE
HEARTLAND

ONE

A Son of the Middle West

By late autumn the brilliant skies and painted forests of October in Iowa yield to the icy mists and sepia landscapes that portend the imminent arrival of winter. The desolate days of November in the upper Midwest at times weigh as heavily upon the soul as upon the body, and those of 1862, the year of William Ashley Sunday's birth, seemed especially bleak. The Civil War which had begun nineteen months earlier had lasted longer and gone less well than most Americans had anticipated. Many an Iowa homestead was now without one or more of its adult male family members, and not a few wives and mothers anxiously awaited word of the fate of their husbands and sons. The pall that the great struggle for the Union cast across the land was in marked contrast to the optimism that had characterized Iowa's early history.

In 1862 the state was only sixteen years old, but those years had witnessed remarkable growth. During the 1840s and 1850s, the fertile soil of the prairies and river valleys between the Mississippi and Missouri Rivers enticed tens of thousands of immigrants westward in search of a better life. As settlement spread steadily westward, the Iowa legislature established a succession of new counties. Among them was Story, a 576-square-mile tract in the heart of the state. Although its population grew rapidly, increasing from a mere 214 people in 1852 to 4,051 in 1860, life in the county in the early 1860s retained much of its frontier quality.[1]

Settlement was only beginning to extend beyond the banks of rivers and streams with their readily accessible supply of water and timber. Tall prairie grasses swaying in the summer breeze dominated most of the landscape. In the fall, these vast expanses of vegetation sometimes yielded a spectacular harvest of flame that left the earth scorched and desolate. Coyotes roamed the prairies. Timber wolves ranged the groves and thickets along the river bottoms, and an occasional black bear raided a settler's farm in search of food. Pioneers seeking to supplement their often meager fare could usually find an ample supply of game, including geese, ducks, grouse, wild turkeys, squirrels, rabbits, deer, and, now and then, an elk.

Residents were just emerging from almost complete dependence upon supplies from more settled parts of the state. As late as 1857, settlers in some areas found it necessary to import corn from Marion and Mahaska Counties, a trip which required as long as four days. Small wagon trains loaded with corn, flour, and bacon rolled into Story County from communities to the east and south. Necessities such as iron, nails, hardware, stoves, and salt, as well as a few luxuries, came from Keokuk and other Mississippi River ports. The terrain over which these supplies were transported was crossed by only a few rough roads that became treacherous in winter, with hilltops deceptively barren of snow and low places clogged by impassable drifts several feet deep. Heavy snows and frigid winds also meant that the weekly or semi-weekly mail from Des Moines, thirty miles south, was sometimes delayed by fifteen or twenty days. Spring flooding, coupled with the poorly drained soil of the region, created almost impenetrable marshy barriers to travel in the wet season.[2]

Although small-scale commercial agriculture was beginning to appear, subsistence farming remained the economic mainstay of the county. In 1860, a patchwork of 471 farms of varying size dotted the landscape. Well over half of them, 272, were fifty acres or less in size; 148 ranged from 50 to 100 acres; and fifty-one exceeded 100 acres. The primary staple was grain. Corn was the largest crop, but significant quantities of wheat and oats were also grown. In addition, farmers produced flax, maple sugar, sorghum, peas, beans, potatoes, and a variety of fruits and vegetables, as well as cattle, horses, and sheep.[3]

Among the first settlers of the area that became Story County was Martin Cory. Born in Ohio of English and German descent, he moved with his wife and children from Syracuse in northeastern Indiana to Iowa in 1848 and began farming about a mile south of the site that would in a few years become Ames. Cory's early arrival on the frontier, coupled with his industriousness and versatility as blacksmith, miller, wagon-builder, carpenter, and farmer, enabled him to quickly emerge as a figure of some affluence and status in his section of the county. In 1860, Squire Cory, as he was known locally, owned real property valued at approximately $5,000, along with personal property worth roughly $700. This made him and his family the fourth wealthiest of Washington Township's eighty-three households. Over the years, as the county economy became more complex and its social structure more strati-fied, Cory's economic position and social status declined relative to the expanding wealth and prestige of his neighbors. For much of his life, however, he was recognized as one of the pioneer figures in his community.[4]

Another early immigrant to Story County was William Sunday. Born of German stock in south-central Pennsylvania near Chambersburg in 1828, Sunday moved to eastern Iowa sometime in the 1850s. After working briefly as a brick mason and day laborer in the vicinity of Cedar Rapids, he moved on to Story County in search of more work and a new start. There he met and, in the fall of 1857, married a girl in her mid-teens, Mary Jane ("Jennie") Cory, the oldest of Martin Cory's eight children.[5]

Although almost 30 at the time of his marriage, William possessed little money and few material goods. The passing years brought no significant

Squire Martin Cory (1812–1882),
Billy Sunday's maternal grandfather.

*From an album at the Billy Sunday Historic Site Museum,
Winona Lake, Indiana. Courtesy of the Farwell T. Brown
Photographic Archive, Ames Public Library, Ames, Iowa.*

improvement in the Sundays' fortunes. Whether because of their lack of land and capital, the depression of the late 1850s, or mere ineptitude on William's part, life was a struggle for the young couple. Over the next five years they had three sons: Albert Monroe, born in 1858; Howard Edward ("Ed"), born in 1860; and William Ashley ("Willie"), born in 1862. Though prized by frontier families, children placed a burden on the Sundays' limited resources. The 1860 census records reflect their precarious financial condition, indicating that William Sunday's real property was worth only $150 and his personal property worth $100. The couple apparently owned no land and never enjoyed any genuine security.[6]

When the Civil War broke out, Iowa, like other states, was expected to supply its share of soldiers for the cause. William Sunday was not among the initial wave of defenders of the Union. At age 33 in 1861, he was considerably older than the average enlistee. With two small sons and financial problems, he may initially have tried to avoid military service. However, in early August 1862, he walked from Ames to Des Moines and enlisted in the army. Perhaps patriotism determined his decision—Union forces badly needed manpower in 1862—or, perhaps, with a third child now on the way, he found appealing the prospect of a regular monthly wage of $13 which might improve his family's meager fortunes. Whatever his motives, in September 1862, he was mustered into Company E of the Twenty-third Infantry Regiment of Iowa volunteers. Sunday expected to serve a maximum of three years, but his term of service lasted scarcely four months. Disease was almost as great a threat to the Civil War soldier as combat, and in the late fall Sunday contracted an illness variously described as pneumonia, inflammatory rheumatism, measles, or chronic diarrhea. Whatever the malady, it proved fatal. He died on December 22, 1862, at Camp Patterson in Missouri and, on a raw winter day, was buried in an unmarked grave.[7]

Jennie was pregnant when her husband left for the war, and on November 19 she gave birth to a son and named him William Ashley, as Sunday had requested in one of his last letters to her. William, who died only a month later, probably knew of his son's birth but never saw the infant.

In the 1860s, the Iowa frontier offered scant security or status to a young widow. After the death of her husband, Jennie Sunday's life was lonely and difficult. With three small sons and little means of support except her parents' largess, it was expected, indeed almost necessary, that she remarry. In August 1864, she became the wife of James M. Heizer, a man roughly twenty years her senior. Jennie may have remarried for love or out of desperation, but in either case she made a serious mistake. Although Heizer became the guardian of his three stepsons and the couple had two more children (LeRoy ["Roy"], born in 1866; and Mary Elizabeth, born in 1868), he was hardly a model husband, father, and provider. In 1870, the combined worth of his real and personal property was about $800, which placed him in the bottom third of heads of households in his township. Jennie had little more financial security in her second than in her first marriage. To add to her troubles, Heizer had a greater passion for alcohol than for familial responsibility.

In 1871, the couple's troubled relationship ended when Heizer abandoned his wife and children. Although the circumstances of this family trauma are not entirely clear, Jennie took the unusual step of securing a divorce in October 1874. Given the social stigma usually attached to such an action in the nineteenth century, she obviously believed not only that her divorce was warranted but also that it would be understood and accepted by her community.[8]

Jennie now found herself with four surviving children and no reliable means of supporting them except a small Civil War orphan's allotment for the three Sunday boys and help from her father and stepmother. During the Civil War, a group of Iowans led by Annie Wittenmyer had organized the Iowa Soldier's Orphans Home Association "to provide a home and education for the orphan children of those who had fallen, or might thereafter fall, in the defense of our country." The association established two homes—the first at Farmington, later relocated to a former army barracks at Davenport, and a second at Cedar Falls. In 1866, the state of Iowa assumed financial responsibility for these two facilities and opened a third at Glenwood in the southwestern part of the state.[9]

Jennie Sunday petitioned for a widow's pension following William's death but withdrew the application after her second marriage. Although she received a few dollars each month from the federal government to support William's orphaned children, the amount was insufficient for her to provide for herself and her family following her abandonment by Heizer. Consequently, in 1874, she placed the two youngest of the three Sunday brothers, Edward and William, in the orphanage at Glenwood. In September of that year, Ed and Willie left their tearful mother in the wee hours of the morning and traveled alone by train from Ames to their new home.[10]

The two Sunday boys' stay at Glenwood was relatively short but not wholly unpleasant. The orphanage was nestled in rolling hills, some heavily wooded, and the children had the run of the fields and forests around the home. On Saturdays, they took their pet dogs into the woods and hunted rabbits and squirrels, gathered nuts, staged footraces, and played ball. These activities were a delight to the Sundays, who had whiled away the meager leisure time they had had on the farm in Story County with just such pastimes. In early 1875, as the need to maintain three separate institutions declined, Iowa closed the Glenwood orphanage and moved the small number of remaining children there to the larger and more commodious facility at Davenport.[11]

Although they had some fond memories of their brief sojourn at Glenwood, these did not mitigate the Sunday boys' longing for home. As the train on which the Glenwood orphans traveled toward Davenport neared Des Moines, relatively close to Ames, the Sundays hatched a scheme that would allow Willie, who now preferred to be called "Billy," the younger and perhaps more homesick of the two brothers, to escape the train and walk home. To their chagrin, the plot was foiled when another orphan disclosed their plan; both boys were soon ensconced in one of the numerous cottages that housed the several hundred residents of the Davenport Orphanage. They found life there much more regimented than at Glenwood, and Billy recalled that none of the children ever liked it as much as their former home.[12]

Nevertheless, many years later, Sunday wrote in his autobiography of the superintendent and matron at Davenport, "If ever the state of Iowa had two public servants absolutely fitted for the responsible position of caring for its orphans, they were Mr. and Mrs. S. W. Pierce." This couple related to the children in very different ways but in a manner consistent with Victorian America's stereotypical understanding of male and female gender roles. Mr. Pierce was a stern and strict disciplinarian. He made the rules and enforced them, sometimes with corporal punishment in recalcitrant cases. Mrs. Pierce, on the other hand, was the nurturer and the instiller of moral sensibilities. She would take the offending child on her lap and explain how sad their conduct would make their mothers. She then prayed with them and, according to Sunday, "No one ever came from an interview with Mrs. Pierce dry-eyed." He recalled that the boys would rather receive a whipping from Mr. Pierce than endure one of these earnest talks with his wife.[13]

Mr. Pierce pursued runaways relentlessly and invariably returned them to the home. Punishment for this most serious of infractions was to walk all day long, with breaks only for meals, around the one-eighth mile cinder drive encircling the lawn in front of the administration building.

The children were subject to a grading scale of one to five, five being the lowest grade. Each child entered the home with a grade of two and could work his or her way up or down from there based on conduct. Almost every aspect of life was graded. Three or more demerits were meted out for such infractions as failure to keep one's hair combed, face washed, or bed made properly. Sunday recalled, "I was never in the bad grade, but I was often near the dead line." Children with grades of three or higher could not leave the grounds. The others could go to Davenport on Saturdays and to city churches on Sundays. Trips into town were especially prized because they often yielded an abundance of treats, such as apples, candy, popcorn, or ice cream, from the compassionate local citizenry.[14]

The residents of the orphanage learned not only to accept responsibility for themselves but also to contribute to the orphanage community as a whole. Each child was expected to work in accord with his or her age and ability. The older girls made the children's uniforms. Other tasks included chores around the farm, washing clothes and linens, scrubbing floors, or working in the kitchen. Jobs were rotated in such a way as to provide a great deal of training for every child; doing one's best at each task was an integral part of the training.

Evangelical Christian values permeated the atmosphere at the home. There were prayers in each cottage once a day, and on Sunday evenings each child had to recite a verse from the Bible. Failure to do so resulted in five demerits; thirty demerits in a month could adversely affect one's grade. Although the discipline was strict and the work sometimes hard, the children were prepared both practically and morally for life outside the home. Sunday recalled years later,

> I never knew a boy from either home to be an infidel or a criminal. Of those of whom I have kept track, some became lawyers, merchants, farmers, railroad men, educators. I was the only one who ever became a big-league baseball player.

Of his own experience he wrote, "What I learned there opened the door in after years that has brought me where I am—I was taught to do my best."[15]

In 1876, Ed reached the age of 16 and was no longer eligible to live at the Davenport home. Billy, who would be 14 that November, could have remained for two more years but chose to leave with his older brother. In June, the two boys returned to Story County to live with their Grandfather Cory. While they were in the orphanage, their mother had married George Stowell of Boone, Iowa, in September 1875, and going to live with her was evidently not an option. Following her marriage, she had placed her oldest son Albert, who was mentally handicapped as a result of a childhood accident, in the care of the county and may not have been living in the Ames area when her sons returned. Ed soon found a job on a neighbor's farm, but his younger brother remained with Martin Cory for several months. According to Billy, this arrangement ended abruptly later in the year when their grandfather asked Billy and his half-brother, Roy Heizer, to harness a horse for a trip into town. The boys were apparently playfully and carelessly struggling with one another for the neck yoke and pulled the rings from it. Cory, who was in a hurry to make his trip, became enraged and swore violently at the boys. Billy, in turn, grew equally angry and resentful at this verbal abuse and, according to his version of the story, decided on the spot to leave the farm, get a job, and fend for himself.[16]

After a brief stay with a neighbor, Sunday borrowed a horse and rode the six miles to the nearby county seat of Nevada. There he got a job as janitor, errand boy, bellhop, and night clerk at a local hotel. After his anger subsided, he was still determined to provide for himself but longed to see his family and make peace with his grandfather. He asked permission of the hotel operator to take a day off to visit the Cory homestead. It proved a costly visit because he failed to return on time and was summarily fired.

Sunday then got a job, with room and board, at the farm of Colonel John Scott, a Civil War veteran, former lieutenant governor of Iowa, and one of the most respected and affluent men in Story County. Among his other enterprises, Scott bred Shetland ponies, and Billy helped with the care of the ponies and attended to a variety of other chores around the farm. The Scotts were fond of their young boarder and hired hand and treated him almost as if he were a member of the family. They encouraged him to continue his education by attending the high school at Nevada. Billy not only acquired more education there but also a steady job as janitor, which afforded him badly needed additional income. He remained at the Scott farm for three or four years, completing most of his high school education. In his senior year, however, he was still a few credits short of those required for graduation and never received his degree.[17]

While living on his grandfather's farm near Ames, Sunday had begun to acquire something of a local reputation as an exceptional runner. Residents of Nevada no doubt noticed Billy exercising the hotel owner's prized horse, a little sorrel trotter with a white face and four white feet. He would put the animal through its paces by taking its halter in one hand and putting the other on its shoulder and running along beside it as it trotted down the street. He later recalled that he sometimes ran so fast he forced his charge from a trot into a gallop. These and other such exhibitions of speed earned for him a local reputation as a fleet-footed athlete.[18]

Sunday's prowess as a runner drew the attention of the fire company in Marshalltown, a thriving farming and railroad center and the county seat of nearby Marshall County. In the rural and small towns of the mid- and late-nineteenth-century Middle West, community competition was an integral part of the culture, offering relief from the humdrum routine of life. Town rivalries frequently included races among fire companies. The men of the Marshalltown brigade were interested in Sunday, less to increase their effectiveness in fighting fires than to enhance their chances of winning contests against other towns. Consequently, they invited him to move to Marshalltown and join their fire company.

Billy was comfortable living with the Scotts, who had been kind to him and had introduced him to the lifestyle of the rural and small-town social elite. Furthermore, he had almost completed a high school education, which many young Americans of his generation lacked. Yet he was on the brink of manhood and experiencing the restlessness that often accompanies late adolescence. The work of farm laborer and school janitor had provided economic security at a crucial moment in his life, but he aspired to more. Marshalltown, with a population of approximately 6,000, was four times the size of Nevada and offered not only the opportunity for athletic competition but also new experiences and perhaps a better job. Therefore, he accepted the invitation.[19]

Since fire companies were volunteer associations, Sunday's first challenge was to find some means of support. On the corner of Main and First Streets in Marshalltown stood "Upson & Wilbur, Dealers in Furniture, Undertakers, and Manufacturers of All Kinds of Upholstered Goods." It was in this eclectic establishment that Billy, with the aid of members of the fire company, found employment. He did everything from finishing furniture and working as a salesman to driving the company's hearse, a task that he passionately hated.[20] It was not, however, his diligence as a laborer, his effectiveness as a salesman, or his skill in handling the team pulling the horse-drawn hearse in funeral processions that earned a measure of fame for Sunday among the citizens of Marshalltown. Rather, it was his speed and enthusiasm in athletic competitions that brought him local acclaim. Not only was Billy a valued member of the fire company, but he also joined the town's baseball team. He became something of a star, noted not for his hitting but for his fielding and spectacular base-running.

Marshalltown was the hometown of Adrian Constantine ("Cap") Anson, one of professional baseball's most outstanding players and manager of Albert G. Spalding's Chicago White Stockings. Anson's parents were among the earliest pioneers in the area, and he was said to have been the first white child born in Marshall County. Many of his relatives resided in and around Marshalltown and were familiar with Billy Sunday's athletic prowess. One of them (stories vary as to whether it was an aunt or a sister) suggested to Anson that Sunday might be a good prospect for professional baseball. In 1883, Anson, who had apparently once seen Sunday in a fire-company competition, invited him to come to Chicago and try out with the White Stockings, which at the time was the premier team in the fledgling National League. Anson was sufficiently impressed with Sunday's enthusiasm and speed to offer him a job with the club, and the elated young Iowan accepted.[21]

In the spring of 1883, Billy Sunday left the rural and small-town Midwest for urban America. Over the next half-century, first as an athlete and then as an evangelist, he became one of the most public figures of his age. He craved and reveled in the attention that came his way and projected to the world a persona calculated to generate interest. Yet this acrobatic apostle, who was at one and the same time outrageous, funny, athletic, militant, and sincerely religious, was essentially a shy and private man. He rarely revealed any more of himself than was necessary for the success of his ministry. In sermons and interviews, he often referred to his boyhood in Iowa, sometimes idealizing his childhood and adolescence while on other occasions stressing the hardships that he had overcome. In both cases, however, his stories were largely anecdotal and illustrative of points he wished to make or moods he desired to create. Sunday's autobiography that appeared initially in installments in the *Ladies' Home Journal* in 1932 and 1933 is illuminating, but also, at least in part, the work of one who has created for himself a usable past. Despite the evangelist's reticence about discussing the more personal and sometimes painful facets of his life, it is clear that the cultural and familial experiences of his first twenty years shaped Sunday's personality and determined his view of the world in ways that would change little over the next half-century.

The sociocultural mythology that developed in the Middle West in the nineteenth century was one that de-emphasized social and economic distinctions. It was a mythology of classless communities strewn among productive farms, peopled by decent, self-reliant, hardworking individualists who feared God, loved their country, respected their fellow man, and were always ready to come to the aid of a neighbor in need. At the heart of this social mystique was an economic creed that stressed individualism, competitiveness, and material success and a moral code that emphasized discipline, decorum, and piety. A blend of yeoman and commercial capitalistic ideals permeated with evangelical morality, this value system, though rarely wholly consistent with reality, was pervasive in the world of Billy Sunday's childhood. He encountered it in church, at public celebrations, and in school.[22]

Indeed, nowhere were such values of middle America more pervasive than in the pages of the William Holmes McGuffey readers, recommended for use in Iowa schools during Sunday's youth. These volumes painted an idyllic picture of life in rural and small-town America. City life, when depicted at all, was usually represented in an unfavorable light. One story described the decline of a country boy who moved to the city and was soon on a path to moral degeneration marked by drinking, gambling, and finally crime and imprisonment. McGuffey's works suggested that community and society rested on religious values. Christianity was not simply a matter of the individual's relationship to God but was conducive to national success. It promoted prosperity, order, and harmony. Civility itself sprang from religious values. Historian Lewis Atherton wrote that in McGuffey's view,

> if you could induce a community to doubt the genuineness and authenticity of the scriptures; to question the reality and obligations of religion; to hesitate, indecisive, whether there be any such thing as virtue or vice; whether there be an external state of retribution beyond the grave; or whether there exists any such being as God, you have broken down the barriers of moral virtue, and hoisted the floodgates of immorality and crime.[23]

In other words, the antithesis of Christianity was chaos; to undermine the former was to contribute to the latter.

In McGuffey's view, a close connection existed not only between Christian values and social stability but also between morality and worldly success. It is, however, unfair to dismiss his attitude as simply a kind of materialistic ethic. To live a moral life was a virtue in its own right, but a life of industriousness, discipline, and piety was also the key to prosperity and respectability. To yield to temptation, to succumb to even the most innocuous of vices, set the stage for potential disaster. Gambling, for example, had insidious effects upon those who indulged, leading to other evils such as drinking, infidelity, or even murder. The consumption of alcohol could have dire consequences both for an individual's health and his ability to earn a livelihood. McGuffey idealized love, marriage, and the family. While he shunned any discussion of sexuality, implicit in his writings was the widely accepted notion that the physical pleasures of sex were to be subordinated if not suppressed, and those who violated codes of sexual purity would inevitably pay a frightful mental, physical, and social price.[24]

McGuffey's texts not only addressed questions affecting the individual and community but those related to national destiny as well. Like the Puritans of the early seventeenth century and millions of Americans since, he believed that the United States had a special mission. It was to be a beacon guiding other countries along the way to a better society. The path toward progress was perilous and occasionally resulted in war, which was not desirable but sometimes necessary. America's wars, such as the Revolution, had been righteous battles against despotism and in defense of liberty. The nation's destiny then was to make the world a better place, and the price to be paid to accomplish our mission might, on occasion, be personal and national sacrifice.[25]

The readers of William Holmes McGuffey reflected and helped to perpetuate the cultural ideology of Protestant, middle-class, mid- and late-nineteenth-century American society. They mirrored a value system that was nowhere more firmly entrenched than in the Middle West. Billy Sunday was born and reared in a region that venerated Christianity, community, family, and nation and extolled the virtues of hard work, individual responsibility, common sense, practicality, and progress. Incongruities between the ideal and the real were either ignored or acknowledged with the caveat that the

ideal was inviolable. While cultural forces are important in shaping personality and character, private circumstances have a far more fundamental
impact. There was a decided dissonance between the orderly, optimistic, and
rather placid sociocultural ideal of the world of his youth and Sunday's own
personal and familial experiences.

The death of his father and problems within the family following his
mother's second marriage meant that Billy spent much time during his early
years with his maternal grandparents, a circumstance that afforded some of
his fondest memories but also some of his saddest moments. Life on the Cory
farm, like that in the majority of frontier households, was difficult. Sunday was
born in a log cabin on his grandfather's farm and lived there until Martin Cory
constructed a water-powered sawmill and cut black walnut logs into boards for
a larger and more comfortable frame house. Sunday remembered his grandfather as a rather rustic figure who

> wore a coonskin cap, rawhide boots, blue jeans, and said "done hit" instead
> of "did it," and "come" instead of "came," and "seen" instead of "saw." He
> drank coffee out of his saucer and ate peas with his knife.

At the same time, Cory also impressed his grandson as a man of extraordinary
versatility and talent, one capable of building houses, laying stone walls,

Sunday family cabin near Ames, Iowa, as it appeared in the 1920s.

making wagons, crafting furniture, constructing water-powered mills, and operating a forge to produce horseshoes and wedges for splitting logs. Sunday credited his grandfather with building the loom on which his grandmother produced most of the family's cloth, including that from which his own homespun garments were made.[26]

Billy also remembered his grandfather as a good provider. Although he was not poor, cash was often "as scarce as mosquitoes in January." Nevertheless, "the cellar was always filled with apples, potatoes, barrels of sauerkraut, salt pork, corned beef, and molasses." The family always had an ample supply of cabbage, parsnips, and turnips buried near the house for winter use. Each summer and fall the garret was filled with such items as rings of dried pumpkin, strings of dried apples, and dried spices, including sage, peppermint, catnip, and red pepper. As he grew older, Sunday was responsible for more and more farm chores. He milked ten cows twice daily, bound grain behind the reaper, and helped with the operation of the crude horse-powered molasses mill in which sorghum was pressed to make syrup that was boiled in kettles over open fires and refined into molasses.

The Cory mill served not only the family but also the neighborhood. Farmers brought their sorghum for processing and paid twenty-five cents per gallon for the finished product or gave Cory half of the molasses refined from their sorghum. The refining process sometimes lasted late into the night, since the boiling kettles had to be constantly tended. It is not difficult to imagine Billy sitting with his grandfather beneath the stars on crisp autumn nights, their faces reflecting the light from the crackling fire while the sweet syrup bubbled and thickened and Martin Cory regaled his grandson with stories of his own boyhood, of the three-month trek west from Indiana to Iowa, or of the earliest days of settlement in Story County. No doubt the old man excited and perhaps frightened the boy by telling him how a few years earlier, as he dozed beneath a tree during one of these nocturnal vigils, a black bear wandered out of the woods and helped himself to the cooling molasses.[27]

Though hard, unpredictable, and sometimes painful, life was not all work. There was time for his grandfather to teach Billy how to ride a horse bareback and do a variety of gymnastic tricks. Over a half-century after the fact, he fondly recalled riding a horse conspicuously down the main street of Ames, standing atop his grandfather's shoulders, to the surprise of local residents.[28]

Not many people would have witnessed Sunday's feat of balance, since Ames was no more than a village. In 1870, it had two small hotels, roughly a dozen stores, and only 636 residents. It was, however, growing steadily and almost doubled in size over the next decade.[29] Its only distinction from other tiny farming communities in the state was that it was the site of the Iowa Agricultural College.

Martin Cory had seen the village rise out of the prairie marsh in the mid-1860s as a stop along the Cedar Rapids and Missouri Valley Railroad as it pushed westward, and he may have been among the town's early boosters. Family tradition contends he was among the group of local residents who donated land or money to secure the college for their community, that he had helped to stake out the initial campus, and was one of the men who determined the site for the first building in the 1860s. While there is no evidence of a donation of land, county land records confirm that Martin and Mary Ann Cory sold the state of Iowa twenty acres for $200 for the use of the agricultural college in 1859. Though no longer readily verifiable, the other stories seem plausible given his early arrival in the county and his proximity to Ames. It is clear, however, that once the town was established, Cory played no significant role in its development.[30]

While they may have been the centers of education, commerce, and society in Billy Sunday's small world, in the late 1860s and early 1870s, neither the college nor the town of Ames was particularly noteworthy. Going into town was perhaps a treat of sorts to a local country boy, but to an outsider, Ames left much to be desired. A professor at the college recalled his first approach to the community in 1870.

> It was a raw February day on which I reached the quite forlorn looking village of Ames. It impressed me with its treelessness and the small houses with no shrubs and no dooryards, as a village which was all out of doors, and lonesome and unprotected. The drive over the rough, mud road, over a rickety bridge and the "bottoms" of Squaw Creek was not reassuring. The mean approach to the college just at the base of the hill, and up through the barnyard, by the old Farm House, and then across the fields to the president's house might well have dampened the ardor of the newcomer. . . . Look back with me, and see this campus as the young botanist saw it. There were no drives, no walks, no paths, no smooth lawn, and only a few small trees.[31]

Small and unimpressive though it was, to Billy, Ames was the center of activity. It was a place where he sold produce from the Cory garden, purchased candy or a rubber ball, and most likely attended church and, for a time, school. On holidays he sometimes joined in community festivities.

Late-nineteenth-century midwestern towns broke the monotony of life with a variety of community celebrations. The Fourth of July, for example, was frequently the occasion for a major holiday. In the 1870s, the celebration at Ames began at sunrise, about 4:30 A.M., when a cannon was fired on the Iowa Agricultural College campus. Soon the streets of the village filled with local residents and country people who came into town for the celebration. Along the streets, vendors sold food, including bologna, cookies, ice cream, fresh lemonade, and a variety of other treats. Competitions of various sorts, including footraces, baseball games, and greased pig chases, were routine parts of the festivities.

At one of these Fourth of July celebrations, probably that of 1876, Billy, only a 13-year-old boy, entered a free-for-all footrace in which he competed against thirteen adult men. The fastest man, Billy remembered, was an agricultural college professor who was shod in running shoes and clad in a rose-colored silk suit. To his delight, Sunday won the race and carried away the $3 prize.

"Bird's Eye View of Ames, Iowa" in the 1870s.

A. T. Andreas, *Illustrated Historical Atlas of the State of Iowa* (Chicago: Andreas Atlas Company, 1875; reprint, Iowa City, Iowa: State Historical Society of Iowa, 1970), p. 324.

Onondaga Street, Ames, Iowa, in 1875.

Farwell T. Brown Photographic Archive, Ames Public Library, Ames, Iowa.

He then entered the greased pig contest. Grabbing the 125-pound porker's neck, he held on for dear life, winning that event with its $1 prize as well. There was not only an element of personal pride in Sunday's victory but also a hint of country-versus-town rivalry. Even residents of villages as small as Ames could sometimes be rather condescending toward their rural neighbors, an attitude that country folk resented. Billy was proud that he and a friend, who had won another contest, both of them "country Jakes" in the eyes of the town boys, had "cleaned up on" their snobbish peers. He celebrated his victory and that of his country caste by using his winnings to treat his friends to ice cream and lemonade.[32]

The recollection of this holiday celebration was the kind of joyous youthful memory to which Sunday clung and which he embellished with the passing years. Many of his childhood experiences, however, were hardly so satisfying as those of riding into town upon the shoulders of his grandfather or winning contests on festive Fourths of July. He often spoke of the hardships he had known as a boy, but he concealed some of the more painful facets of his youth, believing, as he wrote in 1887 to his future wife, Helen Thompson, "Every heart guards its own bitterness, so I will let mine keep its own."[33] Yet it is clear from the glimpses of his past he gave in sermons and writings and from other extant sources that Billy's early years were marred by family tensions and disruptions that contributed to recurring feelings of loss, loneliness, inadequacy, and perhaps rejection.

As a boy, illness and death seemed the most threatening and destabilizing forces in Billy Sunday's world. His mind was filled with images of both. From the time he was able to comprehend them, he heard stories of his own frail condition as a toddler, when, at times, he was so ill and weak he could scarcely walk. His health did not improve significantly until an itinerant physician, Alexander Favre, a native of France and the first doctor in Story County, stopped by the Cory cabin and asked whether anyone needed his services. When told of 3-year-old "Willie's" condition, he went into the nearby woods; gathered roots, leaves, and berries; and concocted an herbal remedy which invigorated the child and set him on the road to recovery. Billy remembered the illnesses and injuries of his own family members, some of which proved fatal. He also recalled friends and neighbors appearing at his grandparents' door and asking Martin Cory, who possessed a spring lance and steel nerves, to come and bleed some stricken member of their family.[34]

Death was an imminent reality on the frontier. Disease, accidents, and occasionally violence, coupled with only the most rudimentary and sometimes detrimental medical attention, meant that nineteenth-century Americans in general, and pioneers in particular, understood clearly the fragility of life. The open grave, wooden coffin, and sight of mourning dress were commonplace in rural and small-town Iowa in the 1860s and 1870s. According to an early local history, Martin Cory hewed with an ax the first crude coffin ever constructed in Story County. Billy recalled that his grandfather donated land on a beautiful spot along a stream for a community cemetery.

The Corys also had their own private graveyard on the farm where a number of family members were buried.[35]

From his earliest childhood, therefore, death was a familiar part of Billy Sunday's world, but he never became inured to it. Indeed, because of the way in which it affected his life, he seems to have been extraordinarily sensitive to death and its consequences for the living. In his autobiography, he recalled the many sorrows of his young life, including the losses of his childhood pets.

The Corys had a pet otter named Jeannette that was trained to catch fish and bring them to the riverbank. After her fishing expeditions, the otter would come into the house and stretch herself across a bed to dry. During one of these visits to the family cabin, the otter attempted to take a piece of meat off a shelf and upset a flatiron that fell and broke the animal's back. Billy had a pet rooster named Bill, which, he claimed, could whip any rooster in the flock. The big red-and-black fowl roosted in a tree near the Cory house. One night an owl attacked and attempted to fly away with the rooster. Sunday, aroused by the commotion, ran into the yard and blasted the offending predator with a shotgun, but the trauma of the struggle with the owl plus the damage done by Billy's undiscriminating weapon resulted in the rooster's death the next day. The grief-stricken boy buried his pet beneath an apple tree.

The rooster was not the last of Billy's animal playmates to meet an untimely end. He had a pet pig, a Chester White, also named Billy, that lived in a special pen and followed Sunday about like a dog, even coming into the house. The boy sometimes lay in the straw with his pig and fell asleep while scratching the animal with a corn cob. One day, when Billy returned home from school, he could not find his prized pig. Then he noticed a carcass hanging in a tree and surmised with horror that in his absence the family had used his pet to replenish its larder. The distraught child refused to eat pork the rest of the winter out of fear he would be devouring his friend. While such losses were a normal part of life in rural areas and may seem inconsequential or even ludicrous in retrospect, to a child like Billy, living in a precarious world, pets afforded security and companionship, and their loss intensified his loneliness and apprehension. The vividness with which he recalled these incidents more than sixty years later suggests their emotional impact upon him.[36]

Other deaths and separations in Sunday's early years were far more traumatic and threatening. Having spent so much time in the care of his grandparents, Billy was deeply attached to his grandmother. When he was about six years old, she died of consumption. Some time later, he lost an aunt to the same disease. Billy's memory of this second death was vivid, and his recollection of it illuminates some of the frontier folk beliefs of the era.

> When my aunt Elisabeth—we called her Libby—lay sick, one day she aroused herself from a comatose state and said, "Oh, I have looked into heaven and I saw Mother." That evening at dusk, a whippoorwill flew down in the yard. It was the first and last one I have ever seen. It was in the early spring and the door was open.

The bird fluttered into the house and perched upon the head of her bed and sang "whip-poor-will, whip-poor-will, whip-poor-will" and out through the door it flew, and off into the darkening woods. From the depths of the gloom we heard his "whip-poor-will, whip-poor-will, whip-poor-will," and everybody trembled with dread and said, "That is a sure sign of death."

The bird sang "whip-poor-will" three times while sitting on the head-board of the bed and three times from the depths of the forest. "Libby will die in three days," they said; and sure enough, on the third day after the visit of the bird, and at the same hour, she died.[37]

It was not only adults who succumbed to disease or accidents. When Billy's half-sister was about 3 years old, her clothing caught fire as she dumped leaves on a bonfire. Before the flames could be extinguished, she suffered extensive and severe burns that proved fatal.[38]

By the time he was roughly 10 years old, Sunday had lost his father, grandmother, half-sister, and an aunt, as well as several other friends and relatives. These losses engendered in him an extreme awareness of the precariousness of life and relationships. It is hardly surprising that he was haunted throughout his life by an ever-present awareness of death.

Mortality troubled him less than did the separation and loneliness that were its corollaries. The loss of his father created a permanent void in Sunday's world. In May 1887, just after Decoration Day and twenty-five years after the death of a man he had never known, he wrote from Detroit to Helen Thompson,

The streets here were thronged with people all going to Decorate the Graves of Loved ones. I wondered as I see them going if they thought that soon some kind loving hands would place Garlands of Flowers on their Graves and I thought of my Fathers Grave and wondered if some kind hand would drop a rose on his Grave. I hope they did.[39]

Years later, in an effort to make some kind of connection with the unknown figure who loomed so large in his psyche, Sunday tried in vain to locate his father's unmarked grave. In 1932, just three years before his own death, Sunday began his autobiography with the revealing words "I never saw my father."[40]

The persistent longing for his father was in part the result of a natural curiosity about the man of whom he had only a fading photograph and some family stories and in part because of the fact that no one in Sunday's life ever satisfactorily took his father's place. The void might have been partially filled had his relationship with his stepfathers proven fulfilling, but his memories of James M. Heizer were of poverty, tension, alcoholism, and eventual abandonment. On those infrequent occasions when he wrote or spoke of him, the only emotion he ever revealed was dislike. Billy was in the orphanage at Davenport when Jennie married George Stowell and was never part of the couple's household. While there is no overt evidence of intense antagonism between Sunday and his second stepfather, neither is there any hint of an emotional bond. The fact that the evangelist never acknowledged Stowell in his autobi-

Only known picture of Billy Sunday's father,
William Sunday (died 1862).

*Billy Sunday Archives, Grace College and Theological Seminary,
Winona Lake, Indiana.*

ography is an omission that may bear silent witness to misgivings about his
mother's third marriage.[41]

By far the most important familial male role model Sunday had as a child
was his maternal grandfather. Yet his relationship with Martin Cory was
complex and not wholly satisfying. Cory appears to have been an essentially
industrious and decent man who loved his grandson but was also prone to
periodic bouts of heavy drinking. His penchant for drink may not have
significantly damaged Cory or his family financially, but it did create an
unpleasant and sometimes menacing atmosphere for members of the Cory
household. Sunday clearly suffered occasionally at the hands of his drunken
grandfather. Either out of embarrassment or because it was such a painful
memory, he generally concealed this part of his boyhood experience, but he

confided in a letter to Helen Thompson in the late 1880s, "My poor dear old Grand-father used to drink oh so much and abuse me and when sober he would feel so sad about it."[42]

Sunday loved his grandfather, who in some ways had been a surrogate father during his early years. He respected him as one of that hearty breed of frontiersmen whose toughness and tenacity had built the nation. He admired him for his many skills and was proud of the success he had achieved as a substantial farmer and well-known member of his community. Yet Sunday struggled to reconcile these aspects of Cory's life with the weaker and more destructive side of his nature.

A recurring pattern of drunken abuse may have ultimately contributed to Sunday's seemingly precipitous departure from his grandfather's farm following the incident with the yoke rings. There may also have been other sources of tension. It is probable that Cory, then in his mid-sixties, was not happy about having his two teenaged grandsons return to his farm after they left the orphanage in 1876. He was now less prosperous by comparison with many of his neighbors than he once had been and was no doubt concerned about providing adequately for himself and his second wife in their old age. Even though Ed and Billy could have helped with the farm work, they were two more mouths to feed and their presence added an unwanted element of parental responsibility.

Financial entanglements may also have caused problems between Martin Cory and his grandson. The three Sunday brothers, through no fault of their own, had complicated their grandfather's life. Martin Cory had acted as James Heizer's bondsman when the latter assumed the guardianship of his stepsons in 1866. After Heizer abandoned his family in 1871, the county appointed a new guardian, Walter Evans, to be financially responsible for the welfare of the heirs of William Sunday. In 1872, Evans sued Heizer and Cory to recover funds due the Sunday estate and won a judgment on behalf of his wards. Since Heizer apparently had little of value, Cory now found himself liable for a claim of more than $700, but he pled inability to meet the obligation without undue hardship. Evans and the court, perhaps recognizing the merit in Cory's plea, chose not to press the issue until a more opportune moment. The upshot was that for roughly the next decade the succession of guardians of his Sunday grandsons held a lien against Martin Cory's homestead. This circumstance, coupled with the fact that he appears to have already been helping to support Roy Heizer, a grandson by Jennie's second husband, and now was at least partially responsible for two additional youths, may have been an irritant to the aging Cory and a contributor to familial conflict. Whatever the case, since any change of residence was probably subject to the approval of the Sundays' guardian, it seems unlikely that a single outburst of temper by the elderly and perhaps crotchety Martin Cory would have been sufficient to cause Billy's dramatic departure had there not already been strains between him and his grandson.[43]

The Civil War not only deprived Sunday of his father but also, in some respects, of his mother as well. His relationship with her during much of his childhood was punctuated by periodic painful separations. After she married James Heizer, Billy spent much of his time with his grandparents, a fact which he later attributed to his dislike of his stepfather. This explanation is probably true but incomplete. It is unlikely that a child under the age of 6 would have been allowed to leave the care of his mother without her consent, and such consent must have been based on more than her son's attitude toward her new husband.[44]

Tensions between children and a stepparent are not uncommon but usually do not result in their leaving home. It is possible that the Sunday boys regarded Heizer as something of an intruder in their world and rival for the affection of their mother and thus disliked him. The situation, however, was probably more complex. Heizer may well have had no emotional attachment to his stepsons and perhaps even regarded them as a burden, especially after the birth of his own two children by Jennie. He was clearly something less than a model spouse. He was never more than a mediocre provider, suffered from alcoholism, and eventually abandoned his wife and children, leaving them in desperate straits. Whatever the exact nature of its problems, there is little doubt that the family was, in modern parlance, dysfunctional. It seems likely that both the Corys and their daughter believed it best to get Billy out of this environment and back into a familiar one where he had been comfortable before his mother's marriage.

Even though Sunday's return to his grandparents' home was in his best interest and something he apparently desired, the separation from his only surviving parent was undoubtedly wrenching. He had never known his father and now, although he saw her frequently, he was, in a sense, separated from his mother as well. In his early years, at least, Billy felt loved and was relatively happy and secure in the familiar surroundings of the Cory farm; yet from a child's perspective, this separation from his mother must have seemed a kind of rejection. She had chosen to remain with a man he disliked while allowing him to spend much of his time elsewhere. Billy was extremely attached to Mary Ann Cory, his maternal grandmother. This strong emotional bond may well have been the result of the fact that he found in her some sense of stability and security that he had been unable to find in his mother's world. His grandmother's death when he was 6 years old was a shattering experience for him. He later recalled that he stayed by the side of her coffin until forced to leave. He was so upset at his separation from her that his family found him two days after her burial lying in the snow atop her grave. Her death threatened the only real stability and security he had ever known and may have forced him to return to the uncertainty and turbulence of the Heizer household.[45]

If his grandmother's death was traumatic for Sunday, his world was shaken to its foundations when Jennie Heizer prepared to formally dissolve her second marriage in the fall of 1874 and sent Billy and Ed to an orphanage. Within a year, she married for a third time, and shortly thereafter she placed her son Albert in the Story County poorhouse. Jennie's actions raise some interesting and potentially troubling questions. Did poverty alone compel her

to send her sons to Glenwood, or was she motivated by more selfish considerations? Did the Sunday brothers' guardian force her to commit them to the
orphanage because he thought it in the boys' best interest? Why did she place
Albert in the care of the county around the time of her marriage to George
Stowell in 1875? Why did Billy and Ed go to their grandfather's farm in 1876
rather than to their mother's household? Was Stowell unwilling or unable to
accept responsibility for rearing the boys? Did his stepchildren resent him or
disapprove of the marriage and want nothing to do with him?

We can never answer the majority of these questions with certainty because
of a paucity of extant family sources from these years. A century and a quarter
after the events it is difficult to breathe life into the dry bones of the handful
of relevant legal documents surviving in the Story County courthouse, but the
fragmentary evidence that remains provides some intriguing clues.

Court records make it quite clear that at least the last two of Jennie Cory's
marriages were less than ideal. James Heizer was an irresponsible alcoholic
who failed to provide for his wife and children, misused or stole money
belonging to his stepsons, and eventually left the family impoverished.
Whether it was their mother or guardian who ultimately decided to place Ed
and Billy in an orphanage, the decision was probably in the boys' best interest
even though they may not have appreciated it at the time. Jennie's relationship with George Stowell may or may not have been emotionally satisfying,
but he evidently afforded little more financial security than had James Heizer.
Stowell was apparently an itinerant laborer whose income was at best meager
and whose trade took him from home much of the time. Although there are
no contemporary corroborating county birth records to substantiate the fact,
it appears that the Stowells had a child in 1876. An 1885 court document
mentions a younger child and in an 1887 letter Sunday makes a reference to
his 11-year-old brother.[46] The birth of another son might, in part, explain why
Jennie decided to place Albert in the care of the county. Little money, an
absent husband, and a disabled teenaged son may have been more than she
could manage with the added responsibility of an infant. This may also help
to explain why, when Billy and Ed left the Davenport orphanage, they went
to live with Martin Cory rather than with their mother.

The passage of time does not appear to have eased Jennie Stowell's plight.
In 1885, claiming that she had no home because of the itinerant nature of her
husband's work, she petitioned the court to remove Albert from the poorhouse. She asked to become his guardian and to be allowed to use his share
of the Sunday brothers' estate (apparently a portion of his deceased Grandfather Cory's farm), to make a home for him, herself, and her youngest child.
Although the matter is not entirely clear, it appears that she did become
Albert's guardian and may have removed him from the county poorhouse. It
is certain, however, that she received little or nothing with which to establish
a home for him. Her son's previous guardian, J. A. Fitchpatrick, under order
of the court, liquidated the property he held for his ward, which after taxes and
other fees were deducted left a cash balance in the estate of only $509.63. In

an age that believed that honest debts should be repaid whenever possible, Story County immediately demanded $1,000 in compensation for the nine years of care it had provided Albert Sunday, thus leaving nothing for Jennie's use. She thereafter joined her husband in western Kansas, where she eked out a modest living on a small farm while George sometimes supplemented the family income with other jobs. The Stowells never really escaped from their marginal existence, and Jennie was partially dependent upon her children for support throughout much of her later life.[47]

Although Sunday's mother's choices of mates and her actions regarding her children admittedly could be interpreted in such a way as to raise some troubling questions about her judgment or character, there is no conclusive evidence that she ever intentionally rejected any of her offspring or acted out of motives other than a desire to provide as best she could for herself and her children. In nineteenth-century America, options for women, especially single women who were poor and possessed little education, were limited. Widows with dependent children often found themselves in dire straits and desperate for security, a condition that probably goes far to explain why Jennie Sunday Heizer Stowell made the choices she did.

Regardless of their cause, these childhood separations from his mother undoubtedly engendered in Billy a variety of complex and dimly understood emotions. He may well have believed that she had been driven to her actions by economic conditions and by loneliness. Yet he must also have felt some resentment, rejection, anger, and inadequacy. His mother had sent him away, first to her parents and then to an orphanage. Both her second and third marriages, rather than creating opportunities for the reunification of the family, resulted in further disruptions. There must have been times when he felt himself an unwanted burden, while at other times he experienced guilt because of his inability to help her through her difficulties. Even if warranted and justifiable, to a fatherless child whose world was repeatedly wracked by death, poverty, alcoholism, family strife, and separation from those whom he loved, rational explanations of his mother's behavior were much less significant than was the pain of separation and loss.

Though emotionally scarred by his childhood experiences, as an adult Billy seems to have harbored little if any conscious resentment or bitterness toward his mother. On the contrary, he apparently concluded that she was a victim of circumstances over which she had little or no control. He took considerable pride in the fact that he was able to help support her for the last thirty years of her life.[48]

Billy Sunday was born in and spent most of his childhood in central Iowa at a time when the area was making a rapid transition from frontier to established society. It was a land of possibilities but also of disappointments, as his own family history proved. In his early years, life was hard, labor long, luxuries few, and pleasures modest. In time, the region grew more stable and comfortable but also more economically complex and socially stratified, which limited mobility and undermined the status of some residents. The dominant cultural mythology of Iowa and the Middle West was optimistic, egalitarian, democratic, Christian, and patriotic. It stressed piety, discipline, practicality, hard work, and individual responsibility, as well as the importance of family and community. Like most mythologies, this one was not wholly consistent with reality.

Certainly there was some dissonance between this cultural ideology and Billy Sunday's own experience, but it was the belief system to which he was exposed at home, at school, at church, in the orphanage, and eventually in the workplace. It was these values that he took with him out of the towns of the nineteenth-century Midwest and into the tabernacles of twentieth-century urban America. He also took with him something else; a profound sense of insecurity and inadequacy born of the personal traumas of his childhood and youth. These feelings of insecurity and inadequacy contributed immeasurably to his nervous energy, drive to succeed, determination to prove himself a man, and uncompromising hostility toward any attitudes or practices that contradicted the religious and social belief system that had helped him to integrate his life and that he thought responsible for his triumph over adversity.

TWO

The Diamond and the Cross

Early on a spring morning in 1883, a train pulled into Chicago carrying an excited but apprehensive and travel-weary Billy Sunday. At roughly 6:30 A.M., the young Iowan stepped off the train and began exploring the unfamiliar streets in search of A. G. Spalding's sporting-goods store, headquarters of the White Stockings. To someone who had never seen a town larger than Des Moines, the city was an enormous and perplexing place.

Chicago in the early 1880s was growing rapidly, already well on its way to becoming Carl Sandburg's city of the "big shoulders." Its population had increased from 300,000 in 1870 to 500,000 in 1880 and would reach more than 1 million by 1890. Its streets teemed with horse-drawn vehicles and diverse throngs of pedestrians. Its smoke-shrouded skyline was punctuated by multistory masonry buildings, many of which had risen out of the ashes of the disastrous fire of 1871. From the tops of nascent skyscrapers one could view a murky panorama of expansive lumberyards, massive grain elevators, sprawling stockyards, decaying slums, mushrooming suburbs, a ship-laden waterfront, and a web of rails that disappeared into the hinterland. The city had already emerged as the hub of commerce, the nexus of East and West, which at the turn of the century Frederick Jackson Turner would describe as the place where "all the forces in the Nation intersect."[1]

Lying along the southwestern shore of Lake Michigan, roughly 300 miles to the east of Billy Sunday's Story County birthplace, Chicago was almost as far removed from the bucolic "heartland" of popular imagination as if it had been in another country. Yet this vibrant world of commerce and chaos was as logical a product of the expanding Midwest as was the agricultural frontier, and it was to play as important a role in Sunday's life as had his experiences on the farms and in the small towns of Iowa. It was in this raw, burgeoning metropolis that Sunday first achieved a measure of popular acclaim as a second-string member of the renowned Chicago White Stockings and there too that he found fulfillment and purpose in religious conversion and marriage.

The base paths were Billy's avenue into the strange new world of urban, industrial America. Although there had been precursors of baseball in both

Britain and the United States, the game as we know it today was just coming of age during Sunday's boyhood. In 1845, Alexander J. Cartwright of the New York Knickerbockers, a middle-class men's club in New York City, the members of which regularly played baseball, codified the rules of the game. Cartwright's codification served as the basis for the standardization of the sport, first in New York City and then in other parts of the East. By the late 1840s and 1850s, baseball had begun to spread out of the Northeast. The convergence and dispersal of hundreds of thousands of men in military service during the Civil War accelerated the dissemination of the game.[2]

By the time Sunday was old enough to participate in team sports, baseball was thoroughly, if often informally, established in many of the small towns of the Middle West. According to local tradition, the first official baseball game in Story County was played in August 1867, when Ames defeated the county seat of Nevada by a score of sixty-six to fifty-five. Thereafter, Ames frequently fielded a team against nearby communities. The Ames squad ordinarily consisted of young men or adolescent boys from the town or from the faculty and student body of the fledgling Iowa Agricultural College. Although Ames in the late 1860s and 1870s was no more than a village, its residents, like those of other midwestern towns, sometimes viewed the nearby country folk with condescension. Thus, it is not surprising that more than a half-century later Sunday recalled with pride that because of his athletic ability, he had been one of the few country boys occasionally invited to join the town nine.

Billy apparently first became acquainted with baseball while attending a one-room school near the Cory homestead. The teacher, C. G. McCarthy, taught his students the rudiments of the game and is said to have sometimes dismissed class early in order to allow the boys to play ball. Sunday honed his skill as a fielder by taking advantage of spare moments on the farm to toss a rubber ball high into the air and then sprint after it. At the Glenwood and Davenport orphanages, he and the other boys had played baseball with a homemade tightly wound twine ball. Since he was only 11 years old when his mother sent him and his older brother to Glenwood, it was probably after his return to his grandfather's farm as a teenager in 1876 that he played occasionally for Ames. Late in life, he claimed to have been such a valued player that the community team had sometimes hired someone to do his work on the farm if he was busy when his services were needed. It is likely that the aging evangelist embellished his importance to his local team, but there is little doubt that by the time he reached his late teens his reputation as a runner was instrumental in his move to Marshalltown. As we have seen, his speed with the Marshalltown fire company and notable play with the local baseball team drew Adrian Anson's attention and launched Sunday's baseball career.[3]

When Sunday arrived in Chicago, he found himself in a city obviously vibrant with economic energy. What was less immediately apparent to him was that he was about to enter a profession that in many ways was becoming as businesslike as any of the commercial and manufacturing enterprises he saw around him. One of the significant cultural developments of post–Civil War America was the growth of organized amateur and professional sports. The phenomenon was largely a product of the rise of the city, the expansion of the rail network, and the revolution in communications. An important result of the growing enthusiasm for sports was the birth of professional baseball. The first league, the National Association of Professional Base Ball Players, was established in 1871, twelve years before Sunday joined the Chicago White Stockings. Plagued by a lack of organization, rowdy players, disorderly fans, and problems with gambling and drunkenness in the ball-parks, the Association lasted only until 1875.[4]

William Ambrose Hulbert, a Chicago businessman, member of the Board of Trade, and an executive with the White Stockings, one of the principal teams in the Association, scorned the chaos characteristic of the league. He envisioned the creation of a new, more stable professional organization. Motivated in part by an eye for the bottom line, Hulbert was also a shameless promoter of his beloved city of Chicago. He allegedly proclaimed, "I would rather be a lamp-post in Chicago than a millionaire in any other city."[5] He recognized in baseball both the possibility of a profitable commercial venture and a means of helping to revive the fortunes of the Windy City following the great fire of 1871. In order to build as strong a team as possible, in 1875 Hulbert began to raid other teams for their best players. His two most notable acquisitions were Albert Goodwill Spalding and Adrian Constantine Anson, from the Boston and Philadelphia clubs respectively.

Spalding became president and a principal owner of the White Stockings after Hulbert's death in 1882. He was not only a fine pitcher and extraordinary baseball executive who was instrumental in building Chicago into a strong team but also an astute entrepreneur who eventually made a fortune in the sporting-goods industry. Adrian "Cap" Anson, among the best players of the age, batted more than .300 in all but two of his twenty-two seasons in the majors and won the batting title on four occasions. Furthermore, he became the most successful player-manager in the game in the 1880s and early 1890s, leading his team to five pennants in seven years.[6]

Naturally, clubs that lost players of the caliber of Spalding and Anson were angry at Hulbert. At least one scholar has suggested that the White Stockings president may have initiated the creation of a new league in part to thwart other teams' efforts at retaliation against his player raids. While there may be some truth in this supposition, his primary objectives were greater stability and profitability in professional baseball. The National League that he and several other team owners formed in late 1875 and 1876 was much more highly structured and businesslike than had been the Players' Association.[7]

The new league permitted only one member team in a city, establishing what amounted to a franchise. No club could reside in a city of less than 75,000 people. The league carefully regulated its teams' contests with inde-pendent clubs or those of other leagues, eventually barring non-league teams from National League ballparks.[8]

Increasingly, owners dealt with players in ways similar to those in which other late-nineteenth-century businessmen dealt with employees. They competed in the marketplace for labor and strove to keep salaries as low as competition and player morale would permit. After 1879, they began trying to bind players to specific teams through the reserve clause and developed mechanisms, including fines and expulsion from the league, to discipline insubordinate or unruly team members. Players were subject to penalties for infractions of rules both on and off the field.[9]

The founders of the National League justified their new creation on the grounds that it had saved professional baseball from ruin by imposing order and morality upon the clubs, the players, and even the fans. In using such a rationale they were attempting to address one of early professional baseball's most persistent problems—its image. Many middle-class Americans, schooled in the Protestant ethic, found it difficult to accept the notion that playing a ball game was work and that those who played it were worthy of respect for anything other than athletic prowess. The gambling, drunkenness, and corruption that characterized much of professional baseball's early days had further undermined the public's perception of the sport. From the outset, Hulbert had determined to make the National League, of which he was president after 1877, acceptable in middle-class circles. Within a few years of its creation, the League, in addition to trying to improve the deportment of players, had banned Sunday games as well as liquor sales and gambling in its parks. It established a minimum admission price of fifty cents, designed to exclude ne'er-do-wells and encourage a better class of fans.[10]

Despite its efforts to establish a businesslike and respectable organization, the National League was unable to completely dominate professional baseball. In the late 1870s and 1880s, several competing circuits emerged, including the International Association of Professional Base Ball Players, the American Association of Base Ball Clubs, and the Union Association. These leagues, most notably the American Association, competed for players and fan loyalty and tended to drive salaries up. The National League ridiculed, warred against, and, when necessary, reached accommodation with its rivals.[11]

Billy Sunday's initial contact with the world of professional baseball suggested a casualness on the part of players and management seemingly inconsistent with the business practices beginning to dominate the game. After wandering the streets of Chicago for about half an hour, the aspiring National Leaguer reached his destination. Accustomed to stores opening early in the small towns of Iowa, he was bewildered by the locked doors of A. G. Spalding's sporting goods emporium, which did not open until eight o'clock. To his further surprise, the first member of the White Stockings did not appear for nearly two more hours. Finally, Abner Dalrymple, Chicago's left fielder, arrived, followed shortly by other team members.[12]

In the presence of what was already emerging as professional baseball's most distinguished club, Billy was self-conscious about his rustic appearance. He wrote years later, "My hair was long, and I sure looked like the hayseed that

I was, compared to those well-groomed men, members of that famous old team." When Anson arrived he was anxious to see again, and to have his players see, an exhibition of the newcomer's speed and agility. He asked Billy to race against Fred Pfeffer, the White Stockings' fastest runner. The team went to the ballfield on the lakefront, where Larry Corcoran, one of Chicago's pitchers, lent the newcomer his uniform. Sunday had no athletic shoes, so he ran barefooted. The shoeless Iowan lived up to his reputation, beating Pfeffer handily. Anson was impressed with Sunday's speed and offered him a position with the team. Billy recalled, "Winning that race opened the hearts of the players to me at once, and I'll always be thankful to Cap for giving me that chance to show off to the best advantage." Anson further endeared himself to the neophyte big-leaguer on his first morning in Chicago by inquiring whether or not his new team member had any money. Billy confessed that he had only a dollar. "Cap," as he was known to his players, responded by handing him a $20 gold piece.[13]

When Sunday joined the White Stockings, he, like most of the players of the day, had no formal training in either the skills or the strategy of baseball. There were no minor leagues in which players could be schooled in the fundamentals of the game. Scouting was more serendipitous than systematic, and players were picked up from sandlots, schoolgrounds, or community teams. Professional clubs had no coaches, athletic trainers, or doctors to develop players' talents or attend to their injuries. Newcomers trained themselves by observing veteran players or, if they were lucky, teammates took an interest in them and shared the benefits of their own experience. Sunday was fortunate because he was popular with his teammates. Stars such as the legendary Mike ("King") Kelly and Anson himself worked to cultivate the ability they recognized in him.[14]

Even with the instruction of his experienced teammates and manager, Sunday never became a skilled batter. During his first year with Chicago, he batted .241 in 14 games. The following year he appeared in 43 games, but his batting average slumped to .222. In 1885, he had a somewhat better season, hitting .256 in 46 games, but the next year he played in only 28 games and hit .243. His last year with the White Stockings, 1887, was actually Sunday's best. That season, he played in 50 games and hit .291, his career high.[15]

Cap Anson liked and probably identified with this raw, young midwesterner, but Anson was a manager and keen competitor whose goal was above all to field the best possible team. He did not retain Sunday on the White Stockings roster simply because of sentimentality. Rather, he recognized that to a considerable extent, Billy made up on the base paths and in the outfield for his deficiencies at the plate. His talents were well-suited to a club that emphasized speed and strategy as well as hitting. In his memoirs, the Chicago manager wrote:

> He was, in my opinion, the fastest man afterwards on his feet in the profession, and one who could run the bases like a scared deer. The first thirteen

times that he went to bat after he began playing with the Chicagos he was struck out, but I was confident that he would yet make a ball player and hung onto him, cheering him up as best I could whenever he became discouraged. As a baserunner his judgement was at times faulty and he was altogether too daring, taking extreme chances because of the tremendous turn of speed that he possessed. He was a good fielder and a strong and accurate thrower, his weak point lying in his batting.[16]

Anson also recognized that, unlike some of his teammates, Sunday was essentially a responsible and trustworthy young man. Consequently, he made him a de facto business manager for the team on road trips. When playing in opponents' parks, the White Stockings received a percentage of the gate receipts. Anson assigned Sunday to watch the turnstile, count the tickets, and secure the team's share of the revenues. He also paid the hotel bills, purchased railroad tickets, arranged Pullman reservations, and occasionally provided salary advances to players who were short of funds. Whenever the White Stockings returned to Chicago, Sunday accompanied Anson to settle accounts with Spalding. Honest, reliable, and careful, Billy was always proud of the fact that even though this was his first experience with money management, he was never short a dollar.[17]

Yet it was not the business dimension of baseball that captured Sunday's imagination. Rather, it was the competition, camaraderie, approbation of the fans, and opportunities for broadened horizons that he found appealing. Even though White Stockings' president and owner A. G. Spalding was professional baseball's most talented and aggressive entrepreneur, Sunday never seems to have been particularly interested in or impressed by the fact that he was part of a game that was emerging rapidly from the status of sport to that of big business and, as such, was beginning to exhibit many of the characteristics of late-nineteenth-century American capitalism. To be sure, he was sufficiently aware that players' options were increasingly circumscribed by management to join the fledgling Brotherhood of Professional Base Ball Players organized in 1885. He abandoned it, however, in 1890, when, in response to the growing arbitrariness of team owners, the Brotherhood became the nucleus for the Players' League. Judging from Sunday's sermons, interviews, and writings after he left the game, one would scarcely know that professional baseball was a business except for occasional references to salaries or the sale of a player.[18]

During his years with the White Stockings, two events occurred in Sunday's life that changed it forever. The first, his religious conversion, gave new meaning to his experience and shaped his professional destiny; the second, his marriage, profoundly altered his personal life and provided the emotional support he would need to pursue his goals over the next half-century.[19]

In the decades after the Civil War, Chicago's religious community struggled desperately to keep pace with the city's rapid growth and the problems that were its corollaries. The ranks of those professing allegiance to one or another of the city's numerous religious bodies steadily increased, as did the number of churches, synagogues, and other places of worship. Yet, Protestants, Catholics, and Jews alike worried that they were failing to stay abreast of the change swirling about them. Evangelical Protestantism, with its tradition of hegemony within American culture and inherent impulse to proselytize, was especially alarmed by its failure to keep pace with population growth. By the late 1880s, according to one estimate, there was only one Protestant for every nineteen residents of Chicago. Part of the Protestant leadership's difficulty was that its understanding of the gospel had relatively little appeal for the increasingly large numbers of immigrants pouring into the city from abroad, and part was due to the fact that most Protestant clergy were unable to identify with the problems and aspirations of the mass of workers. Thus, they had only limited success among them.

In the 1880s, Chicago was a city of opportunity and hope but also one of dislocation, poverty, and despair. The roar of the machine and cacophony of the stockyards threatened to drown out the voices of the disinherited. The dazzle of a city on the make often obscured the plight of the desperate men and women on the margin.

Evangelical churches tried to address the religious needs of the populace through an active Sunday school movement, youth programs such as Christian Endeavor or the Epworth League, and revivalistic crusades, but these efforts drew support and new converts primarily from the middle and upper classes. Some work, however, was oriented specifically toward the unchurched masses. Between 1883 and 1890, the Chicago City Missionary Society organized twenty-four churches with approximately 1,550 members and established twenty-seven Sunday schools, with roughly 7,650 people attending regularly.[20]

Nonsectarian groups, such as the Young Men's Christian Association (YMCA), Young Women's Christian Association (YWCA), and Salvation Army, made a concerted effort to reach the lower strata of society. The YMCA began its work in Chicago in 1858, and by 1873 it had around 1,000 members. Supported by some of Chicago's most affluent citizens, it maintained branches throughout the city and regularly sponsored religious, cultural, educational, and recreational activities for both middle- and working-class young men. The YWCA began its work in the city in 1876 and tried to create a secure and wholesome atmosphere for young working women by helping them find suitable jobs, decent lodging, a place to worship, and various other forms of assistance. The Salvation Army arrived in Chicago in 1885 and soon established its martial ministry among the city's down and out.[21]

Groups such as the YMCA, YWCA, and Salvation Army generally couched their efforts in traditional terms, focusing on the individual rather than the socioeconomic or cultural context within which impoverished and bewildered people struggled against adversity. Another less institutional and more local expression of this essentially conservative impulse to assist the city's masses was the Urban Rescue Mission. The men and women who worked in these facilities sought to meet people at the point of their need. Operating out of storefronts, they offered a variety of services, ranging from a simple cup of coffee to a hot meal, clothing, or temporary lodging. Religious services, however, were always an integral part of their work, for they believed ministering to the soul to be ultimately more important than caring for the body.

Typical of these facilities was the Pacific Garden Mission, one of the oldest rescue missions in the Midwest. Colonel George R. Clarke, a successful businessman and born-again Christian, and his wife, Sarah, established Pacific Garden in 1877. It was housed in what had once been a beer garden on Van Buren Street, known by the respectable as "bums Boulevard." Workers in this nonsectarian mission ministered to the denizens of one of Chicago's seamiest neighborhoods. They sponsored a Sunday school and operated a kindergarten for the children of the disinherited, but their primary goal was to bring the gospel to the destitute.[22]

Among those whose life the mission touched was Billy Sunday. Although the date of his conversion at Pacific Garden is a matter of some dispute, according to one of the evangelist's most familiar stories it occurred in 1886. Following an afternoon of drinking on a summer Sunday, he and several other baseball players emerged from a saloon and sat down at the edge of a vacant lot on the corner of State and Van Buren Streets. As he and his teammates

Pacific Garden Mission, Chicago, Illinois, in the 1890s.

Billy Sunday Archives, Grace College and Theological Seminary, Winona Lake, Indiana.

lounged on the curb, the sounds of music from a "Gospel wagon" parked on the street attracted Billy's attention. Men and women, accompanied by a ragtag brass ensemble, were singing traditional religious songs that reminded him of mother and home. Moved to tears by the music of the little band from the Pacific Garden Mission, Sunday accepted a general invitation from Harry Monroe, former gambler and passer of counterfeit money and now dedicated Christian worker, to come to the mission that evening to hear stories of wretched lives transformed by Jesus Christ.[23]

Precisely what circumstances brought Billy Sunday to this point of transformation in his life is unknown, but several factors may have played a part. The season of 1886 was not an especially auspicious one for his career. In his fourth year in professional baseball, he remained a second-stringer, appearing in only 28 games and batting less than .250. These statistics may have been symptomatic of a player whose performance on the diamond was impeded by personal problems; more likely, they resulted from the fact that the White Stockings roster was so laden with talent that there was only limited need for Sunday's services as a utility outfielder.

In either case, Sunday must at times have pondered with considerable anxiety his future in the game that had brought him a measure of success and self-confidence. Would he be traded from the team and the city where he had found acceptance? How much longer would he be able to play ball? What would he do, where would he go, once his playing days were over? His grandfather had died in 1882, and his mother and her husband were struggling to survive in western Kansas, where George Stowell served as postmaster in Syracuse and Jennie tended a hardscrabble farm near Horace. Although he maintained some ties to the state, Iowa no longer afforded any significant semblance of home. At the same time, although Chicago had its attractions as long as he was a professional athlete, it promised no long-term financial or emotional security. Always prone to bouts of depression and self-doubt, he now must have felt keenly his rootlessness and alienation.[24]

Sunday also seems to have been plagued at times by a profound sense of moral deficiency. In 1887, he wrote to Helen Thompson, soon to be his fiancée, "Nell if I could lift the Mantle that God has spread over my sins and allow you to look you would see sins that would almost put Satan to shame."[25] Granted, he was now writing from a post-conversion perspective that may have intensified his sense of former sinfulness, but this passage probably illuminates his general feeling of inadequacy during these years. There is no evidence that he had lived an especially dissolute life prior to 1886, although as a youth his temper and restlessness had sometimes resulted in errors in judgment.

As a young man, Sunday had made his share of mistakes. His need for companionship and acceptance undoubtedly led him at times to join in the revelries of friends or his White Stockings teammates, but he was hardly a reprobate. Yet something troubled him deeply. Perhaps, as he matured, he experienced some residual guilt from childhood over ways in which he believed himself to have failed his mother and family. Perhaps his fatherlessness left such an enormous emotional emptiness at the core of his being that he ultimately turned in desperation to religion to fill it. Whatever its source, he seems to have felt a void in his life and a conviction that he had fallen far short of the standard of righteous conduct inculcated in him as a child back in Iowa.

All that we can know with certainty is that on a summer evening in the mid 1880s, a depressed and anxious Billy Sunday felt drawn to the worship service at the Pacific Garden Mission. As he listened to the simple message of forgiveness and hope preached by Harry Monroe and sang the songs he remembered from his youth, he struggled to cope with the flood of memories and emotions that swept over him. He longed for the forgiveness and uncon-ditional love promised by Monroe to those who would commit their lives to Christ. However, his conversion was not immediate. Perhaps he had difficulty reconciling his own painful experiences and those of others he had known with the notion of a just and loving God. Without question, he was hesitant in part because of self-consciousness and uncertainty about the way in which his less-than-pious teammates might react to the reorientation of his life. Only after a number of visits to the mission did he yield to the preaching of Monroe and the compassionate ministrations of Sarah ("Mother") Clarke and accept their gospel of salvation.[26]

After his conversion, Sunday began attending worship services at the Jefferson Park Presbyterian Church in a respectable middle-class part of Chicago's west side. It was near the neighborhood where most of the White Stockings rented rooms and within walking distance of the club's home field. Jefferson Park offered Sunday a place to worship and associate with like-minded young Christians and an opportunity to escape what he now regarded as his teammates' unwholesome leisure-time activities. At a social gathering at the church one evening in 1886, a friend introduced him to Helen Amelia Thompson, an attractive 18-year-old who was active in the youth work of the church. She was the daughter of William Thompson, owner of one of Chicago's pioneer dairy-products businesses.

Sunday was instantly smitten, but Helen, or "Nell," as she was known to her friends, was not initially attracted to him. She was already dating another young man and attempted to deflect Billy's interest by introducing him to a friend. She tried to nurture the relationship by inviting the couple to join her and her date for Sunday-night suppers at the Thompson home, after which the four of them adjourned to the Christian Endeavor meetings at the Presby-terian Church. One Sunday evening, when neither of their companions was able to attend Christian Endeavor, Billy took advantage of an apparent rift between Nell and her beau and escorted her home from church. Such walks home became routine and were the genesis of a romance that eventually culminated in engagement and marriage.[27]

At first, their relationship was handicapped by parental opposition and by Sunday's sense of inferiority. Nell's mother quickly grew to like Billy, but her

Helen Thompson Sunday as a young woman.

Billy Sunday Archives, Grace College and Theological Seminary,
Winona Lake, Indiana.

father frowned on the couple's courtship. He undoubtedly considered Sunday, who still bore much evidence of his rural Iowa heritage, to be beneath his middle-class, urban daughter. His misgivings were compounded by the unsavory reputation of professional baseball players. Billy recalled, "When her father learned we were engaged, he 'shelled the woods,' declaring no daughter of his should ever marry a ball player."[28] He was so hostile to the relationship that the couple had to correspond covertly and meet in secret for the first several months of their courtship.

To some degree, Sunday understood Mr. Thompson's reservations. The Thompsons were solidly middle class and were respected members of their church and community. Though he was attracted to Nell, Sunday sometimes felt unworthy of her. He was sensitive about his impoverished background, his ungrammatical speech, and his lack of polish. He wrote to her in November 1887, "Nell why is it that you [*sic*] Father don't like me. I don't blame him much. I am not worthy to have any one like me." Yet, Sunday's interest in Helen was stronger than his self-doubt, and he was determined that she would become his wife. Eventually, the persistence of both Nell and her mother, coupled with Billy's obvious sincerity and decency, transformed Thompson's misgivings first into acceptance and then enthusiastic support.[29]

Sunday benefited much from his association with the Thompsons. They were, by comparison with Billy, educated and refined and possessed the middle-class respectability to which he aspired. He also found in Nell and her family a psychological anchor that gave him the sense of emotional security he had lacked throughout much of his life. In the spring of 1887, while the couple's relationship was still in the friendship stage, he lamented to Nell,

> Well honest Nell I really do feel sad. I can't help from crying just thinking about home and my dear Mother since I was almost as young as Willie (Nell's younger brother) I have been among Strangers and with no home since Grandpa died and honest Nell my heart is almost broke.

Billy, whose own family life had been marred by separation and instability and which had now virtually disintegrated, longed to become a part of the warmth and happiness he found within the Thompson family circle. Nell, her mother, and her siblings quickly became a surrogate family for him. As early as late 1886, only a few months after meeting his future wife and well before their engagement, he was writing to her mother as "mama" and referring to her household as "home."[30]

In addition to providing a measure of acceptance and security, the Thompsons' involvement in the activities of the Jefferson Park Presbyterian Church undoubtedly strengthened Sunday's interest in and commitment to it. He attended services regularly, apparently sometimes sang in the choir, and became rather active in the young people's programs. Such personal and community ties were important to him because they ameliorated his loneliness and nurtured his new and fragile commitment to Christianity.

In November 1886, while spending the off season in Iowa, Sunday wrote to Helen, "Well Nell, you don't know how much I miss you and your mama and the meetings." Without the support system he had known in Chicago, he clearly struggled to conduct himself in a way consistent with his understanding of a Christian life. Living in Iowa among old friends and acquaintances was difficult because they expected him to behave as he always had, and he no longer found his pre-conversion lifestyle satisfying. Furthermore, his winter job as a locomotive fireman brought him into daily contact with men who he believed "ridiculed religion" and for whom "profane language" was the norm, an environment not especially conducive to piety. He confided to Nell, whom he considered his moral superior, "I am not as good as I should be, it is so much harder for me to be good out here than it is there." Likewise, he confessed to her mother,

I am not as good as I was when I bid you all good bye. The influence here is much different. No one here who talks to me as you used to but I shall try and come back as good if not better than I was.

He concluded the letter with words that suggest the degree to which bonds of affection and religious beliefs had intermingled to create a balm that would begin to heal some of the deep emotional wounds in his life. "I miss you all and do Pray we may all be with Jesus some time. Then we will not have to leave each other."[31]

At the center of the web of relationships that began developing in Sunday's life in the fall of 1886 was Helen Thompson herself. Intelligent, strong-willed, practical, and stable, her personality complemented perfectly his rather insecure and mercurial disposition; no other person would be as important in his life. Billy and Nell were married at the Thompson family home in Chicago on September 5, 1888, and they remained together for nearly half a century. Over the years "Ma," as he called his wife, would play the role of surrogate mother as much as that of lover and companion. She coached her husband in the manners of the middle class, managed his business affairs, shielded him from many of the stresses of everyday life, and brought order, security, and a measure of tranquility to his world. Initially, however, that tranquility was disturbed by the challenge of protracted separation.

The years during which Sunday played in Chicago coincided with those in which the White Stockings were baseball's premier team. With an abundance of extraordinary players, led by Anson and Mike Kelly, there was little opportunity for him to be more than a popular and valued second-string player. In 1888, the Pittsburgh Alleghenies sought to acquire him from Chicago.[32] Sunday later contended that Spalding and Anson left to him the decision of whether to go to Pittsburgh. While it would have been unusual to give a utility outfielder complete control over a personnel move, Chicago's management in this instance may have allowed Sunday at least some role in determining his future. His speed and fielding ability were of value to the White Stockings, especially after Spalding sold several star players following the 1886 season, yet Billy was more than a capable second-stringer. He was an asset in two other important respects. He appears to have been generally loyal to the club's ownership, always playing to the best of his ability and never causing trouble. He also represented, especially after his religious conversion, the epitome of the image of the wholesome American ball player that Spalding wished to propagate.

As we have seen, National League club owners were especially concerned with the deportment of players. They were motivated in part by a determination to maintain discipline among often spirited and sometimes insubordinate employees, whose dissipation might undermine productivity and profits. Penalizing players for drunkenness, gambling, and unruly behavior was undoubtedly warranted on occasion. The saloon and its corollary vices were genuine social problems in late-nineteenth-century urban America, and baseball players were often among the clientele of the barroom.

Copyright by *Goodwin & Co., N. Y.*
BILLY SUNDAY IN NATIONAL LEAGUE UNIFORM.

Billy Sunday as a Pittsburgh Alleghenies team
member in the late 1880s.

Farwell T. Brown Photographic Archive,
Ames Public Library, Ames, Iowa.

Ironically, the players' rather unsavory reputation was sometimes useful to team owners. By questioning their rectitude and undermining popular sympathy for them, management denied them an important source of leverage in salary negotiations and strengthened the owners' control over their employees. In other words, just as late-nineteenth-century capitalists tarred organized labor with the brush of radicalism, baseball club owners, seeking public sympathy for their increasingly stringent labor policies, tarred players with the brush of moral laxity.[33]

While the attention paid to player conduct was in part a product of the effort to establish tighter control over personnel, there is no reason to doubt that establishing an aura of propriety about the game was an important consideration as well. The ownership and management of the Chicago White Stockings were in the forefront of efforts to improve the popular perception of professional baseball. While some teams cut costs by securing the cheapest possible railway fares and hotel accommodations, Spalding always provided sufficient funds for his players to ride in Pullman cars and stay in respectable hotels when on the road. His players wore attractive, clean uniforms and were expected to be well-groomed when they appeared for games.

For reasons of productivity, discipline, and image, Spalding kept a watchful eye on his players off the field. In the mid-1880s, he ordered Anson to administer a "bone-dry" oath to players in an effort to stem the abuse of alcohol. Concerned with many team members' penchant for vice, he hired a detective agency to shadow them at home and on the road and urged other team owners to do likewise. When in 1886 this surveillance revealed that seven of the famed White Stockings had violated club strictures against carousing, the embarrassed players, anticipating management's wrath, suggested that they each be fined $25, which would cover the cost of the detective agency's $175 retainer. Even Anson, an aggressive competitor with a booming voice, occasionally found himself in trouble with his boss, usually for some vociferous confrontation with an umpire or a player from an opposing team.[34]

Spalding sometimes chose to rid himself of difficult players, even good ones, if they seemed incorrigible. In 1887, for example, he sold Mike Kelly, a gifted athlete with a flair for the theatrical, to Boston for $10,000. Chicago fans thrilled to Kelly's daring style of play and he became the subject of a popular song of the day, "Slide, Kelly, Slide!" The public may well have also gotten vicarious pleasure from the stories of his escapades off the field, but the Irish wonder's bouts of dissipation with liquor and gambling were not consistent with club discipline or middle-class mores. That fact probably contributed to the team owner's decision to sell Kelly's contract. Billy Sunday, on the other hand, with his clean-cut lifestyle, open commitment to Christianity, and talks to church and YMCA groups in various major-league cities, conformed perfectly to the aura of professionalism and propriety that Spalding wished to cultivate. He was, therefore, of considerable value despite his deficiencies at the plate.[35]

Regardless of whether or not Sunday had a voice in the decision to sell or trade him, he found himself playing for the Alleghenies in 1888. With the exception of the protracted and deeply depressing separations from Nell, the move to Pittsburgh proved fortuitous. There he was a popular starter. No sooner had he joined the club than the *Pittsburg Press* was commenting upon the fact that his batting and base-running had strengthened the Alleghenies, while his work in center field was "all that the most fastidious could desire." Over the next three seasons, though not an outstanding player, Billy proved a reliable and productive member of a rather undistinguished team. This was good for both his ego and his bank account. In 1888, he played in 120 of Pittsburgh's 134 games, getting 119 hits and stealing seventy-one bases. His batting average, however, remained low at .236. In 1889, he played in eighty-one games, got seventy-seven hits, stole forty-seven bases, and batted an average of .240. In 1890, Sunday had one of his best years in the major leagues, playing eighty-six games and batting .257, before Pittsburgh traded him to Philadelphia late in the season, where he appeared in thirty-one more games and batted .261. That season was also one of Billy's best on the base paths. He stole eighty-four bases and was sufficiently well-known as a base stealer to be interviewed for a baseball manual published that year.[36]

While not the most talented player on the team, Sunday quickly became one of the most respected and popular. Local newspapers gave as much attention to his character and activities off the field as to his work on the diamond. Early in the season of 1888, the *Pittsburg Press* reported that Billy and his former White Stockings teammate, Abner Dalrymple, shared a room on a quiet street in Allegheny city and that their presence in the neighborhood was likely to alter the public's perception of professional baseball players, for according to the paper, "two quieter or more gentlemanly men in any line of business it would be hard to find."[37]

Journalists frequently commented upon and complimented Sunday for his devotion to Christianity. Shortly after his arrival in Pittsburgh, *The Press* reprinted an article from the *Chicago Interocean* that not only extolled his virtues as a ballplayer but also made much of his character.

> Chicago sends to Pittsburg[h] one of its best and most exemplary ball players, a young man of irreproachable habits and morals, by name William Sunday, who used to chase after sky-scrapping [sic] flies and daisy-destroying grounders for the White Stocking team and never utter a "cuss word" when the ball slipped through his fingers; who under no circumstances dallied with red liquor nor looked upon beer except with abhorrence; who knew not the taste of "the weed" in any form whatever; who played good ball on week days and attended church and Bible class on the Sabbath; who ran bases with such race-horse speed that a two-bagger usually landed him on third.[38]

Billy apparently made a similar impression on the people of Pittsburgh. A couple of weeks after its reprint of the *Interocean* article, *The Press* reported that

> Billy Sunday's consistent walk in the straight and narrow path which leads to life everlasting has already won him a host of friends among the church-going people of the North Side. The roughest ball player on the diamond respects his scruples and will stifle an oath in his presence. If caught, unwittingly, they have been known to apologize in a shamefaced manner for their language. He usually acts as a peacemaker in factional contests, but when the war becomes too hot will quietly slip away. It is his unpretensions [sic] manner more than anything else that has won their respect. More like him would be a credit to any club in the country, even if they did not possess his ability.[39]

Sunday's reputation as a professional athlete whose speed on the diamond was equaled by his common sense, piety, and probity was such that he was considered an exemplary role model. There was speculation late in the 1889 season that he might become manager of the Alleghenies. According to at least one newspaper, this prospect gave "general satisfaction all around," because Sunday had "the respect of the entire team and the confidence of the public." He did not become leader of the Alleghenies, but he was held in such esteem that a local baseball team was named for him, and several Pittsburgh city councilmen were reportedly seriously considering naming a newly opened street in his honor. Newspapers gave his religious talks in Pittsburgh and elsewhere around the National League circuit extensive and laudatory coverage. Even before he left the Smoky City, he was already being referred to as "the Allegheny club base ball evangelist."[40]

In August of 1890, the Alleghenies traded Sunday to Philadelphia. At the end of the season, his new employer offered Billy a contract for what he claimed was the highest salary he had ever been offered. Many years after the fact he recalled that Philadelphia was willing to pay him almost $400 a month for his services over a seven-month season. The Sunday family papers contain an unsigned copy of a contract for 1891 offering only $2,200, which suggests that the aging evangelist's memory may have been somewhat inaccurate. Nevertheless, there is no question that for little more than half a year's work Billy would have earned an income several times higher than the wage of the average laborer for an entire year.[41] As attractive as the offer was, he had serious misgivings about signing the contract.

After becoming a Christian, Sunday joined a Bible study class at the Chicago YMCA. Soon he began serving as a volunteer in the "Y's" evangelistic program. In the late nineteenth century, the Association was very evangelical. A well-known athlete who was also a Christian was an almost perfect apostle to the young men the "Y" sought to reach. Consequently, first in Chicago and then in other cities around the major-league circuit, Sunday spent a good deal of his spare time speaking to church and YMCA groups. Although hardly eloquent in those early years, his obvious sincerity and commitment to the gospel he preached, and his own testimony of how it had changed his life, made him a popular and persuasive speaker.[42]

Sunday's volunteer work with the YMCA set the stage for his subsequent religious endeavors. As early as August 1887, he had begun to consider leaving major league baseball for Christian work.[43] This idea was no doubt in part a result of his maturing faith but also in part related to his growing commitment to Helen Thompson. Evangelical Christianity had provided him with a sense of meaning and purpose in his life and had, at least partially, helped to fill the long-standing void in his psyche. Furthermore, after their marriage, he found the separations from his wife increasingly onerous. Religious work was consistent both with the sense of fulfillment he found in his faith and his desire for a more stable family life.

When Pittsburgh traded Sunday to Philadelphia, there were newspaper reports suggesting that he might retire from baseball at the end of the season to become an assistant secretary of the YMCA in Chicago. It seems plausible that the possibility of such an arrangement had already been discussed with Billy, but it is not clear whether any offer had actually been tendered. It is certain that he was as yet ambivalent about his plans for the future. *The Philadelphia Inquirer* labeled stories of his impending retirement "fakes pure and simple," and Philadelphia's management clearly executed the trade with the Alleghenies expecting that Sunday would be available to play for the next several years. Colonel John Rogers, president of the Philadelphia club, told *The Inquirer* that Sunday had signed a contract "at a liberal salary" for the remainder of the 1890 season with the right of renewal on Philadelphia's part for the next three years. Indicative of Philadelphia's desire to have Sunday on its team was the fact that Rogers reported that even though it was likely that salaries would drop in the coming season, the club had agreed to continue its new outfielder at the same liberal terms it had offered in his 1890 contract. His remarks made it clear that Sunday had given no indication that he intended to leave baseball. Rogers concluded:

> I do not believe that Mr. Sunday, in view of his high character as a Christian gentleman, could be a party to such a deception. I presume that if it is true that Mr. Sunday is to be secretary of the Young Men's Christian Association in Chicago his duties will be so arranged as not to conflict with his contractural [*sic*] obligations to us.[44]

Given his essential integrity, it is doubtful that Sunday was duplicitous in his negotiations with Philadelphia. Although he was certainly contemplating a career change, he had probably not yet made up his mind whether he would remain in baseball or abandon the game for full-time religious work. Whether a definite offer from the Chicago YMCA was on the table in the late summer of 1890 is not clear, but by the following winter Billy was definitely considering joining the Chicago "Y" as an assistant secretary. The decision was an extremely difficult one because economic and emotional forces pulled him in different directions. The $1,000 salary offered him by the "Y" was less than half that promised by Philadelphia. He now had not only to support his wife but also an infant daughter, Helen, born in 1890. Furthermore, his disabled older brother and mother were apparently also partially dependent upon him. He was, therefore, reluctant to forego the higher salary offered by professional baseball. Being of a practical bent and aware of the financial demands upon her husband, Nell cautioned against forsaking such a lucrative career. She too, however, was deeply religious and understood her husband's commitment to his faith. Convinced that God would reveal His will in their lives, she supported Billy's decision in the late winter of 1891 to ask Philadelphia for his release. The club ownership responded initially with a prompt and unequivocal refusal. Sunday interpreted this response as a sign from God that he was to continue to play professional baseball, and he prepared to do so. In March 1891, however, he received a letter from Colonel Rogers releasing him from his contract. Cincinnati, hearing of Billy's release, made him an attractive offer, but after consultation with family and friends, Sunday concluded that it was God's will that he dedicate himself to religious work.[45]

Professional baseball had been good to Billy Sunday. When Adrian Anson added him to the White Stockings roster, he became a member, albeit a second-string member, of what sports historian Benjamin Rader has described as "one of the most powerful teams in big league history." To be sure, he was a batter of only modest ability, but he was an exciting though erratic outfielder, an exceptional base runner, and a member of an elite group. He enjoyed an excellent rapport with players, fans, and management alike. He had gratifying relationships with Anson and Spalding, who trusted him to attend to the club's financial interests on the road. Even though Billy had been traded to Pittsburgh, Spalding and the White Stockings honored him and his new bride with special recognition at a home game in Chicago following their marriage in September 1888, a fact that is indicative of his widespread popularity.[46]

While the Pittsburgh and Philadelphia clubs lacked the prestige of Chicago, Sunday usually found himself in the starting lineups there. That fact, coupled with Philadelphia's offer in 1890 of a very lucrative contract, suggests that these teams' ownership recognized and valued his talent.

The world of professional sports in urban, industrial America was far removed from the prairie villages and country towns of Sunday's youth. The farm boy from Iowa had traveled a great distance both geographically and culturally since that spring day in 1883 when he boarded a train in Marshalltown for Chicago. In those eight years, he had become a competent and well-known member of the nation's most popular sports elite. Covered by reporters, admired by fans, well paid by the standards of the day, he was in many respects a success.

Steven Riess has found that, contrary to popular mythology, professional baseball did not guarantee the majority of lower-class players opportunities for a more rewarding life after leaving the game.[47] For Billy Sunday, however, baseball was an avenue toward upward social mobility. The game had given him a measure of self-confidence he had not known before. It had acquainted him with a side of American life very different from that of his boyhood experience and had indirectly created the circumstances that led to his religious conversion and his marriage. Through his acquaintance with Spalding and the Thompson family, it exposed him to an urban, middle-class style of life that he found appealing and to which he aspired. Finally, baseball gave him a credibility with all sorts of people, which would greatly facilitate his religious work.

Yet there remained within Sunday a feeling of emptiness, a longing, an uncertainty that success in professional sports had failed to allay. It was this deep-seated void that the apostles of the Pacific Garden Mission began to fill. The preaching of Harry Monroe and the tender warmth of "Mother" Clarke offered a simple and appealing message of God's unconditional love and acceptance of the repentant sinner. For one who had never known the affection of his biological father, whose stepfathers had taken little interest in him, whose mother had left much of his early care to his grandparents and placed him in an orphanage when he was 11 years old, and whose life thereafter had been largely a matter of fending for himself, such a gospel addressed the deepest anxieties of one profoundly lacking in both security and a sense of acceptance.

After 1886, the baseball diamond and the rescue mission constituted two complementary points of orientation in Sunday's life and work. The evangelical worldview rooted in his Iowa heritage, reaffirmed by the Pacific Garden Mission and nurtured by his membership in the Jefferson Park Presbyterian Church, marriage to Helen Thompson, and association with the YMCA, furnished the moral and theological basis of his revivalism. His career in baseball contributed to the rapport with audiences, the athletic quality of delivery, and the familiar sports imagery that gave to his evangelism its unique character.

THREE

Entrepreneurial Evangelism

When he joined the staff of the Chicago Young Men's Christian Association in the spring of 1891, Billy Sunday felt certain that he was answering the call of God to dedicate himself to a career in Christian service. Yet there were moments during the first few years after his departure from professional sports when his confidence in that calling faltered. His occasional doubts appear to have had little to do with either his dedication or his effectiveness. Though inexperienced and untrained, evidence suggests that he was good at his job. L. W. Messer, secretary of the Chicago "Y," recalled that the Association never had a man on its staff "who was more consecrated, more deeply spiritual, more self-sacrificing." He reported that Billy was "especially strong in his personal effort among men who were strongly tempted and among those who had fallen by the way."[1]

Sunday's occasional misgivings about his work stemmed not from a lack of skill or commitment but from an excess of stress. He found many of his activities with the YMCA emotionally taxing and lacking in the physical or psychological release that came from sprinting after fly balls or sliding for second base. The assistant secretary labored 14-hour days, six days a week. He roamed the dingy bar- and brothel-lined streets of Chicago's seamier neighborhoods, distributed tracts in saloons, spoke on street corners, conducted prayer meetings, prayed with and ministered to the needs of the down and out, and secured speakers for local YMCA programs.[2]

When he was not on the streets, a good deal of Sunday's time was consumed with sedentary and tedious office work, the very antithesis of his physically active routine as a ballplayer. The restless and energetic former athlete found the depressing surroundings and dramatic alteration of lifestyle so stressful that he nearly broke under the strain. In search of a rehabilitating change of pace, he temporarily left his position and worked for a short time at the YMCA camp at Lake Geneva, Wisconsin.

Some "Y" leaders, recognizing the value of his reputation as a clean-living professional baseball player and his talents as an athlete, encouraged Billy to devote himself exclusively to the increasingly popular physical culture program of the YMCA. As tempting as this must have been, Sunday felt drawn to the more overtly evangelical dimensions of Christian service. He knew what the gospel espoused by apostles to the desperate and disinherited had meant in his own life, and he was soon back in the office and on the streets of Chicago.[3]

The financial rewards of his new job were modest by comparison with Sunday's former income. He would have earned well in excess of $2,000 with the Philadelphia ball club during the season of 1891. His initial salary with the YMCA was $1,000 a year, and he never earned more than $1,500. The decline in donations to the "Y" resulting from the depression of 1893 meant that his monthly checks were often in arrears. Years later he recalled with considerable pride that to cut expenses he walked to and from work, went without lunch, had his clothes made over and dyed to look new, and wore a celluloid collar to avoid laundry costs. Such sacrifices not withstanding, he claimed to have turned down an offer from Pittsburgh in 1892 to come out of retirement and play for three months for $2,000.[4] At the height of his success, when critics attacked him for his substantial income, tailored clothes, stylish cars, and expensive lifestyle, he pointedly reminded them of the hardships he had experienced more than twenty years earlier when he gave up the rewards of baseball for the sake of the cross.

During his third year with the Chicago YMCA, Sunday's career took a decidedly different turn. The well-known Presbyterian evangelist J. Wilbur Chapman was looking for an advance man and assistant who would do such things as organize pre-revival committees, put up tents, sell books at his meetings, and speak to overflow crowds. Peter Bilhorn, a gospel singer who sometimes worked with Chapman, told him about Sunday. During a visit to Chicago in 1893, the revivalist talked with the YMCA assistant secretary about joining his evangelistic team. Satisfied that Billy was a capable and dependable young man, he offered him the job. At the time, Chapman, an Indiana native, was preaching mostly in the towns and cities of the Middle West. Sunday found the chance to work with this rather refined and educated evangelist an appealing prospect for two reasons. The position afforded an opportunity to become affiliated with a man widely respected in regional religious circles, and it offered an escape from the seamy streets, office routine, and financial uncertainties that were integral parts of his "Y" work in Chicago. He accepted the job and found himself on the road once again.[5]

The two men worked together for more than two years. During that time, Sunday learned much about the construction and delivery of sermons, the organization and administration of revivals, and the most effective means of working with local pastors. This rewarding relationship came to a sudden end during the Christmas holidays of 1895, when Chapman sent his protégé an unexpected telegram. He informed Sunday that he had decided to abandon evangelism for the parish ministry and had accepted the pastorate of the Bethany Presbyterian Church in Philadelphia.[6]

The Sundays were stunned. Chapman's decision left Billy without employment and uncertain about his future in religious work. He prayed for guidance regarding what he should do and even toyed with the idea of returning to baseball. Then he received a telegram from Garner, a small farming community of roughly 1,000 people in north-central Iowa, inviting him to conduct a revival there in early 1896. This invitation, proffered at Chapman's suggestion, and the events of subsequent weeks convinced the Sundays that God had ordained Billy's religious vocation after all.

Before the completion of his meeting in Garner, Sunday received a letter inviting him to conduct services in Sigourney, another small town in the southeastern part of the Hawkeye State, and before that revival was over there came yet another invitation. Ultimately, the neophyte evangelist visited five small midwestern communities before returning to Chicago.[7] Though launched in modest surroundings, this series of revivals began an extraordinarily successful evangelistic career that lasted until his death in 1935.

Throughout much of the first decade of his ministry, Sunday toured what he dubbed the "kerosene circuit," preaching in churches, opera houses, tents, and the occasional tabernacle, in dusty or mud-spattered small midwestern towns of no more than a few thousand people, where electric lighting was as yet merely a dream and the most effective illumination was the pallid glow of the kerosene lamp. Those early years were difficult. Traversing the prairies in rickety coaches, lurching behind lumbering smoke-belching steam locomotives, was a slow, dirty, uncomfortable, and exhausting means of travel. Accommodations in private residences or small-town hostelries were often modest at best. The erection and maintenance of revival tents that were vulnerable to rain, snow, and wind was a problem and often required Sunday to spend sleepless nights in his canvas tabernacles to forestall disaster. Financial

The Opera House in Garner, Iowa, the site of Billy Sunday's first revival in 1896.

Billy Sunday Archives, Grace College and Theological Seminary, Winona Lake, Indiana.

contributions for the support of meetings were sometimes frustratingly meager. Protracted separations from Nell and his children left Sunday lonely and
depressed. Nevertheless, the evangelist persisted, buoyed by the conviction
that he was doing the Lord's work and by the increasingly receptive crowds
that flocked to his services.

By the turn of the century, Billy Sunday had lived in Chicago for almost
half his life. He may well have felt a touch of good-natured urban condescension toward the rustic quality of life in some of the towns in which he
preached, but he had not forgotten his Iowa origins or lost his ability to relate
to small-town folk. An observer in Humboldt, a community in the evangelist's
native state, captured something of the revivalist's congenial demeanor in
those early years when he wrote,

> Mr. Sunday is a hearty, healthy and happy Christian. He laughs and chats
> and enjoys the beauties of nature just as any other mortal. . . . When he
> preaches he preaches with all his might, and he preaches plainly.
>
> His manner is magnetic, and his smile so winsome that the heart of a
> misanthrope would go out toward him. When he reaches out to shake
> hands, and gives that firm, hearty grip, it is time to surrender. Talk with him
> five minutes, and you will feel that he is an old friend.

Such accounts make it quite clear that Billy's early success did not stem from
the careful orchestration of his meetings or the theatrical style of preaching
for which he would later become famous. Rather, it resulted from his ability
to empathize with the hopes and fears of the people, his earnestness in the
pulpit, and his talent for walking the town square, talking farming with
farmers and business with businessmen. Inspired and talented though he may
have been, he was one of them. He worked alongside local residents as they
erected a tent or constructed a tabernacle for his meeting, and when the job
was done he put on his old White Stockings uniform and took the field with
men and boys who had only dreamed of the National League.[8]

The Presbyterian Church licensed Sunday as an evangelist in 1898 but did
not ordain him as a clergyman until 1903. The absence of this ecclesiastical
status symbol seems, however, to have had no significant impact upon his
burgeoning career. Ministers and laity in town after town invited the young
preacher into their communities. During the first decade of his ministry, more
than half of Sunday's roughly 100 revivals took place in his native Iowa, while
the remainder, with one or two exceptions, occurred in other midwestern
states. The majority of these meetings were in towns of less than 2,500 people.
Sunday's infrequent early forays into larger cities, such as Lincoln, Nebraska,
or Elgin, Illinois, were generally unsuccessful. Gradually, however, as his
confidence grew, as he perfected his evangelistic technique, as he developed
the increasingly businesslike methods that characterized his later crusades,
and as his reputation spread, he began receiving invitations to preach in ever-
larger towns and cities across the Midwest and nation. In 1907, the average
population of cities in which he preached was around 10,000, while the

following year the mean rose to roughly 20,000. A 1909 revival in Spokane, Washington, his first in a city of more than 100,000, marked the beginning of a new and more dramatic era in his evangelism. During the 1910s, he preached to millions in most of the nation's largest cities, reaching the zenith of his popularity with a 10-week crusade in New York City in the spring of 1917.[9]

Sunday's campaign in New York provided the evangelist with a vista from which he could observe the course of his life over the previous fifty-four years. The vantage point from the nation's premier city offered the most satisfying panorama of his past that he was ever to have, for what Billy saw was success, and he was unabashedly proud of his accomplishments. He reminded his audiences of what most of them already knew. It had been a long way from a 2-room log cabin on the Iowa prairie to a 20,000-seat tabernacle on Broadway.[10]

The distance had indeed been great and the journey had been long and sometimes difficult. Billy had not swept like a meteor out of the West. He had not suddenly and brilliantly illuminated the nation's religious landscape with an innovative message couched in spellbinding oratory. By the time he achieved the status of national sensation during the teens, he was more than fifty years old and had been preaching for close to two decades. How, then, had the evangelist finally reached the pinnacle of his profession? According to his own understanding and that of millions of his admirers, he had done so by working hard, living cleanly, and making the most of his God-given talents. Along the way he had risen, if not from rags to riches, at least from poverty to prosperity, from obscurity to renown.

Sunday's contemporaries admired nothing so much as the man who reached the top, especially if he seemingly overcame daunting odds to do it. While they might be ambivalent about or even hostile to big business, late-nineteenth- and early-twentieth-century Americans were nevertheless intrigued by the success of the entrepreneurs who were the architects of the new economic order. Sunday, of course, was not a businessman in the usual sense of that term, yet a part of his appeal stemmed from the fact that there was much about his life and evangelism that was congruent with the materialistic, success-oriented ethos of the day.

In the absence of an established church, the various expressions of Christianity in America have, to some degree, been forced to compete in the cultural marketplace both against one another and against a variety of secular forces. From the Great Awakening to the present, revivalism has been one of the most visible, most controversial, and, some would argue, most effective agencies by means of which evangelical Christians have sought to sell their faith and their vision of American society. In the nineteenth and twentieth centuries, there was an increasing tendency to measure evangelism's success in the same quantifiable and material terms that have been applied to business. Nowhere was that tendency more apparent than in the ministry of Billy Sunday.

Devotees and critics alike saw the charismatic preacher as a kind of religious entrepreneur who approached his work with the same competitive zeal;

who employed the same principles of efficiency, marketing, and economies of scale; and who measured his success in the same quantitative terms as an Andrew Carnegie or John D. Rockefeller. This popular perception of the evangelist is accurate but somewhat surprising given his initial experiences in baseball and religious work.

As a player for the White Stockings, Sunday had sometimes acted as a kind of de facto business manager for the team on road trips, and he was evidently conscientious and reliable in the exercise of his responsibilities. Yet he appears to have had little interest in or affinity for the routine tasks of business. Furthermore, in the beginning, there was nothing in his evangelism to suggest that he would someday become the most successful revivalist of his day. His early campaigns in the farming towns of Iowa and the Midwest were small-scale affairs, conducted in traditional fashion in cooperation with local clergy. His style was simple and direct, borrowing heavily at first from what he had learned from Chapman. He traveled alone, made few if any demands, paid his own expenses, and received in payment whatever an appreciative citizenry felt moved to contribute on the last day of the meeting.[11]

After the turn of the century, as his reputation grew and the demand for his services increased, the tenor and structure of Sunday's ministry began to evolve. He became more interested in the statistical measures of his revivalism. He longed for ever-larger crowds, more public affirmations of faith, more laudatory press, and more contributions for the support of his work. Some of this emphasis on the quantifiable was a matter of ego, some a product of his need to stifle self-doubt, but much of it was a reflection of his recognition that success breeds success. If he was to broaden his appeal and continue his work, he had to demonstrate that he could produce, and productivity in evangelism, like that in manufacturing, was measured in terms of volume and cost.

One of the first tangible signs of growth and change in Sunday's ministry came shortly before the turn of the century. Billy spent the early years of his career preaching in local churches, opera houses, and tents that were often too small or (in the case of tents) problematic. In 1898, he conducted his first revival in a wooden tabernacle constructed especially for his meeting in Perry, Iowa. Other evangelists, such as Dwight L. Moody and Sam Jones, had sometimes housed their revivals in tabernacles, but no one had ever made such extensive use of these structures as would Sunday. They not only accommodated the crowds but their construction attested to community commitment and generated interest in the meeting. Within a few years, the graceless but cleverly designed and exceptionally functional turtle-back tabernacle, with its sawdust-strewn floor and barn-like doors, would become the hallmark of Sunday's evangelism.

The revivalist's raw materials are people. Therefore, it was essential for Sunday to develop the techniques that would enable him to attract as many worshipers as possible and to have the maximum effect upon them. Through imitation, trial and error, and receptivity to the advice of friends and associates, he slowly forged a style of evangelism appropriate to his personality and to the times in which he worked.

Worshipers at a Sunday revival service in Carthage, Illinois, 1903.

Billy Sunday Archives, Grace College and Theological Seminary, Winona Lake, Indiana.

Music has traditionally been an integral part of American evangelism and despite the fact that he claimed not to know "a note from a horse fly," no revivalist made more effective use of it than Sunday. In the late 1890s, an associate, French Oliver, sometimes traveled with Billy, helping with the work of the meetings and leading the singing. As he began building his evangelistic team, Sunday hired Fred Fischer in 1900 and Homer ("Rody") Rodeheaver in 1910, each of whom skillfully utilized the musical part of the service to relax and warm up an audience. In the midwestern towns of the "kerosene circuit," Fischer, borrowing techniques from Chicago's Moody Bible Institute, introduced the piano and brass instruments as unconventional accompaniments for hymns and created a spirit of camaraderie among worshipers by encouraging good-natured singing competitions among different groups in the congregation.

Rodeheaver, Sunday's chorister during the heyday of his career, was a handsome, talented musician with a keen sense of crowd psychology. He served as master of ceremonies, played the trombone, did magic tricks for the children, engaged in friendly banter with audiences, conducted massive choirs of as many as 2,000 people, and directed congregational singing. He carefully chose music, ranging from such selections as the quasi-popular "Brighten the Corner" to the martial "Onward Christian Soldiers" to the devotional "Softly and Tenderly Jesus is Calling" or "Just As I Am." Each piece set the tone of a specific part of the worship service. Rody's relaxed, good-humored charm was a useful counterpoint to the rapid-paced intensity of Sunday's sermons, and the chorister was an invaluable asset to the evangelist.[12]

While music was important, no facet of his revivalism contributed as much to Sunday's success as his spectacular style of preaching. In the early days of his ministry he tried to imitate the rather polished and staid preaching of his mentor, J. Wilbur Chapman, but Chapman's style, informed by his education and middle-class heritage, was one with which the novice preacher was not comfortable. By nature, Billy was emotionally intense and gifted with a flair

Billy Sunday's chorister, Homer Rodeheaver.

Postcard in possession of the author.

for the theatrical. It was these inherent qualities that would ultimately give his revivalism much of its unique and appealing character. In time, he developed a style that he described as "[putting] the cookies and jam on the lower shelf." The evangelist delivered his sermons in the everyday speech of the common people, lacing his rhetoric with slang and descriptive language that some considered coarse. He elevated the epigram and the use of invective against evil to the level of an art. He illustrated his points with vivid anecdotes that were by turns humorous, poignant, and sentimental and punctuated his words with an extraordinary display of athleticism that impressed and amused those who came to hear him preach. Once he had perfected the techniques, by means of which he could instruct, entertain, and manipulate an audience's emotions with consummate skill, Billy's sermons were in a very real sense a marketable commodity calculated to attract consumers.

In the world of religion, as in that of business, having a viable product was, however, no guarantee of success. Therefore, like the entrepreneurs of the age, Sunday endeavored to secure his position in the marketplace. In the early years of his ministry, he had made few if any demands on local sponsors of his revivals. As he grew more popular, he began to insist that his campaign be the center of religious activity whenever he was in town. Among the conditions he imposed on those who would have him preach the gospel in their midst were the unanimous support of evangelical ministers, the construction of a strategically located tabernacle under the supervision of his own architect, and pledges of financial support to underwrite the cost of the campaign. To minimize competition and maximize his effectiveness, he asked local churches to suspend any services that would conflict with those scheduled as a part of his meetings. Although this practice was controversial and the source of resentment on the part of some local clergymen, he was generally successful in securing their cooperation. At the zenith of his popularity, he went even farther to assure that his efforts yielded the most favorable results by refusing to hold a crusade in any city in which another major evangelist had recently conducted a revival. Such a policy was undoubtedly motivated in part by his deep-seated fear of failure, but it was also perfectly consistent with his understanding of sound business principles.

By the 1910s, there was no question that Billy Sunday had developed a style of revivalism calculated to appeal to large numbers of Americans. Yet no matter how good the product, success would remain elusive without effective promotion. It is axiomatic that the best advertising is by word of mouth, and the early days of Billy's ministry seem to verify the axiom. Initially, his reputation spread from town to town as satisfied citizens told friends, relatives, and fellow clergy of his work in their midst. Religious conferences and Prohibition conventions also served as conduits for news of his triumphs in city after city.

As his fame grew, Sunday became newsworthy. The local press began devoting an increasing number of column inches to his work. After 1907, national papers discovered Billy. Coverage was at first sporadic but by the teens had become extensive as he rolled out of the Midwest, through one metropolitan center after another. Newspapers in cities where a campaign was underway printed the texts of sermons, reported attendance and contribution figures, described the evangelist's antics, and recounted the impressions of those who attended his meetings. Meanwhile, journalists in areas where Billy was slated to visit in the near future relayed accounts of his work elsewhere, heightening anticipation of his arrival in their locality.

News of the revivalist's success in one community often served as a challenge to the competitive spirit of another. It became a matter of civic pride for the next city on Sunday's schedule to surpass the reception shown him by the previous one. Thorough news coverage was the best advertising Billy could have had. It was both comprehensive and free. The evangelist appreciated this fact and actively courted journalists by providing special press sections in his tabernacles and copies of sermon texts for their benefit. Even when articles were critical, as they sometimes were, they generated interest and swelled the crowds who flocked to see the controversial preacher.

In addition to newspapers, religious and secular periodicals carried stories about Sunday's work. Denominational publications such as the *Lutheran Reporter* and popular magazines such as *Harper's Weekly*, the *Literary Digest*, and the *Metropolitan Magazine* ran articles ranging from the unabashedly laudatory to the hypercritical.[13] This publicity made Billy Sunday one of the best-known men in the United States. It is not surprising, therefore, that when the *American Magazine* conducted a poll in 1914 to determine the nation's most outstanding citizen, Billy ranked eighth, along with Andrew Carnegie and Judge Ben B. Lindsay.

One of the corollaries of Sunday's growing popularity was the evolution of a sophisticated organization to facilitate the revivalist's work. Like many successful businesses of the day, Billy's evolved from the small and simple to the ever larger and more complex.

In 1900, Sunday took the first tentative steps toward assembling an evangelistic team when he hired Fred Fischer as a gospel singer and song leader. Three years later he added an advance man, Rev. I. E. Honeywell, who for a short time did for him the kinds of things he had once done for Chapman. In 1905, Fred Siebert, a graduate of the Moody Bible Institute who was known in the Midwest as the "Cowboy Evangelist," joined Sunday as general factotum and custodian of tents and tabernacles.

Meanwhile, in Chicago, Helen Sunday, who by 1901 had given birth to a daughter and two sons, tried to juggle the responsibilities of motherhood and household management with increased attention to some of the business details of her husband's expanding ministry. Billy loved to preach and to perform but detested the minutiae of revival planning and execution. On the other hand, his wife not only enjoyed but was good at the kinds of administrative and financial tasks her husband loathed. Sunday's reliance upon Nell was not, however, simply a matter of delegating to her the tasks he disliked or for which he had insufficient time. It was also a function of his profound psychological dependence upon her for support in making the routine and major decisions of his life. As Billy's ministry grew and it became more and more difficult for Nell to attend to his needs from afar, Nell encouraged him to hire more staff members and sometimes accompanied him herself. In addition to attending to many details behind the scenes, she conducted Bible classes and prayer meetings, spoke to women's groups, and occasionally even helped to lead the singing.

Finally, after the birth of their fourth and last child in 1907, the couple concluded that it was imperative that Nell devote more of her time and energy to the work. Thereafter, she began traveling more or less regularly with her husband's evangelistic team. She quickly emerged as the chief administrator of the Sunday ministry.[14]

Between 1906 and 1912, the Sunday party expanded steadily. Rev. Elijah Brown assisted with the preparation of sermons and handled a variety of literary tasks for the evangelist. Two dedicated women, Grace Saxe and Frances Miller, hired at the instigation of Helen Sunday, specialized primarily in work among women. They conducted Bible classes and eventually began establishing religious study groups that sometimes survived for years after the revival had ended. Charles Butler joined the staff in 1907 to assist Fischer with the music and was replaced the following year by Charles Pledger. That same year Sunday hired

Billy Sunday and his family
(front row, left to right: Helen, Billy holding Paul, Bill, Nell, George)
with members of Sunday's evangelistic team, Marshalltown, Iowa, May 1909.

Billy Sunday Archives, Grace College and Theological Seminary, Winona Lake, Indiana.

Bentley D. Ackley as his confidential secretary. Later, Ackley assumed Brown's role in the preparation of sermons and acted as public relations manager. The construction of tabernacles involved considerations of cost, efficiency, functionality, and safety. To see that these structures were built according to exact specifications, Sunday hired first A. P. Gill (1908) and later Joseph Spiece (1912) as tabernacle architect. Homer Rodeheaver, the best-known and most talented of Sunday's associates, joined the evangelistic team in 1910, replacing Fischer as chorister. William and Virginia Asher, longtime acquaintances of the Sundays, came on board in 1912. This attractive and able couple were well-suited to the turn toward urban evangelism that Sunday's career was taking. Urbanites themselves, they were comfortable with the vagaries of city life. William Asher acted as an advance man, associate evangelist, and leader of men's Bible-study groups. Virginia, a former Catholic drawn to Protestantism by the preaching of Reuben A. Torrey and Dwight L. Moody, was a talented singer, articulate speaker, and skilled administrator who did much to expand the work among women.

As he moved into larger urban centers and his entourage grew, Sunday began insisting that host cities secure a house for his evangelistic team. The residence served both as a dwelling and as nerve center for the campaign. When members of the staff gathered for meals, they not only dined together but shared information. With the Sundays seated at the head of the table, various associates reported on different facets of the work. Billy, whom his staff always referred to as "Boss," was responsible for the major decisions, but he devoted the bulk of his time and energy to preaching and meeting with civic and religious leaders, public delegations, and representatives of the press. Therefore, Nell often directed much of the day-to-day operation of the organization. Dedicated, hard-working, and pragmatic, she demanded that others be as tirelessly committed to the work as she was. As a result, she commanded the respect, if not always the affection, of the staff.

At times during the peak years of his ministry, Sunday's evangelistic organization numbered more than a score of regular workers, but it generally consisted of nine or ten associates and shrank to around five as the revivalist's popularity declined in the 1920s.[15] After a city was selected and guarantees of financial support arranged, Sunday's highly specialized team of associates carefully orchestrated publicity; pre-revival prayer meetings; the recruitment and training of choirs, ushers, and a tabernacle staff; the establishment of ancillary religious work targeted at specific populations, such as students, businesswomen, or children; and all the other innumerable details of modern urban revivalism. Perhaps their greatest challenge was the mobilization and coordination of the activities of hundreds, or even thousands, of local residents whose efforts would make or break a campaign. In Boston and New York, for example, 35,000 and 50,000 resident workers respectively labored to make the revival a success.

An appealing product, extensive advertising, and a sophisticated organization were as essential to success in evangelism as in commerce and manufacturing. Some observers scorned the commercial quality of Sunday's ministry, but others admired the way in which it reflected the business ethos of the day. William McLoughlin has suggested that Sunday was sometimes more appealing to business-minded laity than to tradition-bound clergy. The former, steeped as they were in the capitalistic values of their era and in the routine challenges of making a living, understood and appreciated his aggressiveness and the skill with which he marketed the gospel. While they might have had misgivings about his theology or his pulpit sensationalism, they were enormously impressed by the solvency of his campaigns and the substantial dividends his revivals appeared to yield in the form of new converts, changed lives, and social stability.

Even in the early years of his ministry, observers in the small towns of Iowa noticed that Billy did not quite fit the stereotypical image of a clergyman. In 1902, the *Audubon Republican* characterized the revivalist as "an up-to-date man," not mired "in no old rut." Another paper reported that the preacher rarely wore the "conventional garb of the pulpit." On the contrary, he was

Billy Sunday as the dapper evangelist.

Postcard in possession of the author.

conspicuous in any group of clergy because of his stylishly tailored clothes that made him look more like "a dapper man of business" than a minister. A journalist in New Hampton reported that Sunday did not look like a preacher but "would more likely be taken for a speculator on the stock exchange, or a prematurely old young business man."[16]

As Sunday became better known outside his native Midwest, observers in other parts of the nation frequently commented favorably upon his business-like style of evangelism. A newspaper in Wilkes-Barre, Pennsylvania, described his message as traditional, his delivery as "racy," and his methods as consistent with "up-to-date business principles."[17]

The commercial aura that surrounded Sunday's evangelism was perhaps enhanced by the fact that as he moved into the nation's major urban centers, members of the country's business elite were often among his most ardent champions. Those whose names were associated with his revivals included John D. Rockefeller, Jr.; John Wanamaker; Albert H. Gary; Henry Clay Frick; Lewis F. Swift; A. J. Drexel-Biddle; J. Ogden Armour; S. S. Kresge; John M. Studebaker; Henry Leland; and H. J. Hunt.[18]

Sunday basked in his reputation as an evangelistic entrepreneur. He enjoyed the company of the rich and powerful, possessing what Homer Rodeheaver called "a curious penchant for what might be termed 'officialdom.'" He had no qualms about drawing upon the expertise and support of the business community to maximize the effectiveness of his revivals. He saw no reason why the techniques responsible for the nation's material progress should not be called into the service of its spiritual growth, and he was critical of the church's failure to do so. The evangelist was convinced that "if you used such methods in business as you do in the work of the church the sheriff's sale flag would soon be hanging outside your door."[19]

Billy was determined that no such fate would befall his ministry. He built upon the evangelistic methods of revivalistic giants such as Charles G. Finney and Dwight L. Moody as well as those of lesser figures such as B. Fay Mills, M. B. Williams, and Reuben A. Torrey. He combined what he had gleaned from their experience with the advice of businessmen to create a sophisticated and efficient organization.

Sophistication and efficiency notwithstanding, urban evangelism was an expensive proposition, even in Sunday's day. The high cost of his campaigns was frequently a source of criticism. Billy, however, considered his revivals models of efficiency and economy. He estimated the per-capita cost of each "trail hitter" (one who answered his altar call) to be only about two dollars. William McLoughlin has suggested that this figure appears to have been relatively accurate if only the expense of a campaign and not the free-will offering, which went directly to Sunday, was included in the calculation. This, Sunday argued, was a far better bargain than that offered by any other evangelist or by local pastors. At least some contemporaries, applying only quantitative measures, concurred in Billy's assessment of his work. One professor of economics ranked the revivalist's operation as one of the five most successful businesses in the country, along with such giants as Standard Oil, United States Steel, and National Cash Register.[20]

Nowhere was Sunday's inclination to portray himself as a businessman in the service of the Lord more apparent than in the New York campaign of 1917. On the day following his first sermon, Billy joined General Leonard Wood and Theodore Roosevelt for lunch at the home of John D. Rockefeller, Jr. After dining with this elite trio, he went to the Marble Collegiate Church for a conference with ministers who were supporting his revival. He introduced his staff and began to explain his strategy for evangelizing the city. Press accounts of this meeting illuminate the way in which Sunday and his team conceived of their work. According to the *Literary Digest*,

> As he presented his staff there gradually took form in the minds of his hearers a picture of a remarkable religious organization — one which follows the most modern business methods in organization, subdivision of labor, the employment of experts for carefully outlined fields, the development and extension of personal contact with the ideal object of reaching every man, woman and child in New York City, and, above all, an appreciation and practical utilization of the importance of advertizing.
>
> Sunday and his helpers made it clear that they were going after souls as a successful commercial corporation would go after sales. They reminded the clergymen present that they had come, not on their own initiative, but upon the urging of the ministers of New York. They pointed out that, having been called in to remedy an undesirable condition in the religious life of New York City, they intended to go to work in their own way, working like any other consulting specialists, according to their own approved and tested methods.[21]

Although subsequent analysis sometimes called into question Sunday's long-term impact on urban America, at first glance his methods seemed quite effective. The most obvious and often used means of determining the evangelist's success was through a tally of worshipers who "hit the sawdust trail." This term describing the response to Billy's altar calls originated during his revival in Bellingham, Washington, and was derived from lumbermen's practice of finding their way home out of dense forest by depositing a trail of sawdust. Using "trail hitters" as the index of a revival's efficacy yielded impressive results. Between 1906 and 1918, Sunday visited twenty-three cities with a population of more than 100,000, where he averaged 567 "trail hitters" per day, or about 300 per sermon. In the forty-one cities of less than 100,000, he averaged 161 per day. In the 10-week New York City campaign, "trail hitters" numbered 98,264; in Boston 64,484; in Chicago 49,165; in Philadelphia 41,724; and in Buffalo 38,853. Given the great interest in such statistics, at times it seemed as though Billy Sunday's tabernacles were factories producing respondents to altar calls and Sunday was the dynamo that provided the energy. Robert Laurence Moore has written, "Everything that mattered in Sunday's religion could be counted or inventoried." While this observation is not wholly accurate, there is more than a grain of truth in it.[22]

Productivity in evangelism could yield handsome rewards. There is no doubt that even in the earliest days of his ministry Sunday profited from his work. Between 1896 and 1902, offerings ranged from a meager $33 to a remarkably generous $1,536. Over the next four years, Sunday's income averaged $2,000 per campaign and by 1906 had risen to roughly $4,000 per 4-week revival campaign. The latter figure was several times the normal annual salary of most small-town parish ministers and was undoubtedly the source of some resentment and perhaps envy on their part.

Those sums would later seem small by comparison with revival revenues during the 1910s. Lyle Dorsett has estimated that between 1908 and 1920, years when the average worker's wages totaled approximately $14,000, the evangelist earned more than a million dollars. Homer Rodeheaver believed him to be a millionaire by 1920, claiming that Dun and Bradstreet estimated his wealth at $1.5 million that year.[23]

The once-impoverished denizen of an Iowa orphan's home took great pleasure in his unaccustomed affluence. He reveled in fashionable clothes, stylish cars, a rural retreat in the Hood River country of Oregon, and all the other amenities of life his income made possible. There were those then and later who considered Sunday's enormous earnings in the name of religion scandalous or immoral. A headline in the *Philadelphia Public Ledger* in 1916 was typical: "Sunday gets pans filled with money." The accompanying story charged that on one occasion during the campaign in that city, after the offering was taken, a huge galvanized bucket near the altar was so filled with money that Billy's aides had difficulty lifting it.

Even such an essentially sympathetic biographer as Dorsett has conceded that

> there was something fundamentally immoral about asking people to make sacrificial monetary contributions at spiritual revival meetings and then walking away with a large part of the take for personal use. It was especially unpalatable when the evangelist and his wife already had money in several banks, owned their own home plus recreational property, and held the second deeds of trust on numerous farms.[24]

The revivalist himself appears never to have seen any incompatibility between affluence and Christian service. He did, however, bridle at criticism of his lifestyle and was not loath to publicize his charitable contributions in an effort to parry accusations that he was a "grafter." For example, at the beginning of the New York campaign in April 1917, he announced that he would donate the entire free-will offering, which later proved to be $120,500, to the war work of the YMCA and Red Cross. The following year he donated the entire free-will offering from the Chicago crusade, more than $54,000, to the Pacific Garden Mission. While he was never as generous as Dwight L. Moody, who had little interest in money and gave away much of the revenue generated by his revivals, Sunday regularly tithed his income and made contributions to a variety of causes. Despite his gifts to religious and charitable endeavors, he never really succeeded in allaying the skepticism of the cynics.

Sunday left himself open to charges of materialism in part because of the emphasis he placed on contributions for the support of his work. Appeals for money had initially been an inconsequential facet of his ministry but became more important with the passing years. The expenses of large-scale urban revivalism during the 1910s and early 1920s undoubtedly necessitated greater attention to the financial dimension of each campaign than had been the case in the small towns of the Midwest. They did not, however, warrant the sometimes graceless emphasis Billy placed on money. On occasion, he chided worshipers for their lack of generosity, declaring, "Don't let me hear any coins fall into those buckets; I want to hear the rustle of paper." At times in the 1920s, as his popularity declined and his income shrank, the revivalist's calls for contributions grew so unseemly that even such longtime associates as Homer Rodeheaver regarded them as inappropriate and detrimental to his boss's effectiveness.[25] Helen Sunday may have been partially responsible for her husband's increasing emphasis on money. As manager of both evangelistic and family finances, she had a comptroller's appreciation for the importance of the balance sheet and the bottom line. "Ma" kept a watchful and sometimes suspicious eye on the collection and distribution of campaign revenues and made certain that Billy and his evangelistic team got their fair share of the proceeds.

While undeniably important to him, the quest for money and the material comforts it could buy was essentially a secondary consideration for Sunday. As even some of his harshest critics acknowledged, had he merely craved wealth he could have accumulated much more by means other than evangelism. George Creel, who had little good to say about Sunday, acknowledged that

> criticism of him on the score of cupidity is . . . without fair foundation. He has made money, to be sure, but not one-tenth of the money that he could make were he greedy and self-seeking. And there is little doubt that the man tithes his income, giving a tenth of all he receives to the form of charity that most attracts him at the moment.[26]

Despite Sunday's wealth and his concern for money, it was never really avarice but his commitment to Christian service and the closely related need to allay self-doubt that lay at the heart of his work. A profound religious experience informed by fundamentalist theology had brought order, meaning, and purpose to his world. His religious convictions were central to his sense of well-being and he could not have consciously betrayed them for the sake of money without risking his psychological equilibrium. Fortunately, given his appreciation for the material trappings of success, his faith, like that of most mainstream Protestants of his day, did not require him to wholly eschew the profane for the sacred. In fact, the line between the two was not sharply drawn. For Billy, the volume of contributions to his crusades was one of the indices of how well he was doing the Lord's work. God blessed those who did his will. Prosperity was, therefore, a measure of divine favor.

That his affluence was indicative of divine approval would have been contested by many of Sunday's critics, but few could deny that revenue generated by revivals was a fairly reliable measure of a city's receptivity to, if not the gospel, at least to the man who preached it. Billy needed popular approbation almost as much as he needed to serve God and certainly as much as he needed money. He was gratified by the massive crowds that flocked to his tabernacles and by the financial and moral support proffered not only by the masses but also by the social, economic, and political elites of city, state, and nation. To a man with his many insecurities, acceptance by a broad spectrum of society helped to assuage self-doubt. He was doing the right thing. He was prospering. God loved him. The people loved him. The rich and powerful loved him. All the good things that came his way he interpreted as a sign of God's favor, as a reward for earlier sacrifices, as a concrete expression in this life of God's grace. While Billy liked having money and all that it could buy, it was never merely the lure of the almighty dollar to which he succumbed. Rather, money was important to him as a tangible expression of divine approval, human acceptance, and material security.

Billy Sunday did not make his mark in the world of commerce, manufacturing, or finance but in that of religion. Yet to an unprecedented degree he

Billy Sunday and his family in Fairfield, Iowa, 1907.

Courtesy of the State Historical Society of Iowa, Iowa City, Iowa.

brought to evangelism the sophisticated business practices of his day, a fact that contributed immeasurably to his success and popularity. Although he espoused the work ethic of the small-town businessman, he and his staff approached their tasks with an emphasis on efficiency, cost, organization, and productivity worthy of the most astute capitalists of the age.

There were many critics of Sunday's commercialization of religion and of the personal profits he reaped from that commercialization, but there were also a great many people who were intrigued by, and who admired, the way in which this evangelistic entrepreneur went about the Lord's work. A broad spectrum of white, native-born, middle-class Americans related to Billy Sunday because he embodied the myth of success in which they believed and because he had achieved that success by conducting his affairs in accord with the rules of the business world to which they belonged or to which they aspired.

FOUR

Playing the Game for God

If Billy Sunday's revivalism was informed by the business ethos of his day, it also resonated with the values of a culture beginning to become absorbed with sports. By the closing decades of the nineteenth century, the rise of the industrial city, the revolution in transportation and communication, the influence of immigrant cultures, and an increase in leisure time had converged to create a growing enthusiasm for a wide range of sports, the most pervasive of which was baseball. By the 1880s and 1890s, it had already become a passion with millions of middle-class Americans and was well on its way to becoming the national pastime. To be sure, other athletic contests had their proponents. Boxing was popular, but it was not quite respectable in many quarters. Football was gaining enthusiasts, but its audience consisted primarily of a relatively small number of collegians and those living in close proximity to the colleges and universities at which it was played. Furthermore, the game was controversial because of the brutality associated with it. Basketball did not make its appearance until 1892, and most Americans still regarded tennis and golf as elitist and somewhat effeminate. As both a participatory and spectator sport, baseball as yet had no important rivals for the hearts and minds of the populace.[1]

The game's popularity, however, lay not in the absence of competitors but in its own inherent characteristics and the way in which those seemed to reflect the mood of the times. To some extent, baseball bridged the gap between tradition and modernity. Its pastoral motif and potential for drama appealed to people seeking a momentary escape from the routine and stress of an urbanizing, industrializing nation. At the same time, its symmetry, specialization, and susceptibility to statistical analysis meant that it was congruent with the increasingly bureaucratic and technological quality of American life. The fact that victory depended on both individual excellence and team effort was consistent with contemporary individualistic and corporate values. Generally lacking definite ethnic or class associations and requiring little training or expense, baseball seemed accessible to all and thus had a democratic and uniquely American aura. The sport was widely hailed not

only as physically and psychologically beneficial but also as a force for socialization, a builder of character, and a reflection of the American way of life. Yet
above all, the game was fun. For tens of thousands of men and boys in city
parks and country pastures, it had become, as Clarence Darrow remembered
from his youth in Kinsmond, Ohio, "the one unalloyed joy of life."[2]

Although at 28 years of age Billy Sunday had abandoned the diamonds of
the National League, baseball remained an integral part of his life and
ministry for the next forty-four years. Aside from his obvious sincerity and
genuine commitment to his faith, no other single factor contributed more to
Billy's popularity than his career as an athlete. By lending a dramatic quality
to his ministry and providing a familiar body of imagery and wealth of anecdotal material upon which the evangelist could draw, it afforded an important
entree with millions of Americans.

A generation or two earlier, the nexus between sports and religion would
have played a much less significant role in Sunday's ministry than was the case
in the early twentieth century. By the time the Iowa-born evangelist appeared
on the scene, sports had become organized and, in some instances, profes-
sionalized, and the church was seeking to accommodate itself to a society in
which athletic contests were becoming an integral part of leisure-time activities. Contrary to what has sometimes been alleged, American Protestantism
has never been wholly antithetical to sports. Even the Puritans, renowned for
their antipathy to many of the pleasures of this world, did not completely
reject sport. They objected only to those physical or other diversions that did
not in some way glorify God or cultivate useful life skills. Wrestling, horse-
back-riding, swordsmanship, hunting, or fishing were acceptable. Dancing
around a maypole, gambling on horse races, or indulging in any activity for
the pure exhilaration it might provide were not.[3]

Something of this utilitarian justification for sport remained viable in
American society into the late nineteenth and early twentieth centuries and,
in fact, persists to the present in our contemporary notion that participation in
athletics builds character and facilitates socialization. In the late Victorian
era, games on the Sabbath and sports associated with gratuitous violence or
vices were anathema to many Christians and professionalization was suspect,
but in general Protestants in America had begun to make their peace with the
burgeoning culture of athleticism. Indeed, many had concluded that sports
could actually be called into the service of the gospel or, at least, of morality.
Some, such as the YMCA's Luther Gulick, with his emphasis on organized
play, stressed socialization and character-building, while others such as
Dwight L. Moody viewed sports largely as merely another means to the end of
spreading the gospel of personal salvation. Although he emphasized the many
beneficial effects of athletics, especially baseball, Sunday was closer to the
position of Moody than to that of Gulick. Baseball and other sports might
build strong bodies and teach important life skills, but these were essentially
tools to be used in the struggle with the Devil for the souls of mankind. In
Billy's hands, they were tools used with consummate skill.[4]

Given the nation's enthusiasm for baseball, it is hardly surprising that Sunday's initial appeal as a volunteer and later as a salaried worker for the Chicago YMCA lay in part in his reputation as a colorful and aggressive athlete. Early newspaper coverage of his religious activities often linked his baseball career and his Christian endeavors. Yet at first Billy appears to have been hesitant to capitalize on his ties to professional sports. Indeed, he sometimes deflected questions young men posed about baseball and redirected their attention toward spiritual matters. Soon, however, he recognized his years in the National League for the valuable asset they were and began to make the most of them. The association in the popular mind between Sunday and baseball spanned his entire ministry. A contemporary biographer of the revivalist wrote:

> In the early days men flocked to hear Sunday because they knew how well he could play ball, and they probably reasoned that the man who would do that so well would not preach poorly, and in this they were not mistaken.[5]

As Billy traveled about the Midwest at the beginning of his career, a Humbolt, Iowa, newspaper reported that "he carries his baseball suit with him, and plays a game now and then to keep his hand in." As his ministry expanded out of the Corn Belt into urban centers across the nation, he sometimes attended games in cities in which he was preaching. Occasionally, the local citizenry challenged Sunday and members of his evangelistic team to a game. One of the most notable of these events was a benefit performance in Los Angeles in 1917 between Sunday's "Evangelicals" and a group of Hollywood movie stars. The proceeds went to purchase sports equipment for U.S. soldiers serving in World War I. In the teens, as he approached the pinnacle of his popularity, journalists not only queried the evangelist about religious or moral issues but also frequently asked him to comment upon the quality of the teams and players of the era and sometimes to compare them with those of his day. As late as the 1930s, in the twilight of his evangelism and forty years after he had left the diamond, newspapers still remarked upon his career in professional baseball.[6]

Not only the press, but Sunday's own publicists and others who wrote books about him stressed his athletic past. An authorized biography published in 1914 described the preacher in its subtitle as the "Baseball Evangelist." The author, Rev. Elijah Brown, made much of the revivalist's athletic prowess. He recalled Billy's days with the White Stockings, reminding readers that he was the first player to circle the bases in fourteen seconds, and reported that the legendary Adrian "Cap" Anson thought him the fastest base runner ever to play the game. Brown also tried to draw parallels between Sunday's baseball and revivalistic skills, suggesting that he was as determined to win in the pulpit as he had been on the diamond and that some of the "earnestness and precision" with which he preached was due to his athletic training. Another contemporary biographer, William T. Ellis, contended in a laudatory volume that Sunday's days on the diamond had accustomed him to the adulation of the crowd and thus inured him to the potentially detrimental effects of the popularity that accompanied his success as an evangelist.[7]

Some of this emphasis on the popular preacher's tie to sports was, of course, merely expediency on the part of the press, and his publicists recognized it as one of the easiest ways to attract readers' interest. Some of it, however, reflected the widespread faith in the salutary effects of America's favorite game. Given his own experience, it is not surprising that Billy himself believed that athletics was an important part of a man's preparation for life. It was not evangelistic opportunism but conviction that prompted him to repeatedly extol the virtues of fitness and competition. He spoke from the heart when he said, "You can bet your life that sport is a mighty good thing, and it certainly has an influence on religion." He had no doubt that

> Sport teaches a man fair play. He does what is right by his opponent, and if he doesn't he's thrown out of the game—a fit playmate of the devil. To live properly a man must be in good physical shape, and athletic competition, whether public or private, will put a man in shape to live a clean, wholesome, religious life.[8]

As for any qualms the pious might have about professional baseball, Billy vehemently denied that there was anything inherently immoral or corrupting about it. In January 1909, as he was beginning to emerge into national prominence, he told a reporter that he "wouldn't take a million dollars" for his career in baseball and somewhat inaccurately affirmed his pride in having been "one of the best of them" in his day. He contended that baseball was the one sport in the nation on which gamblers had been unable to get their hands, despite thirty years of effort. There was not "the same disgrace attached to a professional baseball player" that attended "other professional athletes." Baseball had "stood the test." It was a "pure, clean, and wholesome game," and there was "no disgrace to any man . . . for playing professional baseball."[9]

Sunday pointed out that he had been "converted in 1886 and lived a Christian life for five years" while in the National League. He affirmed his belief that a man could "be a Christian and decent self-respecting citizen there if he wants to be." One did not have to be a "rounder." Furthermore, "the club owners, the fans generally, and the players themselves" respected "a man all the more for living a clean, honest life."[10]

Billy shared the public's conviction that baseball was a quintessentially American game that instilled important qualities of character and basic national values. He believed the game to be "American to the core," as "distinctively American as are pork and beans and pie." It mirrored the strengths and weaknesses of the nation and its people and was, therefore, sometimes marred by human frailty, but it was not inherently flawed. The game was democratic. There was "the same joy in it for the youngster who hotfoots it five miles to a hole in the fence as for the broker whose six-cylinder totes him to the best seat in the grand stand." It was honest, "clean as a hound's tooth," as far as he knew, and he was prepared to defend its honor almost to the point of violence.

When some withered-up, walrus-jawed, limber-legged, gimlet-eyed, pink-tea-blooded old fool of a pessimist comes to me and tells me in a voice like a dying calf and the gurgle of a wheezy cistern pump that the game is crooked as the devil, and that pennants are bought and sold, I feel like knocking his block into the middle of next week. You can't tell me that hundreds of thousands of shrewd, keen-witted, city-bred American men would give the game so much of their time, and support it persistently and enthusiastically, if it were not clean, open, and on the square.

The sport at its best was conducive to the building of skill and virtue. A player who reached the pinnacle of success in the game could not bask in his fame but was "under deep obligation to the public to conserve and develop character and skill to the best of his ability."[11]

Democratic, honest, character-building, the game, Billy believed, also reflected the energy and enthusiasm characteristic of the American people. "Magnetic" and "fascinating," according to Sunday, baseball had "the power to stand you on your toes and tangle up your diaphragm and larynx in a carnival of noise that you never dreamed possible." With enthusiasm bordering on chauvinism, he declared:

Norwegians have their skis and Spain has her bullfights. In England, if a cricket game is drawn out, they drink a little tea and finish it the next day. Duels furnish Frenchmen with morning exercise. But what other sport could so characteristically serve as the play outlet for the nervous, high-strung, third-rail, double-barreled, greased-lightning, strenuous, hustling, bustling bunch of folks—bless 'em!—that inhabit this country to-day?[12]

During World War I, at the zenith of his success, Sunday elucidated his understanding of the importance of his own baseball experience when he declared,

It has made me fit to play this bigger game I'm playing right now, and I want to tell you that I'm mighty glad I was a professional ball player.

A man out there before a great crowd learns to know the crowd—its heart. He absorbs a complete understanding of their emotions. And he has the opportunity of doing good. And don't you forget that it takes nerve.

Have you ever stopped to consider the feelings of an outfielder waiting for a hard hit fly to come down? Up there in the stands are thousands of fans, with their eyes glued upon him. The ball is but a slight speck, and to a young player just breaking in it seems that every second is an hour. But finally the ball drops down, slowly, ever so slowly. He prepares to catch it. If he lets it get away from him—zowie![13]

For millions of Americans, Sunday's life was a validation of the benefits of baseball. Devotees of the sport and admirers of the revivalist believed, or wanted to believe, that their beloved national game had helped to prepare him for his larger and more important career in evangelism. Both they and he persuaded themselves that it had strengthened his character, taught him to work under stress, accustomed him to the pitfalls of the approbation of the crowd, and instilled in him the value of individual effort and the importance of teamwork. In other words, baseball had, as Billy contended, prepared him for the more significant contests of life.

Perhaps the game had indeed helped Sunday develop the physical stamina, concentration, and poise which later served him well as a revivalist. There is no doubt, however, that his reputation as a professional ballplayer provided him with the means of establishing a rapport with audiences unavailable to other evangelists. Homer Rodeheaver wrote of the role of the sports mystique in the revivalist's ministry:

> Because of his experience as a baseball player, many people sent to the platform balls, bats, masks, gloves, and all kinds of baseball equipment. Usually when I presented him with some item on behalf of one of the delegations he would immediately put it on and go through the movements of a player on the diamond, to the amusement of the whole crowd. If it was a bat, he would grasp it, get into position, and take a swing, all the while making some comment about the club or about some old player who used one like that. If it was a mask or a glove, he would put it on, stand on the other side of the platform, and have me toss the ball to him. He was exceedingly graceful in his movements, and he had the smooth rhythm of the perfect athlete.[14]

Scholarly and popular accounts alike are filled with descriptions of Billy's slides, leaps, catches, judgment calls, and other baseball antics in the pulpit. These provided the color and the semblance of the unconventional for which the preacher was renowned. Yet this emphasis on the dramatic has sometimes obscured the way in which his tie to sports afforded Sunday an even more useful evangelistic tool—a body of athletic metaphors by means of which to convey his understanding of the gospel. He had a keen sense of the theatrical and instinctively grasped what would reach an audience. In an age when both participatory and spectator sports were increasingly popular in America, he often couched his message in the athletic vernacular of the day. For example, God was sometimes the "great Umpire of the universe" who called people out at the end of their lives. The evangelist once described the Devil using imagery from not one but three sports—track, baseball, and boxing. He characterized the "prince of darkness" as a sprinter who could "give a lot of men a head start and beat them to the tape." The Devil was, in his opinion, a "major league sprinter" who was "always in the red of condition." According to Billy, Satan "could pitch with the best of them" and possessed a "spit ball that spits fire." Unless one was "fit spiritually," he would "strike you out every time you come to bat." Switching to pugilistic imagery, Sunday contended that the Devil had "knocked out more men than all the boxing champions put together" and had "a much stronger punch than Jeffries, Fitzsimmons, Corbett and Sullivan put together." He was doubly dangerous because he was also a "bum sportsman" who was "tricky, treacherous and sneaky." A "weak-spined, mush-hearted specimen of manhood" had no chance against him.

Only "a regular fellow, a God-fearing man" could stand his ground in any contest against Satan.[15] To be sure, such metaphors reduced the cosmic struggle between good and evil to the mundane level of the track, the diamond, or the ring, but they also made Billy's message entertaining and comprehensible to the masses. The reduction of complex ideas to the lowest common denominator and the conveying of them in the most appealing manner were the essence of successful evangelism.

In baseball, Sunday found much more than the memorable metaphor. He was a master of crowd psychology and understood the power of a good story not only to entertain but to persuade. His experiences as a ballplayer, or at least his memories of those experiences, provided him with a wealth of vivid and sometimes moving anecdotes upon which he could draw to guide his congregations where he wished them to go. To illustrate the efficacy of prayer, for example, he recalled two incidents that had occurred during his years with the White Stockings. Billy's God was always nearby, ready to help whenever his children asked. No request was too mundane, no appeal too insignificant to go unanswered.

Prayer was an essential but commonplace feature of the dedicated Christian's experience. Billy talked to God spontaneously, in the casual but respectful way one might address a parent. For him, faith was a practical matter that could have immediate consequences, ranging from the ordinary to the profound. He often told the story of one of the first occasions when he called upon God for help and his Lord responded. Shortly after his conversion in 1886, the White Stockings were playing a tough, competitive Detroit team and were leading them three to two in the last of the ninth inning. With two outs and runners on second and third, John Clarkson, Chicago's star pitcher, hurled a pitch that Detroit catcher Charlie Bennett hit deep into right field. Sunday, playing in the outfield that afternoon, watched the ball sail high into the air. Knowing that it was going over his head, he turned to give chase. He described what then happened:

> As I ran I offered up a prayer, something like this: "Oh Lord, I'm in an awful hole, and if you ever help me, please do it now, and you haven't much time to make up your mind."
>
> The grand stand and bleachers had overflowed with people and they were standing along the wall in right and left fields. I saw that the ball was going to drop in the edge of the crowd, and I yelled, "Get out of the way," and they opened up like the Red Sea did for the rod of Moses.
>
> I glanced up and saw the ball coming. I leaped into the air and shot out my right hand and the ball hit and stuck fast as my fingers closed over it. I lost my balance and fell but jumped up with the ball in my hand.[16]

Sunday had no doubt that God concerned himself with such ordinary details of life and that his prayer had contributed to his game-saving play.

The contest with Detroit was crucial because the White Stockings were in a tight pennant race that summer. Before the season was over, Billy called upon his God again for divine intervention on behalf of his team. As the 1886 season drew to a close, the White Stockings and the New York Giants were in a virtual dead heat for the National League pennant. As Sunday remembered it, on the last day of the season Chicago had a 1-game lead. They had one game to play, and the Giants were to play a doubleheader. A Chicago loss and two New York wins would give the championship to the Giants.

Sunday felt that an appeal for divine intervention on Chicago's behalf was warranted. On Wednesday night, before the last day of the season on Thursday, Billy attended a midweek prayer service, as was his custom. Frank "Old Silver" Flint, Chicago's catcher, sheepishly asked if he could accompany him. As the two players walked toward the church, Flint, whose religion had long been more a matter of memory than practice, said to his teammate, "Billy, I ain't prayed much for years, but I was taught to pray. Do you believe God will help us win that game tomorrow, and help New York to lose one?" Sunday replied, "Sure, the Lord will; and you and I, Frank, will do the praying for the whole team." That evening, the two men prayed earnestly for the success of their club. The next day, Chicago defeated Boston and Philadelphia took both ends of a doubleheader from New York, giving the pennant to the White Stockings. Late in his life Sunday reiterated his conviction that "the Lord helped us win that game" and affirmed that he would always believe that to have been the case unless, upon his arrival in Heaven, God told him differently.[17]

A recent study of Sunday's baseball career suggests that the revivalist's memories of his days as a player were not always reliable. The two famous stories related above appear to be firmly rooted in actual events, but the details of the games and the circumstances in which they were played are apparently somewhat muddled. From the standpoint of evangelism, however, accuracy was less important than emotional impact. Post-conversion incidents on the diamond may well have strengthened the neophyte Christian's faith. Later, however, his recollections of them were equally important as a rich source of illustrative material that the creative revivalist could embellish and use to add color and texture to his memorable sermons. Sunday's picturesque baseball stories, permeated with the excitement and competitiveness of the nation's most popular sport, etched into the memory of his audiences concrete examples of the power of prayer and reinforced the notion that God was indeed an ever-present help in time of trouble.[18]

If baseball provided Billy a wealth of material illustrative of the power of prayer and the benefits of faith, it also afforded a repertoire of cautionary tales about the consequences of rejecting God. In spite of his public affirmations of the essential decency of professional baseball and its personnel, Sunday recognized that the game had its share of those whose characters were flawed by the gamut of human failings. Furthermore, just as team management had sometimes capitalized upon the disreputable image of their employees as a means of gaining leverage in the struggle with labor, Sunday found the same negative stereotypes advantageous in his combat with the Devil. During his playing days in the 1880s and early 1890s, Billy liked and admired most of his teammates, but after his religious conversion he increasingly sensed a moral and spiritual divergence between himself and many of them. He privately cautioned Nell against associating with the wives and friends of certain Chicago players and suggested to her that at least some of his baseball companions were men of little principle.[19]

Sunday's often-repeated account of his conversion illuminates both his ambivalent feelings toward his baseball comrades and the way in which he used stories of former teammates in his evangelism. In a 1914 version of this story, published in a slender volume entitled *Burning Truths from Billy's Bat*, he recalled that after deciding to accept the invitation to visit the Pacific Garden Mission, he arose and said to his comrades, "I'm through. We've come to the parting of the ways." Then, as he remembered that summer afternoon, he turned his back on them.

> Some of them laughed and some of them mocked me; one of them gave me encouragement; others never said a word. Twenty-seven years ago I turned and left that little group on the corner of State and Madison streets, walked to the little mission, fell on my knees and staggered out of sin and into the arms of the Saviour.[20]

Given his propensity for dramatization and the changes that had occurred in Sunday's life in the intervening years, this account obviously should not be taken at face value, but his interpretation of the event is revealing. He remembered that summer afternoon in 1886 as marking a dramatic and abrupt break with his former life. As he tells it, he quite literally stood and walked away from his past. His teammates on the White Stockings symbolized that past of sin and sorrow on which he was turning his back.

Yet, as if to remind readers that baseball players were not total reprobates but men capable of honor and decency, Sunday described, with appreciation, their reaction following his conversion. He recalled the apprehension with which he went to the ball park, fearing the ridicule of his teammates. To his surprise and delight, he found not derision but respect.

> Up came Mike Kelley. He said: "Bill I'm proud of you—religion is not my long suit, but I'll help you all I can." Up came Anson, Pfeffer, Clarkson, Flint, McCormick, Burns, Williamson and Dalrymple. There wasn't a fellow in that gang who knocked, every fellow had a word of encouragement for me.[21]

Despite his appreciation of their expressions of support for him, the lives of some of these same men provided Sunday with a point of orientation against which he could measure the spiritual and material distance that he had traveled since that summer afternoon in 1886. In *Burning Truths from Billy's Bat*, he told his version of the stories of three White Stockings teammates— Mike Kelly, Ed Williamson, and Frank Flint. Their experiences afforded vivid contrasts with his own and validated the evangelical worldview to which he had committed himself.

Sunday recalled how Mike Kelly had received $5,000 as his portion of the deal that sent him to Boston in 1887, how fans in the city purchased a house for Kelly and presented him with $1,500, and how within a year Kelly had spent his salary, the $5,000 bonus, the $1,500 gift, and had mortgaged the house. Kelly, who loved to drink and gamble, was, according to Billy, eventually so poor that when he died at the age of 36, friends and admirers had to raise the funds to bury him. He concluded the story of Kelly with the observation, "Mike sat there on the corner with me twenty-seven years ago, when I said: 'Goodbye, boys, I'm through.'"

In the late 1880s, Ed Williamson, the shortstop of the White Stockings, went on a world tour with a baseball team sponsored by A. G. Spalding. According to Sunday, as the team crossed the English Channel, a storm threatened to sink the ship on which it was traveling. Williamson, fearing for his life, fell to his knees and promised God that he would be true to Him if he survived the trip. Williamson lived but forgot his promise. He returned to Chicago and opened a saloon. Sunday recalled,

> I would go there and give tickets for the Y. M. C. A. meetings and would talk with him, and [he] would cry like a baby, I would get down and pray for him. When he died they put him on the table and cut him open and took out his liver. It was so big it would not go in a candy bucket.

Again Sunday ended his story with the observation, "Ed Williamson sat there on the street corner with me twenty-seven years ago when I said, 'Goodbye, boys, I'm through.'"

The evangelist recounted the tale of Frank Flint, the White Stockings catcher, who played for years in the National League at a salary far above that of the average laborer of the day. After his baseball career, however, Flint succumbed to alcohol and fell into poverty. Sunday remembered seeing his old friend sleeping on a table in a "stale beer joint" with scarcely a cent to his name. He described in graphic detail the ultimate consequences of his former teammate's addiction to drink and recalled that as Flint lay dying the old catcher said to him,

> There's nothing in the life of years ago I care for now. I can hear the grandstand hiss when I strike out. I can hear the bleachers cheer when I make a hit that wins the game, but there is nothing that can help me now, and if the umpire calls me out now, won't you say a few words over me, Bill?

Then, as the evangelist recounts the story, "The great Umpire of the universe yelled: 'You're out!'" And again Billy reminded readers and audiences that like the others, "Frank Flint sat on the street corner drunk with me twenty-seven years ago in Chicago when I said: 'I'll bid you goodbye, boys, I'm going to Jesus.'"[22]

Sunday concluded his account of the fate of his three friends of years gone by with the question, "Say men, did I win the game of life, or did they?"[23] There was, of course, no doubt about the answer. Drunkenness, poverty, and sorrow were the result of rejecting salvation. Happiness and success were the benefits of accepting it.

The preacher was certain that his victory over evil and its consequences resulted from his decision to heed the invitation to visit the Pacific Garden Mission and to accept the gospel espoused there, while the failure of his baseball comrades stemmed from their decision to remain behind on the street corner and their capitulation to life's temptations. Sunday's big-league cronies provided the principles in a morality play in which the rewards of salvation were measured against the wages of sin, and sin was found wanting. The years he spent in the National League became a point of orientation against which he and others could measure his growth as a man and a Christian.

Sunday's ties to baseball lent verisimilitude to his sports anecdotes. He was the first major evangelist for whom athletics, amateur or professional, had been an integral part of his life and the first to incorporate the national pastime so extensively into his revivalism. Yet his reliance upon baseball as a metaphor for life and medium for conveying the gospel was by no means unique. When he transformed the problems of life into the struggles of the diamond and reduced the complexity of human existence to the simple symmetry of a game, he was drawing analogies increasingly common in Christian circles.

By the early twentieth century, baseball had become such a pervasive part of American life that people with radically different opinions on all sorts of issues could make metaphorical use of it to convey their point of view. Sunday, for whom everything was personal and experiential, used the game to dramatize his sermons and to illustrate the motif of individualism that ran through his message. His gospel was about personal sin and salvation and the moral consequences of each. To be sure, there were important social implications stemming from whether one did or did not accept God's gift of grace, but the transformation of the heart that had to precede the reformation of society was a matter of individual responsibility.

At the other end of the religious spectrum from Billy Sunday and Evangelicals of his ilk were the apostles of the Social Gospel. For these liberal Christians, with their corporate vision of society, baseball afforded an almost perfect metaphor. Success in the game meant that players had to strive for personal excellence but also subordinate individual achievement to the welfare of the team as a whole.

Washington Gladden, one of the earliest spokesmen of the Social Gospel, did not believe that one was truly converted until "he comprehends his social relations and strives to fulfill them." Commitment to others was a fundamental component of the Christian faith. Gladden urged Protestants to think of their lives as analogous to a baseball game. An individual could not learn or successfully play the game alone. The essence of the contest was teamwork. Likewise, the meaning and significance of life lay in recognizing and acting upon one's responsibility to co-workers, community, and society.[24]

Early in the twentieth century, Henry Pope, president of the Religious Education Association, which in conjunction with the University of Chicago Press produced much of the Sunday-school literature of the day, urged teachers to take advantage of boys' familiarity with and fondness for baseball. The game was as real to them as the workplace was to their fathers and it could be used to examine questions about the importance of skill, discipline, integrity, and cooperation.

Erwin L. Shaver, author of a number of Christian educational pamphlets, believed that participation in sport built character. In A *Christian's Recreation*, he contended that "clean sport, fair play, self-sacrifice, obedience to rules, team cooperation, skill, initiative, a sense of honor, chivalry, generous appreciation of an opponent find expression and development in athletics." Shaver's colleague, Herbert Gates, wrote:

> Many a lad has learned lessons of cooperation with his teammates, of self-denial in training, of persistence, endurance, and courage in turning defeat into victory, only to have the same lessons stay by him in the stern contest of later life and make him a winner there.[25]

Proponents of the Social Gospel shared Billy Sunday's conviction that sport in general, and baseball in particular, could prepare a man for the larger game of life. They differed, however, in their understanding of the nature of that preparation. The former, seeking to accommodate their theology and practice to an urbanizing, industrializing nation, found the game's relevance in its spirit of teamwork and mutual cooperation in the interest of achieving a higher goal. The latter, whose faith remained largely informed by the rural and small-town beliefs and norms of his youth, found the game's significance in its color, drama, and opportunities for individual achievement. Both interpretations of the national pastime were valid and had broad appeal, but one looked more to the America of the twentieth century while the other harkened back to the perspective and values of an earlier day.

Given his drive, commitment, and flair for the dramatic, Billy Sunday would no doubt have achieved success as an evangelist even had he not first been a professional ball player, but his earlier career was fortuitous. It enabled an increasingly sports-minded nation to identify with him and his message in ways and with a facility that would have otherwise been lacking. He had accomplished that of which millions of American boys had only dreamed. He had gone to the city in search of success and had found it racing around the base paths of the National League. It mattered little that his lifetime batting average was only .256 and that for several seasons it was significantly lower. As his fame as an evangelist grew, the nation, and perhaps Sunday himself, forgot that for much of his career he was a second-stringer and remembered only that he had played with the best of his era. That fact alone created a charismatic aura about the revivalist and contributed to his ministry an enviable, if not always warranted, credibility.

Some scholars have interpreted the social significance of sports in terms of their congruence with prevalent values and norms, while others have sug-

Billy Sunday playing baseball with the Kansas City
Rotary Club, 1916.

*Billy Sunday Archives, Grace College and
Theological Seminary, Winona Lake, Indiana.*

gested that they play a compensatory role, allowing an escape from the
routine and rigors of everyday life. Neither interpretation is wholly satisfying,
but both illuminate the operation of sport in our culture. They also suggest
something of the way in which Billy Sunday's evangelism functioned in the
lives of his admirers. For those who attended the revivalist's crusades, the
structure of the services was traditional, the sports imagery familiar, and the
gospel message comforting. The messenger, on the other hand, appeared
unconventional. In the early days of professional baseball, some of its attraction lay in the fact that fans perceived many of the players as nonconformists.
They seemingly refused to fit the mold into which an increasingly urban,
industrial, bureaucratic society tried to place men. Despite the fulminations
of moralists and management against their excesses, the best players were
sometimes colorful, daring, aggressive individualists who challenged authority and bent the rules of both the game and society.

Sunday's appeal as an evangelist was similar to that of the free spirits of the diamond. The revivalist, who ranged the pulpit with the same abandon with which he had once streaked along the base paths and across the outfields, sacrificed contemporary liturgical and theological norms on the altar of showmanship and thereby created the illusion of defiant unconventionality. The rituals of the revival and the content of the message—a simple, practical, evangelical version of the gospel—were familiar, but the preacher was refreshingly, though not disconcertingly, different. In other words, the revival was congruent with socioeconomic and religious norms, but the evangelist's persona and unique style of preaching offered a welcome, albeit temporary, escape from the humdrum routine of contemporary civilization.

This major-leaguer-turned-preacher was well aware that the popularity of baseball and his relationship to it added luster to his ministry, and he used that knowledge to his advantage. Yet the prominence of the national pastime in his revivalism was not simply a matter of pandering to the passion of the masses. To be sure, Billy Sunday's role-playing as he raced across the rostrum, mimicked the impossible catch, slid dramatically for the base, or shouted the umpire's verdict as he called a player out at home plate were tabernacle theatrics, but these athletic antics also enabled him to live again in his imagination the thrill he had once known in the ballparks of Chicago, Pittsburgh, and Philadelphia. His years on the diamond with their camaraderie, popular acclaim, and opportunities to excel had brought him a great deal of personal satisfaction. They had elevated his life above the level of the ordinary, and, in some ways, they remained a high point of his experience. Neither the plaudits of the rich and powerful nor the approbation of the millions who flocked to his crusades ever fully eclipsed for him the sheer exhilaration of a baseball game.

That his career as a professional athlete never lost its allure is obvious in the autobiography Sunday wrote in the early 1930s. In one passage, the aging apostle reflected upon his possession of a silver baseball, a token of one of the White Stockings' league championships in the 1880s. "'Every time I look at it,' he recalled, 'I become young again, and the faces of the old team pass in panorama before my eyes and the scenes of other days flit by like a butterfly.'" He confided to his readers that he occasionally took his old uniform and spiked shoes out of mothballs, looked at them, and fondled them "as though they were the crown jewels of Egypt." Whenever he did so, they seemed to say to him, "Hello Bill, put us on once more and we'll go out and do our stuff and show some of these birds we are not all in yet." He acknowledged that "the old urge" was there but admitted that the "dogs" were "a trifle stiff." Nevertheless, even at the age of 70, the once agile outfielder professed to believe that with a little limbering up he could still do 100 yards in fourteen or fifteen seconds.[26]

Although extraordinarily advantageous, the fusion of sports and religion in Billy Sunday's ministry was not mere opportunistic showmanship. Rather, it was, at least in part, a logical expression of his own experience. In the 1880s, baseball and the evangelical gospel of the Pacific Garden Mission had converged to engender in him a sense of confidence and self-worth at a time when he felt profoundly rootless and insecure. Given the meaningful role they had played in his own personal development, it was only natural for him to weave these two integrating forces in his life into the fabric of his evangelism.

FIVE

Man Enough to Be a Christian

In 1936, Homer Rodeheaver wrote of Billy Sunday, his friend and employer of twenty years,

> His life was lived in that period when emphasis was placed on rugged individualism, wide-open spaces, sleeping porches, and the spirit of the West. Theodore Roosevelt crystallized sentiment with his "big-stick" slogan. Vigor, pep, enthusiasm, vitality, and such double-barreled words as he-man, wild-west, red-blooded, two-fisted, hair-trigger, and hell-bent-for-election were part of the current vocabulary, so that Mr. Sunday fitted into the picture perfectly.

The chorister's observation suggests an extremely important but sometimes underestimated dimension of his boss's appeal, the way in which the virile quality of Sunday's revivalism both reflected and addressed contemporary concerns about what some thought to be the perilous state of American manhood in general and the feminization of American Christianity in particular.[1]

During the late nineteenth and early twentieth centuries, there was considerable anxiety, especially among white middle- and upper-class American men, about both the definition of gender roles and the future of their country. Gender roles are largely culturally determined; consequently, subtly different or even disparate understandings of masculinity stemming from such factors as regional, class, religious, or ethnic considerations may exist simultaneously. In a plausible though limited paradigm, E. Anthony Rotundo has described three conceptions of masculinity prevalent among nineteenth-century middle-class Americans living outside of the South. These included notions of man as masculine achiever, Christian gentleman, and masculine primitive.

The masculine achiever ideal was a corollary of the rise of commercial capitalism. It de-emphasized such traits as emotionalism and a sense of collective social responsibility and "encouraged accomplishment, autonomy and aggression—all in the service of an intense competition for success in the market-place." The concept of Christian gentleman was something of a reaction against the excessive competitiveness and individualism characteristic of the masculine achiever. It stressed "love, kindness, and compassion," virtues that were consistent with a measure of concern for others and which expressed themselves in philanthropy, church work, and an active commitment to family. The masculine primitive ideal, increasingly current in the late Victorian era, reflected a fear in some quarters of a debilitating weakness among American males. It emphasized the importance of cultivating such natural characteristics as instinct, vigor, strength, energy, and determination that were deemed vital both to individual men and to society.[2]

The growing apprehension near the end of the nineteenth century over what has sometimes been called, with more than a little hyperbole, "the crisis of American masculinity" was a reaction to changing social and cultural conditions in the United States. Many people feared that urbanization and the disappearance of the frontier threatened the nation with overcivilization. By this they meant an erosion of the instinctiveness, individualism, competitiveness, and drive for success that had traditionally characterized American life. Furthermore, they were convinced that this process of degeneration was compounded by an infusion of new immigrant stock, which they considered inferior, and by the expanding influence of women, which some believed was contributing to the feminization of society. President Charles W. Eliot of Harvard reflected something of the anxiety of the age when, in response to the growing criticism of football, he declared that "effeminacy and luxury are even worse evils than brutality." In 1893, Theodore Roosevelt, writing in a similar vein, asserted that "no sweetness and delicacy, no love for and appreciation of beauty in art or literature, no capacity for building up material prosperity, can possibly atone for lack of the great virile virtues."[3]

Worries about the deterioration of American manliness and the social implications of that deterioration contributed to the popularity of fraternal orders, the proliferation of boys' clubs, and the establishment of the Boy Scouts.[4] Among American churchmen, such concerns were apparent in the interest in muscular Christianity, the development of the athletic program of the Young Men's Christian Association, and the crusade of the Religion and Men Forward Movement. The modern idea of muscular Christianity originated in Britain during the first half of the nineteenth century. Although the term was never precise and its meaning varied with place and time, in general, those who espoused this notion of manhood, such as the English writer and clergyman Charles Kingsley, envisioned men who would be courageous, moral, devout, and fit. Americans first encountered this image of masculinity in the 1850s in the pages of *Tom Brown's School Days*. This novel by Thomas Hughes presented an idealized portrayal of the process of education and character-building at Rugby.

Educators and intellectuals were generally the first Americans to embrace the concept of virile Christianity, but soon many young Victorian males had accepted the idea that physical fitness, patriotism, courage, and strength of will, along with piety and morality, were integral features of the virtuous life. British proponents of muscular Christianity understood it largely in terms of building character. While this emphasis was not lost in the United States, here it became increasingly associated with the evangelical goal of reaching and converting sinners. During the late nineteenth and early twentieth centuries, this muscular Christian motif was a significant facet of the YMCA's philosophy as it expanded its work among young men and boys to include the propagation of fitness as well as piety. The YMCA's burgeoning emphasis on athletics was a practical response to the growing popularity of sports, but it was also an expression of the muscular Christian principle that strength of body, mind, and spirit were inextricably linked.

The notion of Christianity as a virile faith was also an integral feature of the Religion and Men Forward Movement of 1911 and 1912. This interdenominational, largely middle-class, exclusively male revival was a reaction against the perceived feminization of American Protestantism during the nineteenth century. Movement leaders de-emphasized such traits as emotionalism, intuitiveness, and gentleness, which they deemed feminine and dangerously pervasive in American Christianity. Instead, they stressed such presumably masculine and thus constructive characteristics as rationality, efficiency, and productivity. The movement's goal was to bring more men into organized religion and to extend the influence of a manly, vigorous Christianity throughout society at large.[5]

Billy Sunday was not particularly troubled by the preponderance of women in the institutional church nor was he actively involved in the Religion and Men Forward Movement. In fact, he was rather critical of what he regarded as its liberalism, lumping it with other individuals and groups that were "trying to make a religion out of social service" and charging that its ultimate failure stemmed from the fact that it made "the Christian religion a side issue." He did, however, share with this movement, the YMCA, and certain other expressions of contemporary American Protestantism the conviction that to be effective, Christianity must be a muscular, masculine religion. Through the content of his sermons, his aggressive style of evangelism, and the story of his own remarkable life, his revivalism both reflected and addressed some of the gender-related concerns of the day.[6]

In addition to services for men only, all of Sunday's revivals included special sermons for women only, as well as others on motherhood and the home. Although the evangelist's own experiences were not always consistent with his understanding of gender norms, in most respects his vision of the proper, largely private sphere of women was quite conventional. Indeed, his attitudes were very much like those delineated decades later by historian Barbara Welter in her classic model of the middle-class Victorian female ideal which included such qualities as piety, purity, submissiveness, and domesticity. Billy believed that religion and morality were integral to the fully developed character of women. They had, he thought, a greater capacity for these traits than did men. There was "something unfinished in the makeup of a girl" in the absence of religion. Females were, in most instances, morally superior to males. Sunday explained to tabernacle worshipers,

> Men have done a good deal for the world, but women have done more. Many a man wouldn't have amounted to a hill of beans if it hadn't been for

the little woman behind him nagging him on. How thankful we ought to be that God has made woman for us. She has always been the inspiration of the world, from the making of mittens for the Eskimo and the making of mosquito nets for the Hottentots to going without butter on her bread to send the Gospel to the heathen.

Women, he contended, generally lived "on a higher plane, morally, than men," and "no woman was ever ruined that some brute of a man did not take the initiative."[7]

While women had a larger capacity for good than did men, they also had a greater potential for evil. If "a good woman" was "the best thing this side of heaven," a bad woman was "the worst thing this side of hell," and, given her pivotal cultural position as wife and mother, such a creature was dangerous indeed. Therefore, Sunday expressed considerable uneasiness about what he perceived as the modern woman's propensity for luxury, leisure, and "vices," such as smoking, drinking, card-playing, petting, and dancing, all of which threatened to undermine feminine character and therefore society as a whole. To the women in his audiences, he declared, "Let me tell you, sister, when I see you smoking a cigarette I don't want to know anything more about you— I've got your number." The preacher was certain that "the girl who drinks will abandon her virtue." Dancing seemed to him a "hugging match set to music" and was all too often the first step down the road to a life of immorality. He charged that three-fourths of all fallen women fell as a result of the dance. Contemporary unchaperoned courting practices were nearly as great a threat to female virtue as was the dance. He declared that, "A man would not come to see a girl of mine in the parlor unless I had a hole cut in the ceiling with a gatling gun trained through it."[8]

While he regarded no marriage as preferable to a bad one and warned that women should not go to extreme lengths to secure a mate, Billy shared with most of his contemporaries the conviction that the most desirable role for women was that of wife and mother. They must, however, be careful to marry for the right reasons. The "girl" smitten with a ne'er-do-well who married with the intention of reforming the object of her affection was a "fool." On the other hand, too many girls married "for other causes than love." He feared that "ambition, indulgence and laziness" led "more girls to the altar than love."[9]

Maternity was "the highest possible gift of God to woman." Sunday did not think that there was "an angel in heaven that would not be glad to come to earth and be honored with motherhood if God would grant her that privilege." Yet modern women often failed to appreciate the great opportunity the Lord had offered them. The revivalist lamented that "the average girl of today no longer looks forward to motherhood as the crowning glory of womanhood." Too many married women shrank from maternity because they loved luxury and the "ability to flit like a butterfly at some social function."[10]

Sunday frowned on birth control, regarding its advocates as "the devil's mouthpiece," and condemned abortion as murder, proclaiming that God would have nothing to do with women who were guilty of it. The evangelist charged that even among those who had accepted the responsibility of motherhood, there were some who had done so in name only. This, he thought, reflecting something of a populist bias, was especially true of "society women" who left their offspring in the care of others while they attended to the more frivolous activities of life. Children of humbler origins were usually far better off than those of the affluent because they were under the care of a loving mother rather than a hired nurse.[11]

The home and motherhood were important because together they constituted the cornerstone of society. While this was a rather typically Victorian view, Billy, perhaps in part because of the precariousness of his own childhood, idealized the family and the mother's role in it. The home was not only a nurturing and stabilizing force in the lives of children; it was the primary vehicle through which religious and social values were transmitted. It was also an unparalleled force for good. He argued that

> our homes are on the level with women. Towns are on the level with homes. What women are our homes will be; and what the town is, the men will be, so you hold the destiny of the nation. . . . The devil and women can damn this world, and Jesus and women can save this old world. It remains with womanhood today to lift our social life to a higher plane. . . . The womanhood of the world has to settle the destiny of the world.

He contended that "if every cradle was rocked by a good Christian mother, the devil would bank his fires and hell would be for rent."[12]

While Sunday did not make an issue of women's submissiveness, it was implicit in his message. The place of the pious, pure "little woman" was first and foremost in the home, supporting her husband, nurturing the next generation, and providing a moral compass point for society. The man was the head of the household and the liaison between the family and the larger world. That position, however, entailed certain responsibilities which the evangelist believed many husbands shirked. His mother's struggles had taught him much about the challenges women faced when dealing with insensitive or irresponsible men, while his relationship with Nell had demonstrated the emotional and intellectual, as well as physical and economic, importance of wives to their husbands. Consequently, he had both compassion and respect for women and was highly critical of men who did not share his point of view. The Bible, Sunday believed, was filled with texts that admonished husbands to give their wives a "square deal," and he deplored men's failure to do so. In a sermon directed toward rural families, Billy alleged that "there are thousands of men, many of them with their names on church rolls, who call themselves Christians, who treat the livestock on their farms a mighty sight better than they do their wives." He charged that "many a man's highest ideal of womanhood is to have a wife to patch his pants, darn his socks, cook his meals and bear children for him." All too often, husbands were killing their wives with neglect. They not only ought to lighten the burden of their spouse's daily routine by providing as many modern conveniences as possible, but they also ought to appreciate their wives as companions. He pointed out that many a man had "never even discovered the well of love and good cheer and fun" there was in his wife if only he had been good enough to her to draw it out. Treating women with respect and acknowledging their contributions to family and society was not a threat to manliness but an expression of one's obligation to be a responsible husband. Regarding women as merely means to ends rather than ends in and of themselves was, in his view, shortsighted, unjust, inconsistent with biblical teachings, and indicative of the need for a renewed emphasis on Christian manhood.[13]

The reinvigoration of genuine manliness, as he understood it, was an integral part of Sunday's message. His sermons spoke forcefully and repeatedly to his own and others' apprehensions about the atrophy of contemporary manhood. While he did not perceive an imminent crisis, he did believe that both American Christianity and society were in peril. He considered an erosion of virility, stemming largely from the ravages of sin, a significant contributor to this deplorable and dangerous state of affairs. Nevertheless, throughout much of his career, he seems to have been equally confident that there were few challenges genuinely courageous Christian men could not successfully confront. His task was, at least in part, that of the prophet, to call men to an awareness of and repentance for the sins that threatened their manhood. In every crusade, he preached sermons for "men only," such as "Chickens Come Home to Roost" and "The Devil's Boomerang or Hot Cakes Right Off the Griddle," in which he denounced evils such as drunkenness and licentiousness and related, sometimes in excruciating detail, the impact men's irresponsible way of life had on others.

As we shall see in a later chapter, Billy went to great lengths to explain that the consumption of liquor not only destroyed the body of the drunkard but also impoverished the family, emotionally scarred mothers and children, eroded private and public morality, and weakened the nation. Sexual impropriety, he believed, had similar deleterious effects on the individual and society. Reflecting late-nineteenth-century notions of the enervating effects of masturbation, the preacher declared, "The seed of man is worth twenty times more than his blood as a vitalizing force to his mind and to his muscles and to his heart." It should not, therefore, be wasted in wanton pleasure. He warned his male audiences against the debilitating consequences of the "awful curse blighting manhood" and admonished them to shun "that vile demon" as they would a "vampire or a rattle snake coiled to strike with its fangs!" Failure to do so led to men with a "shambling gait," a "nervous hand," a "fluttering heart," "weak muscles," and "tottering memory." Just as castration diminished maleness in livestock, so too masturbation undermined a man's masculinity. Furthermore, the sin of self-pollution not only robbed a man of his mental and physical vitality, but it threatened future generations by filling the veins of his children with "blood that's like water."[14]

Sexual promiscuity was an even more grievous evil than masturbation. It not only violated various moral strictures of the day, but it also put both the innocent and the guilty at serious risk for venereal diseases. The early twentieth century was an era increasingly attuned to issues of science and health. It is not surprising, therefore, that Sunday utilized medical information, and sometimes misinformation, in the interest of making his points more effectively. In his sermons for "men only," he based his call for masculine purity not simply on morality but on an elaborate exposition of the health risks inherent in sexual vice. Perhaps trying to appeal to chivalry or attempting to play upon guilt, Sunday reminded men that their actions had consequences for all those around them. Wives, mothers, sisters, and children would be grieved by the immorality of men who could not master their lust, and some of them could be damaged physically as well as emotionally.

Billy described gonorrhea and syphilis as the "black plagues of the United States" and provided statistics to corroborate his allegation. Although acknowledging that reliable data was difficult to obtain, he reported that 80 percent of the adult males in the nation allegedly had gonorrhea. Of the 800,000 young men who reached sexual maturity annually, approximately 500,000 had "plunged into immorality," and 400,000 of these were said to have contracted venereal disease. There were reportedly 500,000 prostitutes in the U.S., of whom 100,000 died each year of illnesses peculiar to their trade. Since sexually transmitted diseases were so common among prostitutes, it was highly probable that anyone who frequented houses of ill repute had contracted one. Not only was the health of such men at risk but so too was that of their wives and future children.[15]

Billy related numerous anecdotes and ample statistics illustrating the consequences of licentiousness. He recounted the story of a beautiful young bride fatally stricken with gonorrhea, contracted from her husband who had supposedly been cured of the disease before their marriage. He told of a young man who knowingly exposed his wife to gonorrhea, after which she became infected and died. He reminded audiences that 80 percent of the children born with syphilis went blind within a few days of birth. Eighty percent of the women who succumbed to disease in their reproductive organs had, according to the preacher, been infected with gonorrhea and syphilis. Forty-five percent of childless marriages resulted from the transgenerational effects of venereal disease. Immoral and irresponsible sexual conduct had emotional, biological, and social ramifications that were unacceptable to any right-thinking man or woman.[16]

So vivid were Sunday's portrayals of masculine depravity and its horrifying physical and spiritual consequences that men frequently fainted. Homer Rodeheaver recalled that

> One of these sermons, until he tempered it down a little, had one ten-minute period in it where from two to twelve men fainted and had to be carried out every time I heard him preach it.[17]

Sunday did not, however, confine his exhortations to men to masculine audiences. Even in his sermons for both sexes, the theme of manhood was perhaps second only to that of the "evils of the saloon."[18] Sunday often lamented that too many American males were weak, degenerate, even effeminate beings who at best lacked gumption and at worst were all too often cigarette-smoking, liquor-drinking, self-polluting, wife-abusing, child-neglecting libertines, responsible for the deterioration of the American home and the decadence of much of American society. Such weak men were no match for the ultimate source of evil, which was a very real and personal Devil.

In Billy Sunday's cosmology, the Devil was a formidable foe who through cunning and deceit strove constantly to thwart God's will. To combat the power of evil in the world, God needed "Gospel grenadiers" who would battle for righteousness with strength and courage. Too many contemporary Christians were weak. Sunday prayed on occasion,

> Lord save us from off-handed, flabby-cheeked, brittle-boned, weak-kneed, thin-skinned, pliable, plastic, spineless, effeminate, ossified three-karat Christianity.

He liked men "who can stand up and give battle to the devil," and he sometimes lamented that "many think a Christian has to be a sort of dish-rag proposition, a wishy-washy, sissified sort of a galoot that lets everybody make a doormat out of him." But to those who misconstrued the nature of the Christian life, he declared, "Let me tell you the manliest man is the man who will acknowledge Jesus Christ." Religion was no "dish-rag" proposition. Christianity was "a battle and not a dream," and it was a struggle for which many of the faithful seemed ill-equipped. To be effective, Christians required a virile faith which Sunday described in martial and athletic terms.

> Faith is a warrior invading the enemy's country and burning every bridge behind, for it expects to live there. Faith makes no provision for a relapse. Faith is going to the goal for a touchdown. Faith will put the ball over the fence in the last half of the ninth inning, score 3 to 0 against you, bases full, two men out and two strikes and three balls called on you.

This kind of faith was, he feared, woefully lacking in the America of his day. He charged that "if many armies were officered like some of our churches, they would be defeated at the first pop of a gun."[19]

Sunday's understanding of manhood was imprecise but more inclusive than mere physical prowess or individual accomplishment. If he admired strength and agility, frequently sprinkling his sermons with sports anecdotes and metaphors, he also believed that you "can't measure manhood with a tape around his biceps." Sharing the optimism of Horatio Alger and Russell H. Conwell, he admonished men and boys to strive to succeed, which in the America of his day usually meant success in business. He believed that "God calls men to business" and that righteousness in business led not only to success but "a tremendous influence upon moral character in the community." While he contended that "some of the noblest men and women I have ever met have been men and women of wealth," success did not make a man. Sunday believed true manliness entailed responsibility for family, community, and society. A Christian man must have the courage to confront the Devil and his temptations, be sufficiently responsible to put family before self, and be civic-minded enough to rid community, state, and nation of those influences that would undermine morality and lead to social decay. In his famous "booze" sermon, entitled "Get on the Water Wagon," he challenged the men in his congregation in the name of their manhood to eradicate demon rum and subdue its minions.[20] God intended men to be victors over evil, not victims of it.

Sunday did not consider his emphasis on manliness merely a practical response to deteriorating conditions in the United States. Rather, he believed that it flowed directly from the timeless message of both the Old and New Testaments. He argued,

> Nobody can read the Bible thoroughly and thoughtfully and earnestly and not be impressed with the fact that it makes a great deal out of manhood and holds it up as something that should be sought after with diligence and perseverance.

The presence of so many virile heroes in the pages of the Scriptures was, for him, evidence that "God wants us to see what real manhood and real womanhood is and to become enamored of it."[21]

The evangelist never clearly delineated the traits that constituted biblical manliness, but courage and combativeness were definitely two important components. The Old Testament prophets he admired and often cited in his sermons all "carried a big stick." Although Old Testament heroes such as David and Daniel loomed larger in his message than did those of the New Testament, he regarded Jesus as the personification of true manhood. Sunday's Lord was "no dough-faced, lick-spittle proposition"; rather, he was "the greatest scrapper who ever lived." Furthermore, Billy believed that Jesus Christ intended that his disciples be "militant as well as persuasive" and be prepared "to fight as well as pray."[22] Accepting Jesus as one's savior was itself a manly act because publicly acknowledging one's sin and abandoning the lifestyle emanating from that sin required both self-discipline and the courage to confront the potential ridicule and scorn of former friends and associates. Moreover, conversion not only prepared men for spiritual development but facilitated the cultivation of manly virtues.

Sunday was certain "you never become a man until you become a Christian." Thus, his plea for sinners to accept Jesus as their Savior or for Christians to rededicate their lives to God was in a very real sense a challenge to the males in his audience to be men. "The best excuse," he said, that he ever heard a man give "for not seeking Christ was that he was 'not man enough.'" "It takes courage and manhood," he argued, "but it makes character and strength. It enables one to stand up straight before the world and inspires."[23]

The tone and style of Sunday's revivalism complemented the virile emphasis of his message. He delighted in calling "a spade a spade" and spoke with "short, staccato sentences" that "were like straight-arm blows from the shoulder."[24] Although he offended some worshipers' sense of decorum, his unabashed breach of rules of syntax, frequent use of slang, and forceful delivery generally enhanced the preacher's tough, street-wise image.

Sunday's evangelistic crusades were characterized by a carefully cultivated aura of combativeness, courageousness, energy, and athleticism. His sermons were often accompanied by martial music such as "Onward Christian Soldiers" and the "Battle Hymn of the Republic." He punctuated his oratory with military imagery, such as his designation of Christians as "Gospel grenadiers," his description of faith as analogous to "a warrior entering an enemy's country," or his call for "fighting preachers." He frequently turned to metaphors of warfare to depict the struggles of the righteous. Describing Sabbatarians' determination to resist challenges to the American Sabbath, he declared, "And I will say to the people that try to erase the Sabbath from our statute books, we will swim our horses in blood to their bridles before you ever get us away from it."[25]

As he harangued audiences, Sunday often conveyed the impression that he was something of a prophetic pugilist battling for righteousness. When his preaching grew fervent, he would sometimes divest himself of his collar, coat, and tie; roll up his sleeves; and adopt a truculent stance. He might shake his fist in the faces of local clergymen as he condemned the ineffectiveness of their churches or point an accusing finger at his audience as he recited a lengthy litany of contemporary sins. Rodeheaver recalled that although in private the evangelist was usually "far from pugnacious," on the platform "apparently he was ready to fight all opposition at the drop of a hat, giving no odds and asking none. He seemed to delight in stirring up an antagonist and knocking him into a cocked hat."[26]

At the pinnacle of his career in 1917, Sunday confided to his tabernacle audience in New York City that he had a "combative nature" and "a temper like a sheet-iron stove" that became "red hot" almost instantaneously. These characteristics, he confessed, made it difficult for him to abide by the biblical admonition to "resist not evil" and to love your enemies. As if to prove the point, he related an incident from earlier in his evangelistic career when, in a midwestern town in which he was preaching, he visited the workplace of an abusive husband and rebuked him for his sins. When the husband responded with profanity rather than contrition, the preacher's temper flared:

> I put my hand on the counter and I went over there like a shell out of a mortar, and he jumped backward to grab a 32 calibre gun that was lying there. I jumped between him and the gun and I said, "Don't you move to touch that. If you do they will take you up with a dust-pan and a whisk-broom."

He said to me, "You have no business behind the counter." I said, "You are right. Neither have you any business to call me the infamous names that you have sir." I said, "You get out from behind that counter and come out here on the sidewalk and I'll show you the finest demonstration of muscular Christianity you ever looked at." And if that gink had come out I'd have backslid long enough to have licked him.[27]

On at least one or two occasions, Sunday's pugnacity was put to the test by someone attending a revival service. In his autobiography, he recalled an incident that occurred in Springfield, Illinois, early in his career. As the evangelist preached, a man rushed to the platform and began lashing him with a rawhide whip, yelling as he did, "I have a commission from God to horsewhip you!" Although local newspaper accounts suggest that Billy pursued but did not catch his assailant, in his version of the encounter he gave his attacker a blow to the solar plexus and a left hook to the jaw, shouting as he subdued the irate worshiper, "Well, I have a commission from God to knock the tar out of you, you lobster."[28]

If Sunday's demeanor and rhetoric gave the impression that he was always ready for, perhaps even welcomed, such confrontations, it was at least in part because he wished to make it quite clear that the Christian life had in no way been detrimental to his own manhood. To one audience, he declared forthrightly,

> Before I was converted I could go five rounds so fast you couldn't see me for the dust, and I'm still pretty handy with my dukes and I can still deliver the goods with all express charges prepaid. Before I was converted I could run one hundred yards in ten seconds and circle the bases in fourteen seconds, and I could run just as fast after I was converted.[29]

The revivalist's reference to his skill as a base runner was characteristic of another feature of his evangelism, his frequent allusions to sports and his regular demonstrations of his athletic prowess. As thousands of enthralled worshipers watched, Sunday would run, jump, hurl unseen baseballs, smash imaginary home runs, slide for home plate, and shout in umpire-like fashion "you're out," thus announcing God's judgment on the unsaved. Congregations marveled at the evangelist's remarkable agility and energy, and journalists commented upon his stamina. One reporter estimated that as he preached Sunday traveled a mile during each sermon and more than 100 miles in every campaign. In 1914, the *Des Moines Register and Leader* reported that

> He fully measured up to his reputation for dramatic presentation of his themes. He charged back and forth on the platform, dropped to his knees at times, flopped into a chair, jumped upon it, waved his handkerchief and shook his fists, shouted, laughed, stormed, sweated, and performed a variety of other feats which would put an ordinary man in bed for a week.[30]

Sunday recognized the value of his spectacular athleticism for his image as a manly Christian and took considerable pains to maintain his agility and stamina, although not in the way one might expect today. He did not engage in a systematic aerobic or weight-training routine. In fact, the only vigorous workouts he regularly got were those that he received preaching two and sometimes three sermons a day during his revival campaigns. Among the evangelist's friends was Dr. Howard Kelly of Johns Hopkins in Baltimore. Kelly had impressed upon Billy the importance of extensive rest and of a massage at the end of each day's work, and Billy followed these suggestions throughout much of his career.[31]

Aside from the time spent dining with family and associates, an occasional walk, or an infrequent round of golf, Sunday spent the majority of his private hours relaxing in bed. Visitors to the nation's most famous preacher were often ushered into his bedroom, where they found him propped up against the pillows, draped in a worn robe, waiting to receive them. Those who sought an audience with the evangelist following an evening service might well find themselves in a setting reminiscent of the training room of a prizefighter. Sunday had a small private room constructed beneath the choir platform in each tabernacle. After the last sermon of the day, he retreated to this facility, equipped with a rough pine table, where an associate, such as the former welterweight prizefighter Jack Cardiff, who for a time after his conversion served as Sunday's personal trainer, would administer a massage using a special blend of olive and aromatic oils.[32]

As a result of the friendship that developed between the evangelist and the Mayo brothers, Sunday learned a good deal about the importance of diet to good health. He took considerable care to avoid overeating and to eat foods that he believed to be nutritious. He accused Americans of digging their graves with their teeth and claimed that he always left the table wanting more. Sunday liked plain food, such as "mashed potatoes, boiled beef, codfish, dried beef, smoked herring, stewed tomatoes, hard, dry toast," cereal, milk (sometimes heavily laced with cream), weak tea, and weak coffee. He enjoyed fruit, especially oranges and grapefruit, and avoided most sweets, but for dessert would sometimes have one of his favorite foods, "apple pie with cinnamon sprinkled over it." Despite his belief that he would not live to be an old man because of the pace of his work, with the exception of chronic allergies and asthma, Billy appears to have had remarkably good health and an extraordinary level of energy well into his sixties.[33]

If Sunday's persona conveyed an aura of masculine vigor, the story of his life provided something of a model for manliness. The evangelist's life seemed in many respects a tale of courage, determination, and triumph over adversity. As such, it was wholly consistent with, and an affirmation of, the American myth of success in which both he and his audiences believed. Although he was born in a log cabin on the Iowa prairie, by the 1910s he had become the most sought-after preacher in the nation and held evangelistic crusades in most of the country's major metropolitan areas. At the peak of his career, he was one of the best-known men of his age, received at the White House by Woodrow Wilson, admired and entertained by business leaders such as John D. Rockefeller, Jr. and John Wanamaker, given extensive coverage by newspapers and magazines, and heard

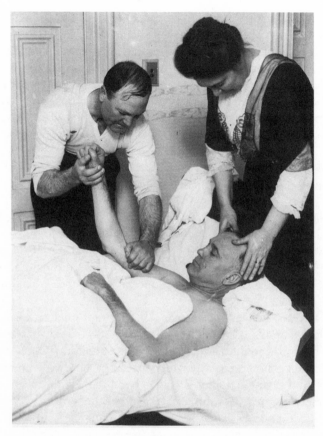

Jack Cardiff administering a massage to Billy Sunday,
with Nell Sunday at his head.

Courtesy of the Billy Sunday Historic Site Museum, Winona Lake, Indiana.

daily by thousands who flocked to services in cavernous wooden tabernacles constructed especially for his campaigns.[34]

To be sure, critics attacked Billy Sunday for his ties to business and his affluent lifestyle and substantial income, but he was for many admirers the embodiment of the American success story. As a child, he was so weak he could scarcely crawl, but by the 1880s he had become the fastest base runner in the National League. Professing to know no more about theology than "a jackrabbit knows about Ping-Pong" and with little oratorical training, he had become by World War I the most persuasive evangelist in the nation. From the confines of a log cabin on the Iowa prairie in the 1860s, Sunday had journeyed by 1915 to preach in the spacious elegance of Carnegie Hall.[35]

Sunday was proud of his achievements. Recognizing that his story captured the imagination of many worshipers, he sometimes referred directly to it in sermons. "I have butted and fought and struggled since I was six years old . . .

and if ever a man fought hard, I have fought hard for everything I have ever gained."[36] His saga affirmed for his audiences that even in an increasingly urban and industrial America, with an ever-more diverse population and an apparently widening gap between rich and poor, there were still opportunities for men to succeed. He had risen from rags to riches, from obscurity to fame, without benefit of father, money, or advanced educational training. Perhaps others could do likewise. The key to success was to follow Billy's example, to confront life with courage and tenacity, to do as he so often admonished — "Be a man."

Sunday's career as an aggressive and flamboyant professional athlete was a facet of his life story that further enhanced his reputation as a muscular Christian. His years with the Chicago White Stockings and Pittsburgh Alleghenies were those during which baseball was emerging as the national game and spectator sports were rapidly gaining popularity in urban America. As we have seen, there is ample evidence that his initial appeal as a volunteer and later as a salaried worker for the Chicago YMCA during the late 1880s and early 1890s was related closely to his performance on the diamonds of the National League.

In recent years, scholars have become increasingly interested in the socio-cultural function of sports. A facet of this interest is the way in which sports provided both an accommodation to change and a reaffirmation of traditional values, including those associated with masculinity. One writer has suggested that baseball was, among other things, "one of the central mechanisms by which masculinity was reconstituted at the turn of the century."[37] Attending or participating in baseball games helped to assure middle- and lower-middle-class white males of the continued legitimacy of such traditionally masculine virtues as aggressiveness, daring, determination, and individual skill and strength while at the same time affirming the worth of characteristics compatible with the new industrial order, including cooperation, discipline, and deference to authority. Thus, baseball was a game well-suited to an industrializing, urbanizing nation.

In the late nineteenth and early twentieth centuries, some argued that sports were "an essential element in the fight against feminization." Sports made men of boys. Theodore Roosevelt, who worried a good deal about American masculinity in particular and the future of the nation in general, included baseball in his list of "the true sports for a manly race."[38] Sunday's ties to professional baseball linked him to what was increasingly perceived as a sport that built character, instilled skill and discipline, and strengthened the nation.

In her book *Manliness and Civilization: A Cultural History of Gender and Race in the United States, 1880–1920*, historian Gail Bederman has described efforts on the part of the middle class to redefine manhood at the end of the nineteenth and beginning of the twentieth centuries. She contends that "manliness," as understood by Victorian America, suggested qualities of character and morality, while "masculinity," which began to appear in the 1890s, connoted physical attributes, such as strength, energy, muscularity, and athletic prowess.[39]

Billy Sunday's gospel message and evangelistic persona combined this emerging notion of "masculinity" with the traditional understanding of "manliness." It is not surprising, therefore, that one observer commented concerning Sunday that "He stands up like a man in the pulpit and out of it. He speaks like a man. He works like a man. . . . He is manly with God, and everyone who comes to hear him. No matter how much you disagree with him, he treats you after a manly fashion. He is not an imitation but a manly man giving to all a square deal."[40]

The author of this observation was correct; Sunday was not an imitation, but neither was he wholly what the public perceived him to be. He was, most certainly, an extraordinary individual who aspired to the ideal of manhood that he espoused. Yet despite his courage and tenacity, he was a fundamentally fragile man who waged a lifelong struggle against loneliness, disappointment, and self-doubt. Over the years, his success in baseball had given him considerable confidence in his physical ability. His conversion experience and commitment to a career in Christian work provided a sense of significance and purpose to his life. It was his marriage to Helen Thompson, however, that furnished the emotional sustenance that enabled Billy to succeed. When he declared, "Many a man wouldn't have amounted to a hill of beans if it hadn't been for the little woman behind him nagging him on," he knew whereof he spoke. Nell hardly fit the stereotype of the "little woman," nor was she a nag, but she, more than any other single individual in the revivalist's circle of family and friends, was responsible for his remarkable rise to evangelistic fame.

Helen Sunday was a bright, talented, and strong-willed woman who in a later era might have made a mark on the world in her own right. She appears, however, to have never directly challenged the prevailing late-nineteenth-century gender norms in which she had been steeped. In many ways, she was at least as strong a figure as Billy, but there is no evidence that she ever contested the principle of male dominance in the family or society. She did not think it necessary that women have the right to vote, scorned many of the innovations in female fashions in the 1920s, opposed birth control, and frowned on women putting jobs or careers ahead of familial responsibilities unless financial pressures made it unavoidable.

Ironically, Helen had what amounted to a career. She spoke publicly about issues that sometimes had political significance and dressed stylishly though conservatively, all of which seemed to belie her words. Yet in her own mind, there were no contradictions between what she preached and what she practiced because she always exercised her influence within the context of her role as wife, mother, and helpmate. She told reporters, "I believe that every married woman should make her husband's career her own, help him to be successful, and take her joy in his accomplishments," and "I never helped Mr. Sunday because I felt I had to have a career. I did it as a duty."[41]

She willingly admitted, however, that she had enjoyed her life on the road with Billy.

That life had begun in 1908, when, after the birth of Paul, the couple's last child, Nell concluded that if her husband's work was to continue to prosper, she would have to devote more of her time to it. With the two oldest Sunday children in school and the two youngest in the care of a nurse, Helen committed herself wholeheartedly to Billy's ministry. For the next twenty-seven years, she acted as ex officio chief of staff, helped promote evangelistic work among women, assisted with public relations, and served as general factotum. Her most important function, however, was as her husband's constant companion and confidant. He made few if any major decisions without consulting his wife.

The indispensable role Nell played in Billy's ministry was recognized by the Sundays' professional associates, the press, and the public. For routine matters, and sometimes for important ones, the evangelist's staff frequently dealt with Nell rather than with Billy directly. In any campaign, reporters gave Mrs. Sunday considerable attention, covering her activities and seeking her opinion on issues of contemporary interest, such as pacifism, the theory of evolution, or current women's fashions. As far as the populace was concerned, Billy was without question the star of the show, but "Ma" played a very prominent supporting role.

The truth was that Helen was even more important to Sunday's success than anyone outside the family knew. The revivalist was profoundly dependent materially and emotionally on his wife. This is nowhere more apparent than in the extant letters between the two dating from the mid and late 1880s to the late 1920s and early 1930s. In the early days of the couple's relationship, when Billy was on the road with the White Stockings or the Alleghenies, Nell repeatedly had to comfort, cajole, and occasionally reprimand the lonely, depressed, and sometimes self-pitying ballplayer. As he began his own ministry and traveled across the Corn Belt, the extended absences from home aggravated his insecurity. In the late 1890s, while on an evangelistic campaign, he wrote to Nell of a dream in which he had returned home and found her in bed with another man.[42] This nightmare, for it was for him just that, was indicative not of concerns about marital infidelity but of his own chronic uneasiness and self-doubt. The loneliness of his travels sometimes became almost overwhelming, and he would ask Nell to join him whenever possible. His persistent appeals for her assistance, along with her understanding of Billy's need for her advice and companionship, eventually persuaded her to begin working with him on a regular basis.

To his credit, Sunday appreciated and acknowledged how much of an asset his wife was to his ministry. He also recognized the degree to which she was a bulwark against the stresses and strains that threatened his equilibrium. He lived and worked in a culture in which men were reluctant to reveal emotions other than those conventionally regarded as manly, but with her he did not have to conceal his weaknesses and his fears. He knew that in moments of indecision or self-doubt she would be there to help him believe in himself and find the strength to do what needed to be done. In 1929, as the couple wrestled with declining popularity and the personal and financial entanglements of their two oldest sons, a beleaguered Billy wrote to Nell, "Dearest on earth, Miss you? does a blind man miss his eyes?" In another letter, he described something resembling an anxiety attack he had experienced after returning to their empty Winona Lake home,

> I couldn't stand it. . . . It's the first time in my life I was at home and *all* the family gone: of course you have been down in the Park but I mean all away. I thought I would faint. I had to gasp for my breath. Oh, oh what a lonely feeling. Say Ma don't you go to Heaven first. I couldn't stay if you were gone and the children gone: I surely love you and home too but rugs and chairs and pictures cant [sic] talk and comfort you.[43]

Companionship and care were what this extraordinarily complex man needed most. Helen Haines, the Sundays' oldest child and only daughter, came as close as anyone to grasping the essence of her father's personality when she wrote to him, "Even with all your wonderful success and high place you always seem like a little boy to me — a little boy, who needs comforting and loving." Helen also understood the degree to which her mother helped her father to function effectively. In 1929, she wrote to her, "You are entirely responsible for making papa what he is."[44]

Perhaps there was an element of hyperbole in Helen Haines's observations, but she was essentially right on both counts. Billy Sunday possessed genuine courage, toughness, tenacity, and a drive to succeed and to serve his God. He was in many ways the kind of man he urged the males in his audiences to become. Yet at the core of his being there was an insecure, lonely little boy who needed mothering, and Helen Sunday fulfilled more of that need than did anyone else. As nurturer, comforter, and protector, she fulfilled a role the evangelist's mother had never really been able to fill and, by doing so, she enabled him to more easily project a manly persona to the world.

Sunday's need for surrogate maternal care throughout much of his life and the absence of a strong father figure during his youth contributed to another chink in the armor of masculinity with which the evangelist tried to gird himself as an adult — his deficiencies as a parent. Despite his idealization of the home and the role of the mother and father in it, Billy's childhood experiences provided only incomplete models of the nuclear family on which to draw. Consequently, although a loving and devoted father, he appears to have never been entirely comfortable dealing with even the somewhat limited routine parental obligations of males in his day. His relationship with his children was further complicated by his frequent separations from them. Although he had missed Nell deeply while on the road as a baseball player, once settled into his new life as an assistant "Y" secretary in Chicago, Billy quickly grew restless. The normal patterns of day-to-day familial responsibility and a relatively sedentary job had never been part of his experience.

It may well have been disquietude as much as his ambition, a higher salary, or desire to serve God and humanity that led Sunday to leave his growing family, first to join the revivalistic team of J. W. Chapman and then to launch his own evangelistic career and begin roaming the Midwest and nation as he had years earlier as a ballplayer. He loved his wife and children very much, but he was not wholly at ease with his paternal role. He missed his family to the point of despondency when he was away but found it difficult to surrender the peripatetic life of first a ballplayer and then an evangelist. Although he remained an important figure in his children's lives, over the years he relinquished an increasingly large part of the parental role to Nell. He justified this to himself and others by saying he was doing the Lord's work while simultaneously providing for his family.

Billy's frequent protracted absences were difficult for his children. In her early thirties, Helen Haines wrote to her mother of the wrenching emotions her father's departures engendered in her as a child:

> It just seems to me I will never get over, as long as I live, that dreadful feeling way down inside of me, when I used to stand out on the front stoop in Chicago and see dad disappearing from view past the arc light and the church, waving us a good-bye. It seemed to me in those old days that my heart would simply burst open with longing.[45]

Add to the periodic separations the fact that his children, to some degree, stood in awe of their famous, successful father who had devoted his life to serving God, and it is not surprising that normal patterns of intimacy were strained.

A letter from George to his father, written sometime in the 1920s, illuminates the complex relationship between Billy and his sons:

> Our dad . . . is rather neglectful of his boys, doesn't come and see us very often but we understand.
>
> Dad you know that sometimes I could just cry to think that circumstances always sort of kept you and I from really knowing each other. In our hearts there is so much love for each other—but it just seems there has been sort of a wall of misunderstanding or rather lack of close heart understanding. I so often want to write you and pour out my heart to you but I am always afraid, or sort of bashful—and I sort of freeze it up. Daddy dear, I do so love you, do so appreciate your wonderful accomplishments in life—your great big heart of love—your great mind and spirit of drive. If ever a father has earned a place of love and respect in the hearts of his sons—you sure have and I want you to know Daddy dear that you have it—and that I am trying hard every day to be worthy of you.[46]

While the Sunday offspring admired their father, they regarded their mother as the "Gibraltar" of stability in their world.[47] Yet as she became increasingly involved in Billy's work, even that anchor of security began to slip. The disrupted patterns of family life and the emotional strains that resulted from being the children of prominent, successful, driven parents were enormous psychological burdens from which Helen, George, Bill, and Paul seem never to have been able to escape. Likewise, the personal and financial problems that plagued their children in adulthood haunted the Sundays and became an increasingly debilitating force in Billy's life.

Millions of Americans, unaware of the evangelist's personal and familial struggles, viewed him as a tough, athletic battler for righteousness who feared only the Lord and who was willing to confront the Devil anywhere, anytime, in any guise. Like Theodore Roosevelt, he seemed to his admirers to embody the strenuous life, but there was more to his appeal than flamboyant aggressiveness. A son of the frontier, an athlete, a man of God, a success in his chosen profession, Sunday personified a variety of characteristics that his contemporaries associated with American manliness. His passion, strength, agility, and combativeness typified the masculine primitive ideal of manhood. His piety, emphasis on moral reform, and belief in the sanctity of the family were consistent with the Christian gentleman's conception of manliness. The sophisticated, businesslike organization of his revivals, his acceptance by many prominent figures within the nation's commercial community, and his ascent from poverty to affluence conveyed the impression of business acumen and worldly success inherent in the masculine achiever ideal.

It is difficult to judge how much of Sunday's aura of manliness was conscious and calculated and how much was an unconscious reflection of prevailing gender norms and an expression of his own emotional struggles. Clearly, the revivalist was a sensitive and shrewd public speaker who could read the mood of the times, knew what audiences found engaging, and understood how to manipulate a crowd. Undoubtedly, he developed a persona that would enhance the appeal of his ministry; however, he most certainly believed in and tried to personify the manly virtues that he espoused. They were consistent both with prevailing cultural ideals and his reading of the Bible. Furthermore, his experiences as he endeavored to cope with the problems of his own life seemed to him to corroborate their validity.

Although his faith, his marriage, and his success alleviated some of the feelings of inadequacy and loneliness stemming from the loss, poverty, and uncertainty of his troubled early years on the Iowa prairie, Sunday was never able to wholly escape the haunting emotions that were a legacy of his past. It is too simplistic to suggest that his flamboyant, aggressive personality was merely a classic case of overcompensation. Nevertheless, attempting to cultivate traits such as independence, self-reliance, and an apparent toughness that were admired in the frontier ethos of his youth most certainly helped him to allay self-doubt and cope more effectively with the vagaries of his unpredictable and sometimes lonely world. His triumph over hardship and adversity coupled with the gospel of muscular Christianity that he imbibed through the YMCA early in his life as a committed evangelical Christian authenticated his understanding of what it meant to be a man. A blend of temperament and experience, accentuated by his sense of what was appealing and his flair for the dramatic, Sunday's virile persona and the resounding affirmation of manliness in his message struck a resonant chord in the hearts and minds of millions of anxious Americans and contributed immeasurably to the appeal of his evangelism.

SIX

Progressive Orthodoxy

For those who admired Billy Sunday, one of the most dramatic and appealing characteristics of his masculine persona was an aura of combative moral courage which suggested that he would take on all comers in defense or advocacy of a just cause. His apparent willingness to campaign, at any cost, for a more righteous nation came at a time when millions of Americans were engaged in a fervent crusade to make their land a better place in which to live. In striking ways, the course of Sunday's evangelistic career paralleled the history of the broad, amorphous response to change known as Progressivism. Each originated in the 1890s, gained momentum in the first decade of the century, reached its zenith in the 1910s, and faded but did not wholly disappear thereafter. That the two phenomena were coterminous does not necessarily imply a correlation between them. Nevertheless, the revivalist's widespread popularity in an era of social activism suggests that his ministry in some way was congruent with the spirit of the times and raises the intriguing question of where, if at all, Sunday fit along the spectrum of early-twentieth-century reform.

The evangelist's contemporaries, as well as subsequent generations of defenders and detractors, have held widely disparate views of his relationship to the efforts to resolve the major problems of the times. During the first and second decades of the century, many admirers regarded the unconventional preacher as both a great winner of souls and a catalyst for progress. They applauded not only the number of "trail hitters" who answered his altar calls but also the way he appeared to rouse people out of their apathy and marshal them against political corruption, vice, and immorality.

In the summer of 1905, an observer in Macomb, Illinois, noted that as a result of Sunday's work, swearing had ceased, there was a "marked change in the men of our factories," and the laws were being enforced. Later that year, supporters in Burlington, Iowa, contended that his revival there had ushered in an era of civic reform. Journalist Ray Stannard Baker reported in 1910 that many midwestern clergy were enthusiastic about Sunday's work because they believed his ministry would in some way improve the quality of life in their communities. In 1914, a pastor in Scranton, Pennsylvania, credited the revivalist's preaching with having had more to do with the revolt against Senator Boies Penrose and his political machine than any other single cause. John D. Rockefeller, Jr. called Sunday "a rallying center around whom all people interested in good things may gather," and Henry Leland described him as "this great plumed knight clothed in the armor of God."[1]

Many other people were, to say the least, unimpressed with Sunday's methods and message. Apostles of the Social Gospel, such as Washington Gladden, scorned what they regarded as the social vacuity and atavistic theology of his evangelism. Secular critics, such as the Progressive journalist George Creel, not only shared the conviction that Sunday's sermons were void of meaningful content but also denounced him as the pawn of special interests and an obstacle to constructive change. In a scathing 1915 article entitled "Salvation Circus" in *Harper's Weekly*, Creel acknowledged Sunday's sincerity and commitment but described him as a "man with the child's mind and the child's faith" who "fits the needs of Big Business as skin fits the hand." He charged that at a time when the "oppressed and disinherited" were no longer "servile" but beginning to challenge the status quo and force alone could not keep them in check, the establishment turned to distraction to defuse their threat, and what better distraction than Billy Sunday. He would

> pack people into a great amphitheater, set their emotions to boiling with music and passionate oratory, and convince them that all poverty, all injustice, all starvation, is due to drinking, dancing, card playing and a refusal to say, "I am for Christ."

Creel was certain that through his revivals Sunday had "dealt the social sense a body blow." The "spirit of service" that had begun "to be a significant feature of modern life" had "been turned into its ancient channels of emotionalism." "Altruism" was being "frittered away" in "'experience meetings' and 'hitting the sawdust trail.'" He had no doubt that big business, which for years had recognized the manipulative potential of religion, was now using Sunday, with his "faith and fervor" and his "power to intoxicate crowds, and the most absolute ignorance of everything pertaining to democracy, industry, economics and politics."[2]

Forty years after Creel blasted Sunday for impeding reform in his day, historian William McLoughlin made a similar accusation. In an exceptionally able study, *Billy Sunday Was His Real Name*, McLoughlin wrote of the evangelist,

> What he did not claim, but might rightfully have, for his revivalism, was a large part in halting, at least temporarily, the trend which began at the turn of the century toward a re-examination of the traditional beliefs and institutions of America. By playing upon the middle classes' innate fear of change, Sunday's preaching blunted and almost destroyed the keen edge of the reform movement which had seemed to promise so much.[3]

It is a measure of Sunday's popularity and apparent powers of persuasion that a well-known contemporary journalist and an astute student of American revivalism of a later generation could consider him a sufficiently potent force to obstruct the broad and diverse currents of early-twentieth-century reform. There is, however, no credible evidence that the evangelist had any negative impact on the overall course of Progressivism. On the contrary, some of his social objectives were wholly consistent with the goals of the more conservative wing of the movement.

Given the cataclysmic events of the twentieth century, the early 1900s seem, in retrospect, an appealingly placid and innocent age. For those who experienced them, however, these years were hardly so tranquil as they appear through the nostalgic mists of our collective national memory. At the time, millions of Americans were apprehensive about the tide of change flowing about them, but they also appreciated the material progress that was its corollary. Their ambivalence meant that few people genuinely yearned for a return to an idealized past. Most simply wanted a way to reconcile continuity and change. This desire furnished much of the impetus for the rise of Progressivism and facilitated the extraordinary success of the most famous preacher of the age.

It would, of course, be an exercise in hyperbole, if not sheer deceit, to argue that Billy Sunday was either a leading theoretician or tactician of Progressivism. Yet it is equally erroneous to exclude him altogether from the ranks of the reformers of his day. Given the optimism, patriotism, businesslike efficiency, aura of democracy, and moral content that his evangelism shared with various facets of the Progressive spirit, it is easy to understand why contemporary admirers sometimes regarded him not just as a revivalist but also as a social activist.

For the most part, Progressives were an extraordinarily optimistic and patriotic lot. They were certain that they could discern what was best for their country and confident that they could achieve it. Implicit in their notion of progress was the assumption that their land was exceptional. Although it was plagued by a myriad of problems, they believed the future of the United States would be bright if men and women set their minds to making it so. For all his prophetic fulminations against the decline of American society, Sunday shared much of this idealism. For him, however, there was one important caveat. The national destiny was tied closely to the citizenry's commitment to Christian principles. As far as he was concerned, loyalty to country and to Christ were synonymous. The United States would progress only to the extent that it remained true to the will of God. Individuals and nations were incomplete and unfulfilled without religion. For Billy to preach the gospel, therefore, was not simply a matter of trying to save souls but also an effort to promote the country's welfare. The evangelist declared,

> There are lots of things that I'm not proud of in my country. I am proud of
> everything that's good and I abhor everything that's evil, and I hope that
> when I stand up here and preach the gospel of Jesus Christ to make

drunkards sober, to make libertines pure, to make blasphemers pray, and Sabath desecrators keep the law of God, I am working for the good of my nation and of my land, and for you.[4]

The challenge for Billy was to help millions of Americans realize their potential. His sermons were, therefore, as much a call to action as a call to salvation. There was no limit to what the Christian men and women of the United States could accomplish if only they would have the courage to stand up for what was right. Tides of change were eroding national life, but courageous action rooted in loyalty to Christ could stem the tide. Douglas Frank has written perceptively,

> The good news, in Sunday's hands, became the proclamation that men and women could be good and strong; and that if enough people were good and strong, politics would be purified, insanity and poverty would disappear, families would be made whole, young people would grow up to be solid citizens, and, in general, America would be saved. . . . What excited Sunday was not that people would hear of the love and merciful forgiveness of God, but that they could use God to make themselves and their country good.[5]

Another characteristic of Sunday's evangelism that was consonant with the Progressive tenor of the times was the air of efficiency and expertise that surrounded his meetings. Many Progressives admired nothing so much as the application of business and scientific methods to any and all problems. As we have already seen in the discussion of Sunday's entrepreneurial evangelism, at its zenith his ministry appeared to operate like a well-oiled machine. Every aspect of a campaign—advertising, financing, organization of personnel, construction of tabernacles, pre-revival meetings, utilization of music, and handling of crowds—was highly orchestrated. Published statistics regarding attendance, revenues, and numbers of "trail hitters" provided detailed and usually satisfying indexes of the economy, efficiency, and effectiveness with which a revival was run. The evangelist and his staff were God's experts, winning souls and championing righteousness with the precision of an engineer and skill of a scientific manager. This lent a very appealing air of sophistication and modernity to his ministry.

At the same time, there were other threads in Sunday's revivalism that were consistent with another somewhat different element within the Progressive movement, that which celebrated tradition and believed that the values and relationships of earlier generations of Americans were relevant to the problems of the contemporary world. One dimension of this effort to call the past into the service of the present was the appeal to democracy. Despite the fact that many early-twentieth-century reformers were rather elitist in their assurance that they knew better than anyone else what was best for those they sought to help, they often used democratic rhetoric in the struggle for the causes they championed. They professed concern for the poor, called for justice for the disadvantaged, and argued that government should be made more accessible and responsive to the wishes of the people. Even though sometimes arrogant in their approach to problems, they believed they were acting in the interest of the masses.

This semblance of democracy was readily apparent in both the substance of Sunday's message and the form of his evangelism. Billy considered himself a man of the people, and for much of his career he related well to the common folk. He believed that the people had it within their power to change the world for the better and that, in general, "You can always count on a decent public to right a wrong." His job as evangelist was, at least in part, to call attention to those wrongs and to rally the righteous of the land to eliminate them.[6]

There was also an appealingly democratic and egalitarian air about Sunday's tent and tabernacle meetings. The rich and poor, the respected and obscure walked the sawdust aisles, sat shoulder to shoulder on rough-hewn benches, gazed at surroundings void of adornment, and heard the preacher talk about God and their souls, not in the sophisticated lexicon of the seminary but in the everyday language of the home, the workplace, or the street. The rustic surroundings, intimate contact, and plain speech, reminiscent of what worshipers believed to have been a simpler time, helped to convey the notion of equality before God and man.[7]

Sunday preached to people about much more than God or their souls. He addressed the quality of their lives in this world as well. The substance of his sermons, like the form of his evangelism, was a blend of tradition and modernity that the more conservative reformers of the day found appealing. For the most part, he taught conventional evangelical theology and social values but couched them in terms designed to make them palatable to a nation in transition. The revivalist championed what he called "progressive orthodoxy," an ill-defined phrase probably intended to give his ministry an air of relevance. Sometimes his words did indeed have a very contemporary ring, as when he condemned political corruption or economic injustice and advocated such reforms as women's suffrage, the teaching of sex hygiene in the schools, and higher salaries for educators. These were not dominant themes in his message and there may have been an element of opportunism in the raising of such issues, but there is no doubt that he sincerely believed that his work had important social implications. As his career unfolded and he began to emerge from the smaller towns of the Midwest into the larger cities of the region and nation, he advertised the salutary effects his revivals would have on community life. Both he and the sympathetic citizenry of the places in which he preached regarded his ministry as a potent force for change.

In terms of philosophy and tactics, Billy Sunday's approach to reform had more in common with the social activism of the nineteenth century than with that of the twentieth. While he shared much of Progressivism's optimism and patriotism and some of its willingness to use legislation as a means of improving the quality of American life, Sunday was essentially an evangelical reformer for whom sin, not society, was the problem and the individual, not the state, the instrument for its solution. He considered the Social Gospel heretical, shortsighted, and materialistic. He complained that some people were "trying to make a religion out of social service with Jesus Christ left out." He thought that by failing to look to the transformation of the human heart through the acceptance of God's gift of salvation, this burgeoning movement within Christianity was neglecting the welfare of the soul and doing little to reform society.[8]

Despite his support of such moral strictures as Sabbatarian or Prohibition laws, Sunday generally had little faith in statutory or economic solutions to most problems. He acknowledged the importance of the social and economic milieu in helping men and women to live better lives, but he believed that social ills originated in flawed human nature. The transformation of society must begin with the transformation of the human heart. Order, stability, and justice rested upon the behavior of individuals. Those with the right relationship to God would have a proper relationship with their fellow human beings and would act in their best interest. He reminded worshipers that "Jesus said, 'out of the heart proceedeth evil thoughts, murders, fornication.' If the deeds of men and women are black it is because their hearts were first black." To try to reform society without first changing the hearts of individuals was futile. To provide people a higher standard of living and to pass legislation curbing their baser tendencies was worthwhile but of limited value. He warned repeatedly that "you cannot legislate men and women out of vice."

> It is not simply a question of a pay envelope, whether anybody be pure or whether they be impure. You can't raise, my friends, the morals by raising simply the scale of wages alone. . . . When the hearts of men and women are right, then their conduct will be right.[9]

Billy's message focused on repentance and the acceptance of God's grace, but the consequences of redemption were clearly social as well as personal. His evangelistic crusades always included altar calls that drew "converts" by the hundreds or even thousands. Yet his sermons were also lessons in his version of applied Christianity rather than mere discourses in a fundamentalist theology or emotional appeals for repentance. He believed his mission, at least in part, to be to "make it easier for men to do right and harder to do wrong."[10]

Doing right was largely a matter of what Sunday characterized as "decency." Billy told his audiences "God wants you to be decent," by which he meant conformity to the rural and small-town evangelical mores of the Midwest of his youth.[11] He never asked probing questions about the traditional moral code of his day. On the contrary, he equated its tenets with Christian conduct. His notion of sin was a matter of personal or societal deviation from accepted norms. He railed against a litany of individual evils, from masturbation to intemperance to gambling to greed, but the evangelist's message clearly went beyond individual piety. Laziness, drunkenness, licentiousness, selfishness, or irreligiousness were unquestionably sinful tendencies that endangered the soul, but they were also sins with broad social implications. Reflecting the ideal (if not necessarily the reality) of community cohesiveness prevalent in Iowa during his early years, Sunday believed such irresponsible habits to be unproductive and a threat to family, church, community, and the larger economic and social fabric of the nation. Although he lacked the experience and sophistication to make such connections in the economic or institutional sphere, Sunday had a profound sense of the interconnectedness of personal and social relationships.

The evangelist's view of society was fundamentally organic. He believed in individual freedom and the right of every person to strive for success. At the same time, he did not think that such liberty should take precedence over the welfare of the collective whole. Individuals had a moral obligation to the community that transcended personal freedom. He told New Yorkers in 1917, "Never in the name of liberty must you exercise your liberty that's going to harm anybody else." He illustrated this point by saying,

> When the citizenship of this city multiplies to 4,000,000 or 5,000,000, you can't make a race track out of Broadway nor Fifth Avenue. You can't build a slaughter house down at the Madison Square. You can't build a glue factory in City Hall Park.[12]

Sunday believed that just as one could not exercise personal liberty if it physically endangered others, so too one could not engage in activities that undermined the morality of another. One could not operate a brothel or saloon or do anything else that was detrimental to the moral welfare of the community. God expected people to live lives that promoted the public good, and society had a right to restrain those who failed to do so. Billy made it clear that because of the collateral effects of a person's actions, "It is everybody's business what everybody does."[13]

Most Progressives had a strong sense of their obligation to take responsibility for the general welfare, a point of view that Billy Sunday and others of his ilk shared. The evangelist believed it unconscionable to perpetuate institutions and influences in society that were detrimental to others even when they did him no immediate or direct harm. "There is my neighbor, and I am not going to be fool enough to let an institution exist that will damn him because it doesn't damn me, and live a life of selfishness, sir."[14]

While the weblike nature of personal and social relationships seemed obvious to Sunday, the economic complexities of his world were, for the most part, lost on him. As far as he was concerned, there was "no prejudice existing between man and men, between masses and classes, between capital and labor, that can't be driven from the world by the principles of Jesus Christ manifested in the lives of man and men, masses and classes, capital and labor."[15]

Although he occasionally spoke out against child labor and condemned the exploitation of industrial workers, Sunday tended to see such injustices as simply the result of sinful conduct. He failed to recognize the extent to which the rise of large-scale capitalism had contributed to growing problems of social injustice. Never especially well-versed in the business complexities of his day, Billy continued to think largely in terms of the commercial and

manufacturing ethos of the Midwest of his youth. He understood only dimly
the way in which the new economic order was becoming ruthlessly competitive, broadening the distance between management and labor, altering the
nature of work, and transforming men and women into depersonalized pawns
in the deadly serious game of making a profit. He acknowledged that many
people were struggling to make ends meet and seems to have genuinely
sympathized with their plight. Yet his own emergence out of an impoverished
background into the ranks of the successful, coupled with the prevailing
notion that individuals were primarily the masters of their own destiny, made
it difficult for him to understand how the economic system and those who
profited from it were victimizing millions.[16]

For Sunday, life was a concrete and personal matter. Abstract complexities
often eluded him. He could see the drunkard or prostitute on the street and
readily grasp the relationship between their condition and the saloon or
brothel because he was predisposed to see these very visible institutions as
detrimental forces in society. He could not, however, easily make the same
kind of connection between the impoverished laboring class and the captains
of industry for whom they worked. In his experience, the businessman was
generally a respected member of and a contributor to the community. Usually, the more successful he was, the greater respect he commanded. The
pervasive power of the American myth of success blinded Billy, as it did
millions of others, to the social costs that were sometimes the corollary of
individual achievement.

Like many of his Christian contemporaries, the revivalist believed that God
intended men to strive to succeed, and he regarded prosperity as a manifestation of divine favor.

> The Bible, my friends, hasn't one word to say against success. The Bible
> applauds success. The Bible has no quarrel with success. The Bible says that
> the man that doesn't provide for his family is worse than an infidel.

He pointed out that such Old Testament heroes as Abraham, David, and
Solomon would have been billionaires had they lived in the modern world.
This was surely proof enough that God rewarded the faithful. If success was a
blessing bestowed on the righteous by the Lord, then what right did men have
to criticize them?

> We have got a lot of guys in this country that stand around on corners and
> loaf around stale beer joints and cuss and damn and whittle and spit and
> condemn everybody that's got an honest dollar, whether the man that had
> the remark made about him was a scallawag [sic] or not, and I notice that all
> these guys that knock the fellow that's got the money would take every cent
> the fellow's got if he'd give it to them.[17]

Sunday saw nothing wrong with material gain, so long as one did not use
crooked methods to acquire it and did not place it above the more important
things of life.

The evangelist's relationship to the business community was also informed by a characteristic rather common among American Evangelicals—a tendency to appraise people almost exclusively in terms of their personal morality and overt religiosity. If, as was the case with many of his business acquaintances, one abstained from alcohol, gambling, dancing, card-playing, sexual impropriety, or other vices; was an active member of the church; and was an upstanding member of the community, he or she was judged a person of good character. The assumption that such people did not take advantage of others precluded more perceptive analyses of their role in the economic and social problems of their day.

The absence of a critique of the economic order in Sunday's message is also not surprising, because he was part of a revivalistic tradition that had usually shunned non-pietistic social issues. Desiring to alienate as few supporters and potential converts as possible, Billy, like other evangelists, avoided attacking that which did not seem directly relevant to the goals of his ministry. The condition of labor, unlike the saloon, brothel, gambling den, dance hall, or other moral threats, did not appear to have direct implications for one's personal salvation. The fact that there was no compelling need to attack the prevailing economic order was, of course, convenient because it enabled the revivalist to avoid antagonizing the business class whose support was crucial to the success of his campaigns. To conclude, however, that a self-serving deference to his patrons determined the tenor of his sermons is simplistic, since it fails to take into account the nature of the evangelical tradition of which he was a part.

At the same time, it is naive to oversimplify the reasons for the economic establishment's support of Sunday's work. Reflecting a Progressive predisposition to think conspiratorially, George Creel viewed the evangelist as a sincere but unwitting pawn of special interests who maneuvered him from trouble spot to trouble spot to quell unrest. While there is a kernel of truth in this, it is somewhat unfair to both the flamboyant preacher and those who sponsored his campaigns. Millions of Sunday's contemporaries shared a nineteenth-century value system that prized individualism and personal piety but, at the same time, placed a premium on the ideal of community peace and harmony.

The middle and upper classes felt increasingly uneasy about the social and cultural changes occurring in their world. Businessmen, like most Americans, loathed discord because it was inconsistent with their social ideology. They understood that a religious revival could act as oil on troubled waters, and they recognized that to be to their advantage. However, when they supported a Sunday campaign, it was not simply a selfish use of religion to stifle economic unrest and protect their own interest; it was also part of an effort to preserve and promote their idealized, and perhaps unrealistic, vision of American life. Given their frame of reference, they found Billy's revivals not merely useful but also comforting, affirming, and even Progressive. In turn, Sunday, chronically plagued by insecurity, was gratified and invigorated by their support, both for him and for the religious and social values that he espoused.

If the nation's most famous revivalist did not join the ranks of those decrying the threat to traditional political and economic values posed by the rise of big business and the injustices inherent in the new economic order, the question then arises, From what sources did his reputation as a reformer spring? The answer lies entangled in a complex contemporary and historical controversy over the nature of Progressive social action. George Creel and William McLoughlin understood Progressivism largely in political, social, and economic terms and refused to acknowledge the legitimacy of a moral component within it. In doing so, they staked out a position in what has become a long-standing debate over the nature of early-twentieth-century reform.

Neither Progressives nor those who have studied them have ever reached a consensus regarding what constituted genuine reform. Much of the debate has turned on questions of individual freedom and the legitimacy of campaigns, such as the push for Prohibition and the crusade against prostitution. Some Progressives embraced these efforts, while others viewed them as ill-conceived or reactionary. In 1912, Charles Beard criticized the "moral enthusiasts" who were "pushing through legislation" that they were "not willing to uphold by concentrated and persistent action." In *The Promise of American Life*, Herbert Croly argued that reformers who functioned as "moral Protestants and purifiers" were engaged in a fundamentally "misdirected effort." Only "personal self-stultification" could result from such an "illiberal puritanism." Croly believed that true reform involved "an intellectual as well as a moral challenge."[18]

In the mid-1950s, Richard Hofstadter condemned Prohibition as "a ludicrous caricature of the reforming impulse," a "'pinched, parochial substitute' for genuine reform, imposed by spiteful rural folk upon the more tolerant and urbane cities." Little more than a decade later, Egal Feldman used similarly derogatory language to describe the coercive aspects of the crusade against prostitution that he labeled "irrational, evangelical, uncompromising, and completely divorced from the humanitarianism of the early twentieth century."[19]

On the other hand, many people who considered themselves Progressives, including such diverse figures as William Jennings Bryan and Theodore Roosevelt, believed that attacks on the saloon or the brothel were integral threads in the tapestry of reform. A number of latter twentieth-century historians have concurred, among them James Timberlake, Paul Boyer, and Norman Clark. These and other scholars have argued that philosophically and tactically, proponents of what is often labeled moral reform had much in common with other contemporary advocates of change.[20]

Boyer contends that "for Progressives of all stripes, as for their predecessors in the 1890s, questions of social injustice, corporate wrongdoing, governmental corruption, and personal morality were inextricably linked."

> Almost every Progressive cause had its moral dimension; almost every condition Progressives set out to change was seen as contributing to a debilitating social environment that made it easier for people to go wrong and harder

for them to go right. Child labor and exploitation of women workers were evil not only because they were physically harmful, but also because they stunted the moral and spiritual development of their victims.

Urban graft and corruption were "evil not only because they wasted the taxpayers' money, but also because they debased the moral climate of the city." Therefore, causes such as Prohibition or the purity crusade, though not universally popular among reformers, were an "authentic expression of the broader Progressive impulse."[21]

It was in the theater of moral reform that Billy Sunday's ministry most obviously converged with contemporary activism. While his success was by no means attributable to a single cause, his popularity was unquestionably related to his social agenda. In times of societal stress, a single issue may become emblematic of a constellation of perceived evils. At such moments, those who confront society's symbolic dragons often assume the mantle of Saint George in the popular mind. Such was the case with Billy Sunday, who challenged what many people perceived as the most sinister threats to the nation—demon rum and its hellish abode, the saloon.

It is one of the ironies of his life and work that the revivalist who hated liquor with a passion owed much of his success to it. His battle against the manufacturers and dispensers of intoxicating beverages facilitated his work in a number of ways. His booze sermon, "Get on the Water Wagon," was the most famous in his repertoire. His graphic exposition of the destructive effects of liquor and his impassioned attacks on those responsible for them added color to his sermons. Audiences long remembered his assertion that "Jesus Christ was God's revenue officer." They roared with laughter when he explained, "I'm trying to make America so dry that a man must be primed before he can spit." His assertion, exaggerated but probably not wholly unfounded, that he had had his "life threatened from the Atlantic to the Pacific" because he had declared himself the "out-and-out, uncompromising foe" of the liquor business lent an air of heroic manliness to his ministry. Furthermore, advocating Prohibition enabled the revivalist to broaden his appeal by weaving traditional and contemporary themes into the fabric of his evangelism.[22]

For generations, Evangelicals and other Americans had regarded alcohol as a corrosive force that ate away at an individual's health and at the cohesiveness of families, thereby undermining the foundations of society. Temperance and its more radical cousin Prohibition were conventional currents within American reform that Billy and millions of people across the nation understood and with which they were comfortable. At the same time, a new generation of activists, such as advocates of social justice for the disinherited, saw the drive against strong drink as a way to remove a destabilizing and debilitating influence from the world of the urban poor, while proponents of efficiency and economy regarded it as conducive to greater industrial productivity. Therefore, as the Prohibition crusade gained momentum, Sunday's willingness to take on what he and others regarded as a dangerous and powerfully entrenched interest made him a valuable ally to a wide range of reformers, some of whom might otherwise have found him only marginally, if at all, attractive. It is no accident that during the 1910s, when the manufacturers and distributors of intoxicating beverages were under siege, Billy was the most sought-after evangelist in America.

John Barleycorn was an almost perfect foe for the revivalist. Sunday's battle against booze enabled him to combine both his own profound convictions and certain attributes of the reform spirit of the age. The litany of evils against which he railed consisted largely of those with which he had direct or indirect experience. His crusade against alcohol affords a case in point. Only death had done more than liquor to destabilize his childhood. The fact that his stepfather James Heizer succumbed to drink and abandoned his family led eventually to Billy's 2-year stint in Iowa's Civil War orphanages. His Grandfather Cory's occasional drunken binges disrupted Sunday's most secure boyhood refuge in an otherwise precarious world. As a young baseball player and later as a YMCA worker in the disreputable districts of Chicago, he once again saw how the abuse of alcohol could destroy lives. It is hardly surprising, therefore, that he passionately hated liquor and those who trafficked in it, believing that they represented the most serious threat to the individual, family, community, and nation.

When Sunday took on the "liquor interests," he was engaging a familiar and hated foe, but he recognized that the age in which he lived, with its growing faith in science and social science, would not be persuaded of the evils of drink or promiscuity or any other "sin" by moral fulminations alone. Therefore, like other Progressive reformers, he felt compelled to provide convincing evidence to substantiate his arguments against the social ills he chose to confront. Although rarely specific about his sources, he assured audiences, "I don't quote any quacks." It was his job, he said, to translate the writings of the experts into language that the "fellow with a dinner bucket" could understand. What he provided was a sometimes shocking but purportedly accurate elucidation of the detrimental physiological effects of alcohol on the drinker. The man who drank might appear healthy, but he was "full of rotten tissues" that had about as much resilience as a piece of dough. He was at a 94 percent risk of dying of blood poisoning if he had an accident that required surgery. Pneumonia had "a first mortgage on a booze-hoister." According to Billy, 82 percent of the men who drank and lived in sin died when stricken with pneumonia. Furthermore, they suffered from weakened hearts and "hobnailed" livers, and eighty-seven out of every one hundred experienced chronic kidney problems.[23]

Booze was as detrimental to society as to the individual. Sunday contended that 75 percent of the country's "idiots" came from intemperate parents, as did 80 percent of its paupers. Eighty-two percent of the crimes were committed by men under the influence of alcohol. Ninety percent of adult criminals were "whisky-made." Demon rum was not only a criminal but also a thief. Billy estimated that the whiskey business cost the United States more than $3.4

billion annually to rectify the damage done by the abuse of alcohol. He claimed that the amount of money spent on drink in New York City each year amounted to $365 million. This, he alleged, was four times the annual output of gold and six times the value of all the silver mined in the United States. He said New York had one saloon for every thirty families and claimed that the money working people spent for drink in ten years would buy every laborer in the city "a beautiful home, allowing $3,500 for house and lot."[24]

If New York City demonstrated the costliness of booze, the revivalist believed that Kansas City, Kansas, offered a vivid illustration of the salutary effects of banning liquor. According to Sunday, in July of 1905, temperance legislation went into effect in that city of 100,000. At the time, there were 250 saloons, 200 gambling halls, and 60 houses of prostitution. Within less than a year after Prohibition began, the benefits of the legislation were already quite apparent. The president of one of the city's major banks found that deposits had increased $1.7 million and that 72 percent of the deposits were from men who had never saved a cent before. The pace of business accelerated, while court expenses decreased. The decrease in crime following Prohibition was so significant that the city canceled plans to expand its jail. The number of elderly committed to the poorhouse because their children squandered money that was needed to care for them decreased. The city had to employ eighteen additional teachers to instruct children between the ages of 12 and 18 who had not previously attended school because they were helping their drunken fathers take care of the family. Given Kansas City's experience, the benefits of Prohibition seemed obvious.[25]

Sunday's appeal to studies and statistics was consistent with the Progressive emphasis upon expertise and made him appear perfectly attuned to the times. However, for those who found the anecdotal more persuasive than the evidential, Billy offered a wealth of melodramatic stories depicting the devastating consequences of strong drink on the lives of individual men and women. He told of the young man who killed his best friend in a drunken rage after whiling away the hours in a saloon and spent the rest of his life in prison. He recounted the fate of a refined young woman of Freeport, Illinois, who was mistakenly shot to death by a drunkard as she walked along a city street with her baby in her arms. He related the stories of intoxicated men who abused or murdered their mothers or wives and left their children impoverished and grief-stricken. All this misery could have been avoided had Jesus replaced John Barleycorn in the affections of men and women.[26]

The target of Sunday's greatest wrath was not the drinker but those who manufactured and dispensed the Devil's brew. For the revivalist and many of his contemporaries, the saloon represented a greater threat to family and society than alcohol itself. It was perceived as at the heart of a constellation of evils, including poverty, alcoholism, gambling, white slavery, theft, radicalism, and political corruption. Billy described it as "the most damnable, corrupt institution that ever wriggled out of hell and fastened itself on the public" and as "the deadliest foe to the home, the church and the state, on top of God Almighty's dirt." Perhaps speaking from the depths of his own child-hood experience, he charged that the saloon came

> as near being a rat hole for a wage earner to dump his wages in as anything you can find. The only interest it pays is red eyes and foul breath, and the loss of health. You go in with money and you come out with empty pockets. You go in with character and come out ruined. You go in with a good position and you lose it. You lost your position in the bank, or in the cab of the locomotive. And it pays nothing back but disease and damnation and gives an extra dividend in delirium tremens and a free pass to hell. And then it will let your wife be buried in the potter's field and your children go to the asylum.[27]

Not only was the saloon detrimental to individuals and their families, it also posed a serious threat to the nation. According to Billy, it was a "hotbed of political damnation, rot and corruption." It was "the nest of anarchy," where Hell hatched "its damnable brood that wave their red flag and sneer and damn the Stars and Stripes" and the country that had given them a home. The saloon had "sent the bullet through the body of Lincoln" and had "nerved the arm" that fired the lethal shots at Garfield and McKinley. Every plot ever conceived against order, stability, and the government of the United States had been "born and bred, and crawled out of the grog-shop to damn this country."[28]

Sunday believed that the pervasiveness and power of the saloon and the liquor interests were in part due to the apathy or actual complicity of America's Christians. He criticized those who tolerated the purveyors of strong drink. The man who voted for the saloon was "pulling on the same rope with the devil" whether he realized it or not. The revivalist was convinced that "when Church members stop voting for the saloon, liquor will go to hell."[29]

For those, Christian or otherwise, who found such legislation as Prohibition statutes an unjustifiable intrusion upon individual freedom, Sunday had nothing but contempt. He regarded the question of personal liberty to be a red herring, benefiting men and women who wanted to drink to excess while offering nothing to the victims of their irresponsible conduct. To those who appealed to civil liberties and constitutional rights, Billy responded, "Our forefathers did not die on the snow-covered hills of New England, sir, and dye the soil of the colonies red with their blood in order to establish personal license—they did die to establish liberty, regulated by law." He recognized the difficulties in making Prohibition work where the legislation was unpopular but was confident that this law, like any other, could be enforced if officials made an honest and determined effort to do so. He acknowledged that it would never be 100 percent effective but that, he argued, was true of any law.

> There isn't a law on the books of the state that prohibits. We have laws against murder. Do they prohibit? We have laws against burglary. Do they prohibit? We have laws against arson, rape, but do they prohibit? Would you introduce a bill to repeal all the laws that do not prohibit? Any law will prohibit to a certain extent if honest officials enforce it. But no law will

absolutely prohibit. We can make law against liquor prohibit as much as any law prohibits.

Of those who advocated licensure, regulation, and taxation of the liquor industry, Sunday scornfully inquired,

> Would you introduce a bill saying, if you pay $1,000 a year you can kill any one you don't like; or by paying $500 a year you can attack any girl you want to; or by paying $100 a year you can steal anything that suits you? That's what you do with the dirtiest, rottenest gang this side of hell. You say for so much a year you can have a license to make staggering, reeling drunken sots, murderers and thieves and vagabonds.[30]

Sunday's attacks on the saloon were perfectly attuned to the mood of the times. While the motives of those who sought to ban liquor from American life varied widely, there was about the Prohibition campaign, as there had been about the temperance movement before it, something of a symbolic character. Though hardly a uniquely urban institution, the barroom and a constellation of supposedly related evils such as prostitution, gambling, and political corruption were associated in the popular mind with the rise of the city. On one level, reforms such as Prohibition were part of an effort to control the rapidly expanding urban centers of America. The Anti-Saloon League, for example, was less concerned about alcohol per se than about the quintessentially urban evil, the saloon. This is obvious in a 1914 declaration of the general superintendent of the League,

> The vices of the cities have been the undoing of past empires and civilizations. It has been at the point where the urban population outnumbers the rural people that wrecked Republics have gone down. . . . The peril of this Republic likewise is now clearly seen to be in her cities. There is no greater menace to democratic institutions than the great segregation of an element which gathers its ideas of patriotism and citizenship from the low grogshop. . . . Already some of our cities are well-nigh submerged with this unpatriotic element, which is manipulated by the still baser element engaged in the unAmerican drink traffic and by the kind of politician the saloon creates. . . . If our Republic is to be saved the liquor traffic must be destroyed.[31]

For some, the battle to curb the consumption of alcohol was nothing short of a struggle for the republic, and the theater of operations was urban America.

Sunday shared many of the popular misgivings about the city. He tended to romanticize rural life and the farmer, whom he hailed as "the best class of men on God's dirt." Yet he left the farm at age 14 and never again earned his livelihood from agriculture. As a ballplayer, he had found urban America exciting and rewarding but not entirely satisfying. Once he was well-established as an evangelist, he left Chicago for the semi-rural confines of Winona Lake, Indiana, which was his primary place of residence for the remainder of his life. He recognized the importance of the city and appreciated the fact that it was the source of his greatest success. At the same time, he also saw it as a

potential threat to the nation's future. It was not necessarily the city itself that
worried him but certain influences emanating from it that seemed to endan-
ger the hegemony of Protestant cultural values. He deplored the squalor,
poverty, corruption, and vice found there. He ridiculed urban society women,
whose lives seemed to him aimless and wasteful. He scorned the young wags
who in his opinion would rather loaf than work and who could do nothing but
criticize the nation that had given them so much. Yet perhaps because of his
ties to the city, the revivalist never wholly lost faith in the heterogeneous
population that lived there.[32]

With a few exceptions, the Progressive era was not especially progressive
regarding issues of race, ethnicity, or religious diversity. Sunday was a product
of his times and shared many of the prejudices of his age, but unlike some
conservative twentieth-century Evangelicals, he generally did not exploit
them for the sake of promoting his ministry. In spite of the fact that his rhetoric
was at times harsh, he was essentially too kind a man to hate on a basis of race,
culture, or sectarian affiliation.

To be sure, Sunday was not wholly free of bias. For example, overtones of
racism were apparent in his revivalism. His occasional use of the expression
"nigger in the wood pile" or the fact that "De Brewer's Big Hosses," a popular
Prohibition song associated with his evangelism, was in African-American
dialect, suggests the degree to which he was immersed in the prejudice of his
times. Nevertheless, he deplored racial hatred and violence, believing that
those of other races should be treated with decency. Without question, the
gospel was to be made available to all regardless of the color of their skin. In
Atlanta, Georgia, in late 1917, he made some white southerners decidedly
uncomfortable by holding special services for black Atlantans and inviting an
enormous "colored" choir to sing at white services. Several years later, he
undoubtedly alienated strict adherents to the color line when he delivered
sermons before integrated congregations during revivals in Kansas City and
Wichita. Some African-American Evangelicals appreciated the fact that he
embraced them in his evangelism, while other sophisticated black Americans
found his ministry disgraceful. The latter most certainly recognized quite
correctly that the evangelist never challenged then or later the fundamental
racial tenets of his day. In fact, by the 1930s, as the tone of his ministry became
more negative, he asserted publicly that "there can be no social equality
between black and white races."[33]

Sunday also did not exploit religious bigotry, even though he was certain
that Christianity was the only true religion and confident that Protestantism
was its highest expression. To be sure, he publicly scorned and dismissed as
foolish groups he thought heretical or heathen, such as Mormons, Unitar-
ians, Christian Scientists, "holy rollers," and adherents to any belief system
outside the Judeo-Christian tradition, but he did not capitalize upon the most
prevalent American religious prejudices. He recognized his faith's affinity
with Judaism and, despite the fact that he accepted some of the stereotypes of
the age, his revivalism appears to have been largely free of anti-Semitism.

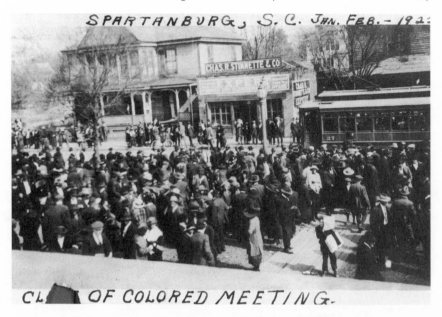

African-American attendees leaving a Sunday revival meeting
in Spartanburg, South Carolina, in the early 1920s.

*Billy Sunday Archives, Grace College and Theological Seminary,
Winona Lake, Indiana.*

Although they undoubtedly reflected his cognizance of the city's growing
Jewish population, his remarks during his 1917 campaign in New York were
probably an accurate reflection of his sentiments.

> The seed of Abraham is the miracle of history. It makes my blood boil to hear
> a man speak of the Jew as a sheeny or a Christ-killer. If ever you walk the
> streets of glory and are kept out of hell it will be because of your repentance
> and faith in the shed blood of a Jew, for humanly speaking, Jesus Christ
> came from the Jewish nation.
>
> Some of the shrewdest financiers of the world are Jews. You pay tribute
> to the Jew for the suit you have on, and the dress you wear, for they control
> the tailor and the custom-made business of the United States. There is not
> a cabinet in Europe that hasn't had its membership of Jews.
>
> If you visit a poorhouse you will not find a single Jew father or mother
> living off of the county. You won't find a Jew among the hoboes or weary
> Willies panhandling for a hand-out.[34]

As for Catholicism, Sunday did not publicly display the anti-Catholic
feeling so prevalent among contemporary Protestants. Indeed, he sometimes
tried, with marginal success, to build bridges to those of the Catholic tradition. He asserted in one account of his courtship with Nell that had she been
a Catholic, he would have become a Catholic. In 1928, when he opposed the

election of Democrat Al Smith to the presidency, he tried to make it clear that his opposition was not based on Smith's Catholicism but on the New Yorker's opposition to Prohibition. In his major urban revivals, he welcomed any Catholic support. His desire to be as ecumenical as possible undoubtedly tempered whatever anti-Catholicism he may have harbored.[35]

The immigrant was a source of concern for millions of Progressive-era Americans, and Sunday was no exception. He believed that ideally his country could function as a melting pot, absorbing and providing opportunities for those with what he would have described as "grit." His vision of national life was inclusive so long as newcomers subordinated their cultural values and practices to those of their new land. He feared, however, that his land was becoming a dumping ground for the world's riffraff, those who could not or would not assimilate and who would become a burden on society.

> I haven't one word to say against any man or woman who is born across the sea. Originally we all came from across the sea and I am proud of the fact that they see within this country the principles which they love and they are willing to leave the Fatherland and cross the waters and come to the land of the free and the home of the brave, to build homes, rear families, if they want to do that, and assimilate to our laws I will be among the first that will stand on the front line and give them the gladhand as they come from Ellis Island, but say! I tell you I object! I object to America becoming the back-dooryard for Europe to dump her paupers and her criminals.
>
> Many have come here with just money and morals enough to escape the pauper and criminal laws, and they settle in our cities and they refuse to assimilate to our laws and they become carbuncles on the neck of the body politic and they have turned the American idea of the Sabbath into a Continental idea of the Sabbath Day.[36]

The greatest urban revivalist of his day was willing to accept the tired, the poor, the huddled masses, as long as their yearning to be free meant a willingness to thoroughly acculturate. He could tolerate the rise of the city and its corollary diversity as long as he believed that any threat these changes posed to traditional values could be contained and eventually quelled. His ministry was in part directed toward that end. Only after the Great War did his confidence in the future of his nation begin to waver, and only then did his message truly begin to grow more negative.

Billy Sunday was born into a nation in crisis and reached manhood in an era of unprecedented change. He launched his evangelistic work in a decade sometimes considered a watershed of modernity, and his ministry spanned an extraordinary epoch of reform. Steeped as he was in the values and patterns of life of the rural and small-town nineteenth-century Midwest, he judged his country's ills and couched his cures for them largely in personal and pietistic terms. Most of the complexities and inherent injustices of life in urbanizing and industrializing America were lost upon him, as they were upon millions of his contemporaries. Yet as the nation's expanding population concentrated in cities, many of the detrimental human consequences of modernization seemed perfectly obvious to Billy and those of his ilk. Therefore, the city, its inhabitants, and its dangers, real and imagined, became the focal point of much of the moral reform effort of the day.

Sunday's revivals, especially during the peak years of his ministry in the 1910s, were part of a campaign against the perceived evils of the city and the threats those posed to the nation. His admirers believed that Billy was rallying the devout and decent to directly confront the erosion of faith, values, and traditional relationships that appeared rampant in modern life. The social implications of his message, the democratic ethos of his services, the highly organized businesslike activities that preceded and accompanied his crusades, and the extensive press coverage with its statistical analysis of attendance, revenue, and trail hitters allegedly verifying the evangelist's successes gave the preacher the aura of a reformer and many within the middle class a sense of empowerment. People convinced themselves that their world, or at least their city, was the better for Billy Sunday having been there. While in some instances he may have played a significant role in securing the enactment of legislation against alcohol and the saloon and perhaps in temporarily raising the moral tenor of some smaller communities, Sunday's impact was generally more symbolic than real. Nevertheless, his devotees perceived him as a courageous and effective champion of reform.

SEVEN

Hero of the Heartland

Billy Sunday reached the pinnacle of his popularity with his 10-week revival in New York City in the spring of 1917. For a time thereafter, the future of his ministry continued to appear bright. In the late summer and fall of that year he conducted successful meetings in Los Angeles and Atlanta. In 1918, he waged relentless war against his notion of sin in its many and varied manifestations in Washington, D.C., and Chicago. The revival in the latter city was, however, to be the last of his great protracted meetings in metropolitan America.

During the 1910s, the evangelist had been a national sensation, preaching to millions in the country's greatest cities. By the 1920s, invitations to challenge the Devil and his worldly minions in their major urban bastions had become infrequent. Sunday continued to tour mid-sized and smaller cities, especially those of the South and Midwest, but the campaigns were shorter, the crowds smaller, the converts fewer, and the press coverage more limited. His revivals retained something of their attraction for the admiring and the curious, but they lacked their former power. Astute observers noted that the preacher's sermons often seemed to have a perfunctory quality.[1]

Sunday's decline in the postwar era stemmed from both personal and sociocultural circumstances. In part, it was a result of the fact that a man in his sixties could no longer sustain the kind of dramatic expenditure of energy characteristic of his earlier campaigns. By the latter 1920s, newspapers reported that while the old fire was still apparent as the veteran revivalist got in his licks against Satan, the athleticism of his earlier years was less evident. At those moments, when the heat of combat tempted the old battler for righteousness to grow more animated, Nell would quietly caution him against becoming overly excited.

By the early 1930s, there were other signs that age was beginning to take a toll on the once remarkably fit preacher. As his health deteriorated, Sunday experienced occasional lapses of memory. At such moments, he relied on his wife, who often sat nearby as he preached, to provide him with gentle reminders of what he wished to say or to quietly correct his more glaring errors of fact. In 1933, while speaking in Des Moines, he became weak and disoriented and had to be escorted from the auditorium and hospitalized. Two years later, in

Billy Sunday and Nell Sunday at their second home
in the Hood River country of Oregon.

Billy Sunday Archives, Grace College and Theological Seminary,
Winona Lake, Indiana.

the spring of 1935, he experienced heart problems during a revival in Chattanooga, Tennessee, which significantly curtailed his work for the remaining few months of his life.[2]

As age sapped Sunday's physical strength, the scandals that swirled about his sons because of their moral lapses and financial difficulties enervated him psychologically. The idea of the troubled and troublesome "preacher's kid" is well-established in American popular culture. More often than not, the facts do not support the perception, but the lives of three of the Sundays' four children lent credence to the stereotype. Their oldest child, Helen Haines, wife of a small-town newspaper publisher in Sturgis, Michigan, was a conscientious and dutiful daughter who asked for little and appreciated anything her father and mother did for her. She appears to have been all that her parents could have hoped for in a child.

The Sunday boys, especially the two oldest, George and Bill, were disappointments. Unwise or unfortunate in both their business and personal relations, they found themselves entangled in a web of divorce, remarriage, allegations of immorality, litigation, and debt. The lapses of Paul, the youngest of the three sons, were perhaps less egregious than those of his brothers, but he was apparently no less spoiled, irresponsible, or dependent upon his parents to bail him out of his difficulties.

Throughout the 1920s and early 1930s, Billy and Nell devoted much of their energy and a substantial portion of their wealth to a futile effort to rescue their sons from their financial problems, help them get their personal lives back on track, and keep their familial crises and real or alleged sexual indiscretions as much a private matter as possible. By the late 1920s, Billy estimated that he and Nell had spent close to half a million dollars to help their children, a level of assistance which the couple's dwindling resources could not indefinitely sustain.[3]

The Sunday boys' conduct strained their parents emotionally as well as financially and made a mockery of the version of the gospel to which their father had committed his life. Billy's letters to Nell reveal a man in agony over his children's failures and worried about the implications of scandal for his reputation and his ministry. In the early 1920s, as George and Bill's indiscretions were beginning to become an issue, the despondent revivalist wrote to his wife,

> The name Sunday God has made famous with his cause and I would die before I would dishonor it and I would rather the boys would die than disgrace it. You and I have kept it clean and bequeathed it to our children and oh I pray God that they keep it clean after you and I have gone west.[4]

Concern over his sons' errant ways made it increasingly difficult for Billy to focus on his work. He confided to Helen that the stress was so great that he became sick to his stomach and sometimes forgot words and had difficulty pronouncing others when he preached. Later he wrote,

> I am so distressed over what Geo. and Billy have done I could cry my eyes out but I must appear cheerful and light hearted when I am broken hearted. Its [sic] so hard but when I get back to my room where I can hide away I give way to my feelings and my imagination runs riot.[5]

Some of this strain undoubtedly arose from a deep-seated sense of guilt. Although at times the Sundays tried to console themselves with the notion that they were not responsible for their sons' lapses, they could not escape the feeling that they were somehow culpable.

In his biography of Sunday, Lyle Dorsett contends that the evangelist blamed the problems plaguing his ministry and his family in the 1920s and 1930s on the work of the Devil. While Dorsett does not offer a great deal of evidence to support his contention, it is a plausible one, given Billy's perspective on life. The revivalist believed that if one lived according to God's will, spiritual and material rewards would follow. When professional and personal problems developed after World War I, he either had to determine how he had failed the Lord or interpret his difficulties as the scourge of the Devil against a godly man. Having always thought of himself as a combatant in a cosmic struggle between good and evil, it is not surprising that he chose the latter interpretation. Believing himself a marked man in the eyes of the Devil enhanced his sense of being a faithful warrior in the army of the Lord.[6] Viewing the circumstances in which he found himself in this way also enabled him to partially evade questions of his own responsibility for the problems besetting his family and to avoid having to grapple with the socio-cultural changes that were beginning to render his ministry less relevant for many Americans.

Yet Sunday held views that were not entirely consistent with the attribution of all of life's problems to the Prince of Darkness. The mainstream American culture in which he was steeped stressed the individual's responsibility for his or her fate and had little patience with those who saw themselves as victims. Furthermore, the evangelical ethos in which he had been reared and from which he drew much of life's meaning included the notion that, at least in moral and spiritual matters, men and women had an obligation to nurture their brothers and sisters and their sons and daughters. These ideas, coupled with Billy's predisposition toward self-doubt, meant that he could never wholly escape the fear that somehow he was responsible for the things that had gone awry in his life and in the lives of those whom he loved.

Years after his death, Helen recalled an autumn afternoon at the couple's Winona Lake home when her aging husband stood looking wistfully out the window at the leaves drifting across the landscape, wondering aloud, "Where did I go wrong?" As she had throughout much of their marriage, "Ma" once again tried to buoy Billy's spirits by assuring him that their boys had brought their problems upon themselves. Yet there is evidence that she, too, felt more than a little responsibility for the mistakes of her sons. Grady Wilson, an associate of Billy Graham, recalled an evening in Atlanta early in the young evangelist's ministry when Graham and several members of his team went out for a snack. Ma Sunday happened to be in the city, and they invited her to join them. According to Wilson, with tears running down her cheeks, she admonished her young friends, "Boys, whatever you do, don't neglect your family. I did. I traveled with Pa all over the country, and I sacrificed my children." Mrs. Danielle Cochrane Brown recalled that when she was a child, the Sundays frequently visited in her home. One of the things she remembered most vividly from those occasions was Ma Sunday's words, "Take care of your little boys. Take care of your little boys."[7]

While the Sunday children must ultimately be held accountable for their actions, Billy and Nell undoubtedly do bear at least some responsibility for their difficulties. The couple genuinely loved and sought to meet all the material needs of their daughter and sons and to nurture them spiritually. Perhaps, as Dorsett has suggested, they were overly indulgent, spoiling their offspring, especially the boys, to the point of damaging their character. But overindulgence affords only a partial explanation of the misfortunes that beset the family. The Sunday siblings faced challenges not uncommon among the progeny of driven, successful parents. Throughout much of their childhood and youth, they lacked the day-to-day parental intimacy and guidance important to a sense of self-worth and well-being. Furthermore, as the children of one of the nation's most famous couples, they constantly wrestled with the enormous burden of having to measure up to their own expectations of themselves and to the public's expectations of them. Just as their father had been scarred by a childhood characterized by death, poverty, and failure, they were impaired by childhoods distinguished by affluence, success, and popular acclaim.

In 1932, after several years of deteriorating health, resulting from what may have been multiple sclerosis, Helen Haines died of pneumonia. The following year George, overwhelmed by familial and financial difficulties, committed suicide. The troubles of their children, especially those of their sons, and the untimely deaths of Helen and George haunted and at times enervated the Sundays and had serious implications for the later years of Billy's ministry.[8]

Beyond the personal impediments to Sunday's work were the larger sociocultural ones. As this study has tried to suggest, one key to comprehending the revivalist's remarkable success lies in an understanding of the way in which his ministry resonated with the mood of the times. Throughout much of his career, in addition to his charisma and the appeal of his conservative evangelical gospel message, Billy's attraction for millions stemmed from the entrepreneurial quality of his evangelism, the role of sports in his ministry, his aggressive masculinity, and the perception that he was a force for constructive social change. After World War I, however, Sunday rather quickly lost his ability to connect with the masses in the way that he had only a few years earlier. To understand both his ascendance and subsequent decline, it may prove worthwhile to examine one other curious phenomenon, the parallel between the popular perception of the evangelist and that of the region from which he came.

The era from the Civil War to the Great Depression was one of extraordinary economic, cultural, and social transformation in the United States. Given the tide of change flowing about them, it is hardly surprising that for many Americans it was also an age of considerable uncertainty and ambivalence. They were generally proud of and welcomed the unprecedented material progress resulting from the enormous expansion that had transformed their nation's economy since the mid nineteenth century, yet they were often wary of the kaleidoscopic cultural shifts that seemed to threaten conventional patterns of life. Millions longed for familiarity and certainty, but few actually wished for a genuine return to an idealized bygone era. Rather, most preferred a new order in which change would be tempered by tradition and progress informed by the past. For a time, the popular image of the Middle West seemed to offer a viable model of such a society.

An ambivalence toward change and the consequent effort to bridge the traditional and the modern is apparent in some of the popular myths and symbols prevalent at the end of the nineteenth and beginning of the twentieth centuries. John Bodnar has observed that the late nineteenth century was an era of considerable competition among local, regional, and national constituencies with divergent, though not necessarily mutually exclusive, loyalties and agendas. He maintains that in public ceremonies commemorating the past, the local populace often stressed a pioneer motif that celebrated the struggles and triumphs of the common people, while cultural or commercial elites frequently emphasized a patriotic motif that extolled national ideals and cohesiveness. Michael Kammen, too, has noted a persistent localism during these years but stresses a "renaissance of patriotism" that began in the late 1880s and surged during the 1890s.[9]

A mythology featuring local custom and tradition affirmed norms and afforded a sense of continuity and security while a mythology emphasizing a national point of view was consistent with the contemporary faith in economic and social progress. These themes were not necessarily incompatible and sometimes converged in myths and symbols that simultaneously acknowledged and preserved elements of local or regional culture while serving national interests. For example, by 1909, the centennial of his birth, the popular perception of Abraham Lincoln as a rail-splitting son of the frontier had merged with his image as president and American messiah to create a heroic figure embodying a broad range of cultural ideals.[10] By that time, too, some Americans had begun to regard the Midwest from which Lincoln had sprung as itself representative of many quintessentially American traits.

Geographer James Shortridge argues that by the early twentieth century, when to many people the South seemed exotic, the West inchoate, and the East in decline, the "Middle West" epitomized traditional, wholesome, vibrant, prosperous, democratic American civilization. For a brief time, in the midst of an era of rapid transition, the region that had been the cradle of Republicanism and now appeared to be the matrix out of which much of Progressivism was emerging constituted, for millions, something of a point of cultural orientation.[11]

As we have already observed, the value system at the core of the Midwest's identity began taking shape in the mid nineteenth century and evolved in response to the changing economic, social, and cultural conditions that were the corollaries of industrialization, immigration, and urbanization. As Andrew R. L. Cayton and Peter S. Onuf have reminded us, midwesterners' sense of who they were was closely related to the ideology that underlay the Republican party. Born in the 1850s in opposition to the spread of slavery, the party emerged from the Civil War as the champion of an economic creed that featured individualism, acquisitiveness, competitiveness, and freedom from governmental restrictions and a moral code that stressed "sobriety, self-restraint, decorum, industriousness, and piety."[12] A blend of yeoman and commercial capitalistic ideals permeated with evangelical morality, this value system retained much of its vitality well into the late nineteenth century.

The rise of large-scale capitalism, with its burgeoning working class and ethnically diverse population, posed a formidable threat to the bourgeois ideology that lay at the core of the identity of midwesterners. By the 1890s, some residents of the region had begun to accommodate themselves to the new and more complex economic order. Others yielded more slowly to change. Most people, however, regardless of their attitude toward the rise of industrial capitalism, retained their traditional faith in the relationship between character and material success. They believed that in spite of the accelerating pace of change around them, their region continued to exhibit those egalitarian, democratic, self-reliant, and volunteeristic values characteristic of American civilization at its best. By embracing material progress while eschewing cultural change, midwesterners created a mythology which suggested that tradition and modernity could in some way be reconciled.

From the turn of the century through World War I, writers such as Edward A. Ross and Charles M. Harger who described the region revealed an evolving conception that linked it with a body of images and ideas epitomizing the essence of American culture. Cullom Davis has argued quite persuasively that parts of the Midwest rather accurately reflect the diversity and complexity of American life, but the early-twentieth-century image of the "Heartland" conveyed something more idyllic. According to Shortridge, the "Middle West" evoked visions of a pastoral paradise strewn with villages, towns, and a few dynamic urban centers. The region supposedly possessed a fortuitous combination of youthful western and mature eastern characteristics. It had advanced beyond the adolescent excesses of the West and had not yet fallen victim to the deterioration, loss of idealism, and decline of vitality that allegedly characterized the increasingly urban, industrial, and heterogeneous aging East. Its people were open, honest, kind, energetic, industrious, self-reliant, moral, and progressive. Society was democratic and egalitarian. The Middle West, in other words, represented a mature Americanism.[13]

Billy Sunday was one of the best-known but most controversial progeny of the Middle West, and there is an intriguing and perhaps illuminating congruity between the course of the evangelist's singular career and his native region's shifting fortunes in the popular mind. People associated the revivalist not so much with the Midwest per se as with the "Heartland" characteristics they believed he and it embodied. In many respects, his prominence as preacher and public figure waxed and waned with the ebb and flow of the potency of the region's cultural mystique. Each emerged slowly into the national consciousness in the late nineteenth and early twentieth centuries. The significance of each peaked during the 1910s and declined thereafter. For millions of middle-class Americans, both Sunday and the Middle West, at the zenith of their appeal, symbolized qualities such as youthful vigor, pietistic morality, democratic egalitarianism, self-reliance, and Progressive idealism. Many considered these traits vital to national greatness, but they appeared in peril after the profound socioeconomic changes that occurred in the years between the Civil War and World War I. As such traits were redefined, or the connection between them and national identity waned after the Great War, so too did the cultural importance of the Midwest and the popularity of Billy Sunday.[14]

Although middle-aged by the time he became a national phenomenon, his career in baseball and his frenetic style of preaching meant that Sunday epitomized for his audiences a kind of youthful, manly vigor associated with the vitality of the Midwest as a region and with American manhood at its best. His evangelistic persona combined the emerging physical conception of "masculinity" with the traditional, more character-oriented understanding of "manliness."

Had there been no more to Sunday's embodiment of manhood than an extraordinary display of masculine vigor, it would have been of little consequence beyond revivalistic theatrics, but he also conveyed an aura of manliness that extended beyond physical agility and endurance to a kind of combative moral courage that would take on all comers in defense or advocacy of a just cause. As he assured one tabernacle audience,

> If I knew that the chief of devils sat out there on one of those benches, and that all the cohorts of hell were in front of me, sneering and leering, I would preach anyway, and I would preach the truth as God has given it to me.[15]

The truth granted to Sunday was that bestowed on his generation of midwesterners. It was more a matter of morality than theology. He clearly believed in the substitutionary atonement of Jesus' death, and his evangelistic crusades always included altar calls that drew "converts" by the hundreds or even thousands. Yet his sermons were also lessons in his version of applied Christianity rather than mere discourses in fundamentalist theology or emotional appeals for repentance. His message was often oriented as much toward social uplift as personal salvation.

The zenith of Sunday's career coincided closely with that of the Progressive era, and some of the causes he championed, especially Prohibition, occasionally converged with those of other contemporary reformers. In the eyes of at least some of his admirers, this fact, coupled with the crusading tone of his evangelism, lent a Progressive aura to his ministry, and he was perceived as a fearless champion of constructive change. Sunday's notion of righteousness was informed by the pietistic norms of the Iowa towns of his youth, and his understanding of evil was a matter of personal or societal deviation from those norms. Reflecting the ideal, if not necessarily the reality, of community cohesiveness prevalent in the Midwest of his youth, he believed personal sins to be both unproductive and a threat to family, church, community, and the larger economic and social fabric of the nation. Yet for all his prophetic fulminations against the decline of American society, throughout much of his career there was about Sunday and his message an aura of youthful optimism and idealism. He thanked God that he was not "one of those who believes that all the young men of America are devoid of virtue and of goodness."[16]

Like many of the Progressives of his age, Sunday had a profound faith in the potential inherent in American society. The challenge was to mobilize that potential. His sermons were as much a call to action as a call to salvation. There was no limit to what the Christian men and women of the United States could accomplish if only they would have the courage to stand up for what was right. Tides of change were eroding American life, but courageous action rooted in loyalty to Christ could stem the tide.

Sunday's social critique was more moral than institutional because his own experience and the ideology of the region from which he came appeared to offer little grounds for socioeconomic criticism. An important feature of the mystique of the Middle West, and one which the evangelist's life seemed to validate, was its alleged blend of socioeconomic mobility, egalitarianism, and democracy. For many, the region epitomized the free play of competition in every aspect of life and the opportunity for the able to succeed by virtue of their ability. Unlike the East, the playing field seemed, for the most part, still level and opportunities abundant. What better example of this reality than Billy Sunday, whose story suggested the extent to which an individual could overcome adversity?

The evangelist understood fully the usefulness of his difficult past. He enjoyed stressing the perils of his youth—his fatherless boyhood, struggles against childhood poverty, years in an orphanage, and self-sufficient adolescence. He took considerable pride in reminding audiences of the social distance he had traversed, as when he declared to New Yorkers in 1917, "I've been thirty years getting here. It's a long trip from a little log cabin out in Iowa to the Tabernacle on Broadway."[17]

Even without a reminder, the point was not lost on those attending Sunday revivals. Frank "Home Run" Baker, a major-league baseball star of the early twentieth century, recalled his experience at a 1916 Sunday revival in Baltimore:

> As Billy Sunday spoke I looked around that vast tabernacle. It appealed to me as a miracle of our country's democracy. The people met to see and hear a man born in a log cabin, trained in professional baseball, converted in a rescue mission, and the most potent single personality in our land to-day.[18]

While the saga of Sunday's life was not precisely a journey from rags to riches, it was clearly one of marvelous mobility. Furthermore, at the zenith of his success, despite his tailored suits and expensive cars, he tried to convey the image of just plain "Billy" Sunday, a man of the people, a son of rural America who had made good but who, like Abraham Lincoln, retained his rural simplicity. He affirmed for Americans that upward socioeconomic mobility was still possible, even in a rapidly changing nation.

Sunday's style of evangelism also heightened the aura of egalitarian democracy that surrounded his religious crusades. He never communicated to his audiences an air of superiority. In 1914, Sunday biographer Elijah Brown reprinted a Humboldt, Iowa, reporter's impressions of the evangelist. "There is none of the puffed-up Pharisee about him, and that is why he is so well liked by those to whom he preaches."[19] His revivalism was open, simple, and direct.

In the plain speech of the common people, Sunday delivered a message free of equivocation and sophistication. In an increasingly complex age in which American society was becoming more impersonal, bureaucratic, and institutionalized, Sunday spoke frankly and personally. As he expressed it, "I put the cookies and jam on the lower shelf so an audience don't have brain fag when they sit and listen to me."[20]

Some equated Sunday's use of the vernacular with the vulgar and condemned his methods. Others, however, appreciated his efforts to preach a gospel which would reach the masses. One contemporary observer wrote:

> It has been our habit for centuries to discuss religion and the affairs of the soul in a King James's vocabulary; to depart from that custom has come to seem something like sacrilege. Billy Sunday talks to people about God and their souls just as people talk to one another six days in the week across the counter or the dinner table or on the street.[21]

Concerning the organization of Sunday's revival services in the Midwest, Bruce Barton observed in the early 1910s that "even the baseball game, democracy's national sport, has its boxes and its bleachers."

> But there are no boxes here. Those who occupy seats do so because they came before twelve o'clock and sat in them: the service was scheduled for two. The president of the First National Bank sits tight pressed between two sooted miners. The Mayor is on the platform—perhaps—that is, if he happens to be a choir singer. Otherwise he takes his chance with his masters, the common people.[22]

Billy Sunday was then, for many Americans, a kind of latter-day Lincoln, a strong, vigorous, self-made, egalitarian hero who came out of the prairies of the heartland to summon the nation back to its highest ideals.[23] Yet neither the man nor his message captured the imagination of the age simply because they represented a nostalgic longing for a bygone era. Rather, by weaving many of the practices and values of both the old and the new into the colorful fabric of his career, Sunday and his evangelism helped alleviate the tension and anxiety that resulted from the transition from the rural agricultural America of the nineteenth century to the urban industrial nation of the twentieth.

Rising out of rural poverty, this orphaned son of a Civil War soldier had become an integral part of the popular culture of the new industrial America by the 1910s. He sometimes railed against the sinfulness of the cities and urged young men to go west or at least seek opportunities on the farms or in the villages of the countryside but was himself attracted to the city, and it was there that he scored his greatest success.[24] He had first achieved a limited measure of fame in professional baseball, a game with a pastoral ethos but a city context. His version of the gospel resembled closely that of the small-town preachers of his youth, but his evangelism was very much an urban phenomenon and, for a time at least, he had a remarkable rapport with the throngs that packed his tabernacles. Although he could claim some identification with the working class because of his humble origins, his greatest affinity was with a sizable segment of the middle class because he affirmed its values and it respected his accomplishments. Sunday's success as something of a religious entrepreneur undoubtedly enhanced his appeal for his bourgeois admirers. His crusades were as businesslike as his sermons were spectacular. Although he espoused the work ethic of the small-town businessman, he and his staff approached their task with the acumen of a Rockefeller or a Carnegie.

Aside from the color and the drama of a Billy Sunday revival, the quality that made the man and his message most appealing was the way the evangelist and his ministry mediated between the past and present. Sunday's life and work seemed to many to demonstrate the continued relevance of traditional ideals and mores for a new era, and he gave people a sense of empowerment. Out of his experiences and those of his audiences, he fashioned a vision of the future that built upon the values of the past and convinced ordinary men and women that they could take control of the present and, with the help of God, shape their destiny and that of their society. Like the region from which he sprang, he represented to an uncertain people the possibility of mutual accommodation between the best of the old and the new.

By the 1920s, the fortunes of both Billy Sunday and the Midwest were beginning to decline. In the aftermath of World War I, the nation's cultural center of gravity was shifting rapidly toward modernity. An increasingly urban, industrial, heterogeneous populace was growing more comfortable with modern America and thus less in need of the sort of psychic linkage between tradition and change that Sunday and his region had afforded. To be sure, there were those, mostly in rural and small-town America, who were unwilling or unable to embrace or even acquiesce in the emerging sociocultural synthesis. These individuals sensed that they were now part of a substantial but declining minority, and as confidence in their ability to significantly shape the nation's destiny ebbed, many grew increasingly shrill in their critique of American life. Some were drawn to one or another of a host of eccentric and sometimes bizarre minor prophets of economic or political salvation. Others donned the regalia of the Klan, while still more rallied beneath the banner of fundamentalism. Most, however, merely retreated into a quiet provincialism that usually welcomed material advances but yielded only grudgingly to cultural change. Such resistance to modernity led only to further alienation, isolation, and social strain. Consequently, during the 1920s and thereafter, the growing urban majority began viewing the Middle West less as a vibrant heartland and more as a stodgy, backward, complacent, declining region, out of touch with the main currents of American life.

As the cultural power of the mystique of the Midwest began to diminish in the postwar era, Billy Sunday's appeal also waned. It was in urban America that the revivalist had enjoyed his greatest success and there that he had his greatest impact. Now, however, his gospel, always social as well as personal, no longer rang true to many of the denizens of the city. At best, his message had never been more than marginally relevant for the ethnically diverse non-Protestant immigrant population. His primary appeal had been among refugees from rural America and established urbanites steeped in the Protestant hegemony of the nineteenth century. For them, his revivalism provided a continuity between past and present and an affirmation of the best of both worlds that facilitated accommodation to the new era in American life. By the 1920s, that kind of affirmation was becoming less necessary and less meaningful. The majority of urban Americans were groping toward a reconciliation with the present.

Through economic regulation and social legislation, Progressivism had begun to confront at least some of the excesses of industrial capitalism and the problems that were its corollaries. The decisive role of the United States in the Great War had confirmed the importance of the new economic order, promoted patriotism, and demonstrated that American manhood had not, after all, succumbed to the enervating forces of civilization. Prohibition had placed demon rum on the defensive. In the National Origins Act, Congress had moved to parry the perceived cultural threat posed by the postwar onslaught of immigrants. Automobiles, movies, and spectator sports provided unprecedented diversions and vents for the tensions latent in the process of modernization. While problems and anxieties remained, millions of Americans were now becoming more accustomed to and comfortable with an urban, industrial society.

Sunday sensed that while once he had, to some degree, been attuned to the pulse of urban life, he was now increasingly out of touch, and that realization was profoundly troubling. In 1921, he wrote to his wife, "I see [sic] more and more afraid to act on my own initiative or Judgement. The big cities scare me."[25] This loss of confidence was apparent in the diminution of the fundamental optimism that had permeated Sunday's evangelism through World War I.

Throughout most of his ministry, Sunday had been able to portray himself as and to believe himself to be a part of the reform ferment of the day. Although Progressivism was a complex phenomenon, it had always included a substantial moral component with which the evangelist could identify. The rising tide of Prohibitionism, for example, had helped propel him to national prominence during the teens, but it appeared, for the moment at least, that that battle had been won and there was no comparable mainstream cause with which Sunday could associate himself.

Historian Lynn Dumenil has argued that in the 1920s, popular interest shifted toward the individual and private sphere of life at the expense of the reform-minded public sphere. This reorientation, like a number of other developments of the postwar decade, adversely affected Sunday's work.[26] His gospel had always had a social dimension and was never wholly personal and otherworldly. In the years after the Great War, it seemed to him that few people shared his vision of society as morally integrated and interdependent.

Political, cultural, and religious heterodoxies were rampant, and the souls of men and the fate of the nation were in peril.

As his country moved toward modernity, Sunday no longer bridged the gap between present and past as he had done at the height of his popularity. Instead, he increasingly took refuge in the social and religious norms of late-nineteenth-century midwestern America. His rhetoric was familiar, but the words rang with bafflement, frustration, anger, and fear. The diminution of interest in moral reform and the decline in the popularity of his brand of Protestantism alarmed the evangelist. He worried that far too many Americans were either blind to or apathetic toward the unraveling of the fabric of their society. At times he retreated momentarily into a biblical apocalypticism, talking of the "Second Coming." More often, however, he challenged his hearers to courageously confront the destructive forces abroad in their land. The constituency to which his moral and social critique appealed was now declining in size and importance; yet if the evangelist no longer had the ear of the majority, his message did ring true to a substantial number of his disoriented and disenchanted contemporaries. Regardless of whether or not they agreed with his theology, they shared his conviction that the world was "going to Hell so fast you can't see it for the dust."[27]

The objects of Sunday's wrath during the 1920s and 1930s will surprise no one familiar with the religious and social conservatism of the era. He denounced movies, dancing, card-playing, birth control, companionate marriage, modern authors, much of higher education, and the lawlessness and gullibility he believed pervasive throughout the land. With the menace of liquor temporarily quelled, Billy targeted other evils which threatened to become monolithic, most notably political radicalism, the theory of evolution, and the nebulous phenomenon of modernism.

Sunday had nothing but scorn for those who failed to recognize the superiority of the country's democratic institutions. He cautioned Americans to be wary of the political heresies filtering into the nation from abroad. With characteristic flamboyance, he declared that if those who were currently criticizing the government "had Emma Goldman for their mother and the devil for their sire they would be a disgrace to their parents." He charged that some of the malcontents were so vile that their souls would cause an eclipse of the sun. Warning against the immorality of godless communism, he alleged that "in Russia there is not a virgin over fourteen years of age" and asked his audiences if they were prepared to tolerate such circumstances in America. For his part, he made it quite clear that he'd "rather be in hell than be in Russia." The ideas of Darwin were, in their own way, equally dangerous. Evolution, he contended, was an immoral and unproven theory, and teaching it was an insult to God. Science should confine itself to the natural world and not interfere with the affairs of the Lord. The tax dollars of devout parents should not be used to support the dissemination of such heretical theories. Those who wanted this kind of science taught could build their own schools.[28]

Another manifestation of the machinations of Satan was modernism. Like most religious conservatives, Billy could never precisely define the term, but he believed it to be merely another word for infidelity and as such he regarded it as a threat. "Modernism," he thought, tended toward "internationalism." "Internationalism" led to "communism." "Communism" led to "anarchy." "Anarchy" led to "destruction."[29]

Nowhere was modernism more of a danger than in the churches. The faith was being corrupted by preachers whose message bore little resemblance to the gospel of Christ. The church was "in the purple folds of a python of modernism" and the truth was "being crushed out of it." The result was the pervasiveness of sin and its destructive consequences.[30]

By the late 1920s, one sign that evil was indeed abroad in the land was the fact that Billy's old nemesis "demon rum" seemed to be rallying for another battle, and the prohibitionist preacher rose to the challenge. In 1928, he threatened to run for president if both parties nominated advocates of repeal. After the Democrats selected Al Smith, the revivalist spoke out frequently against the New Yorker, not for his Roman Catholicism, he assured audiences, but because he was a "wet." Sunday told a crowd of 10,000 in New Jersey that he would be against his own brother if he opposed Prohibition. In the spring of 1929, after Smith's defeat, for which Billy seems to have taken some credit, he hailed the eighteenth amendment as "the greatest blessing, morally and economically, any nation in the world could ever receive." It seemed to him that the evidence of the salutary effects of Prohibition was incontrovertible. He contended that "it not only has benefitted industry and business, but it has benefitted the individual, the small wage earner."

> When prohibition was enacted, there were 6,000,000 autos. Now there are 29,756,000 autos in the world, and of these 24,000,000 are in the United States. That tells a story in itself. Before prohibition the small wage earner did not have credit. With prohibition the small wage earner has become a sober man and has established credit and can buy his car on the installment plan.[31]

Given its benefits, Sunday did not believe that the nation would disavow its great experiment in sanity and righteousness. He saw Smith's defeat as verification of his earlier assertion that "no man is going to roll into the White House on a wine or beer-keg" platform. He recognized that there were problems with enforcement and that some negative consequences had arisen as a result of the law, but he believed that criticism of Prohibition had been grossly exaggerated, primarily by pro-liquor elements in the cities, especially New York. To his chagrin, within a few years, another politician from the Empire State would occupy the presidency and repeal would follow shortly thereafter.[32]

Sunday attributed many of his country's ills in the 1920s and 1930s to two overarching circumstances—immigration and prosperity. Reflecting the recurring nativist motif that ran through the 1920s, he implied that "aliens" were the source of much of the nation's trouble. Noting that America was often called the "melting pot of the world," he observed that it was "time to skim off the scum." The problem was not the immigrant per se but those who seemingly resisted acculturation. He continued, "Let anybody come to our shores that so desires but if they don't like the way we run our own country, then I say let them take their damnable carcasses and get back to where they came from."[33]

Billy Sunday appears not to have been overly concerned by the economic crisis that befell the nation in 1929 and thereafter. His attitude was not an expression of the insensitivity of a man merely enjoying affluence while millions suffered around him. In fact, the dwindling revenues which were the corollaries of his declining popularity and the periodic efforts to bail his family out of trouble meant that his own financial resources had shrunk to relatively modest proportions by the 1930s. Rather, his perspective was informed by his conviction that the prosperity of the 1920s had, in some ways, been detrimental to the nation. Sunday tended to see the post–World War I decades as a kind of morality play in which the excesses of the 1920s were being punished by the depression of the 1930s. He contended that virtue flourished in hard times and lapsed in periods of affluence. In 1930, he told the citizens of Hutchinson, Kansas,

> I'll tell you what's the matter with us. It's prosperity, that's what's the matter. Talk about financial depression. What's hurting us is too much prosperity. . . . That's what's the matter with us. Too much wealth, too much materialism, too much prosperity. . . . One reason of our materialism, our modernism, our falling faith in God, and falling interest in religion is because we are too prosperous, too wealthy. Let me tell you, if America does not turn away from material things and turn our eyes to God, America will sink to the depths of Hell.[34]

With the advent of the New Deal, popular interest in certain kinds of political and social action reemerged, but changing attitudes and innovative policies afforded the evangelist no solace. The reforms of the day were largely institutional and economic, with little in the way of the kind of moral component that Sunday would have found gratifying. Furthermore, after 1932, the programs of the Democratic administration represented for him a disconcerting and unprecedented degree of peacetime governmental involvement in people's lives. The lack of emphasis on a reinvigoration of traditional values and the pervasiveness of government made the New Deal anathema to the lifelong midwestern Republican whose party and whose values were seemingly being steamrollered by the Roosevelt revolution of the 1930s.

The revivalist suspected that leftists were shaping New Deal policies and regarded the National Recovery Administration and most other recovery programs as "the bunk." The onetime Iowa farm boy ridiculed the role of "brain busters" in the New Deal. "Why, I'll bet that not a one of those high-up agricultural experts would know which side of a cow to sit on when milking." He scorned the intrusion of government into people's private lives, telling a Knoxville, Tennessee, reporter in 1935, "If the government continue [*sic*] to extend its control over people as it has done since Mr. Roosevelt came into office, it won't be any time until a fellow can't kiss his own wife without legislative sanction." Repentance, not regulation, devotion, not direction, was the answer to the nation's problems.[35]

The senior evangelist in his study.

Billy Sunday Archives, Grace College and Theological Seminary,
Winona Lake, Indiana.

In the decade and a half prior to his death in November 1935, Sunday struggled with personal and social circumstances that he had not anticipated and that he only dimly understood. His beloved children had proven a source of disappointment and grief. Much of the wealth he and Ma had accumulated was gone. His ministry had fallen out of favor. The armies of the righteous seemed to be in retreat. Nevertheless, Billy preached on valiantly to hold the line and reverse the tide of battle. Now, however, his message grew more defensive and negative, which alienated him from the mainstream and diminished his credibility as role model and symbol.

At their zenith, the constellation of images and emotions evoked by Billy Sunday and his native heartland had provided important linkages between the values and relationships of a once rural agricultural nation and the increasingly complex consumer-oriented ones of twentieth-century America. In bridging the gap between tradition and modernity, the revivalist and the region from which he came offered security and hope in an age of anxiety. Much of his appeal, like that of the Middle West, had lain in the capacity of each to affirm the relevance and efficacy of conventional norms for a nation in transition. By the 1920s and 1930s, that era of transition was nearing completion and, as that occurred, both Billy Sunday and the Middle West seemed to millions increasingly quaint, ludicrous, or irrelevant.

Epilogue

On Wednesday evening, November 6, 1935, Billy Sunday lay resting in bed while his beloved "Ma" sat near him writing letters. Suddenly, at about eight o'clock, the silence of this tranquil domestic scene was broken when he announced, "Oh, I feel dizzy."[1] With those unremarkable words, one of the most colorful and often quoted men of early-twentieth-century American popular culture slipped quietly into the eternity about which he had preached for much of his life.

The scope of Sunday's ministry and consequently his fame had diminished over the previous decade and a half, but his passing was, nevertheless, a notable event. Within a few hours, news of his death had swept the nation, and messages of condolence began pouring into the residence of William J. Thompson, Sunday's brother-in-law, in whose Chicago home he had been visiting at the time of his fatal heart attack. They came from colleagues and converts, from the obscure and the prominent. Some, like the telegram from President Franklin D. Roosevelt, reflected the obligatory courtesy one public figure extends to the bereaved family of another. Others, like that of General Evangeline Booth, commander of the Salvation Army, expressed the genuine grief Evangelicals felt over the loss of an admired fallen comrade. Sentiments similar to those of General Booth were very much in evidence a few days later as Sunday's body lay in state at the Moody Memorial Church in Chicago. More than 3,000 people filed by his casket. The 3,500 mourners who gathered in the church later in the day to pay their final respects to the revivalist heard tributes from friends and associates who celebrated his life as that of one dedicated unequivocally to what he understood to be the Lord's work.[2]

Since the age of 24, Sunday had, indeed, devoted himself to what he considered a higher cause. From his days as a ballplayer who spoke to church and YMCA groups through his association with J. Wilbur Chapman to the heyday of his own evangelism in the 1910s, he preached salvation and championed conventional morality with an abandon rare even among professional revivalists. In the 1920s and 1930s, even as changing times and tastes eclipsed his popularity, age drained him physically, and family problems enervated him emotionally, he remained committed to his task. He crisscrossed the nation preaching the gospel, exhorting sinners to repent and the saved to rededicate their lives to God. The revivalist, who had always wanted to die in harness, was proud of the fact that, even though his fame waned in post–World War I America, he never went without calls to preach. Although serious heart problems in 1935 forced him to drastically curtail his activities, as late as October of that year he honored a request from Homer Rodeheaver to fill in for him at a revival in Mishawaka, Indiana, during which he, for the last time, saw penitents hit the sawdust trail.[3]

In the course of roughly forty years as a peripatetic preacher, Sunday touched the lives of millions of his contemporaries. Some attended his revival services out of skeptical curiosity, others out of sympathetic admiration, and still more because they longed for the peace and assurance they hoped to find in his version of the gospel. The people who journeyed to the tents and tabernacles of a Sunday campaign usually found what they expected to find there and, if testimonial letters are indicative, the lives of some were permanently transformed by the experience. Regardless of their motives, those who attended heard a revivalist who entertained, reproached, exhorted, and astonished his audiences. One moment he spewed forth vitriolic streams of condemnation that seemed void of compassion. The next, he charmed them with a winsome smile and an irresistible wit that neutralized the vitriol and left no doubt that he was there to save them and their nation from the consequences of sin.

Both individual and social salvation were the ultimate goals of a Sunday revival. He did not sharply distinguish between the two because for him the latter followed directly from the former. Any effort to bypass the personal transformation that flowed from the redemptive power of the blood of Jesus Christ was both a corruption of the gospel and an exercise in folly. Christianity, however, was a matter of action as well as of faith. Genuinely Christian men and women should be concerned not only with the state of their own souls but should also work to build a stable and harmonious social order.

Sunday's vision of society had more to do with the mystique of the Midwest of his youth than with thoughtful reflection upon, or analysis of, the complex personal and social problems of his day. The evangelist did not simply try to recreate a lost world, of which he had once been a part, but tried to establish one that he had never fully known. He idealized the rural and small-town cultural norms of late-nineteenth-century Iowa, yet his own experience had never been wholly consistent with those norms. His sermons reflected the dissonance between the ideal and the real in his life. He extolled the virtues of fatherhood and motherhood and excoriated drinking, gambling, philandering, indolence, and any other behavior that eroded the nuclear family. He railed against greed, dishonesty, irreligion, gossip, stinginess, pettiness, and all other conduct that undermined church and community. In a very real sense, in addition to preaching personal redemption, he spent his entire career trying to realize for others the familial and community values of his youth. The social vision he espoused was one with which many Americans were quite comfortable. It was, however, one that seemed in peril in their rapidly changing nation. The evangelist's life story, public persona, and successful ministry enabled him to package conventional norms in a way that made them appear relevant to the new economic and social realities. Thus, many in his audiences found solace in his message.

If the ability to bridge the gap between tradition and modernity was an important source of Sunday's appeal as an evangelist, it also flowed directly from some of his personal and professional shortcomings. Because of the way in which he had resolved many of his own doubts and fears in terms of the religious and social values of the American heartland and because of the limits of his educational experience, he lacked the will or ability to disassociate himself from the culture in which he had been steeped. His prophetic voice was, therefore, limited to a condemnation of individual and collective failings within the context of prevailing norms. He could not or would not step outside that context to question the dominant economic, social, or political assumptions of the day. Consequently, he manifested and perpetuated many of the weaknesses that were a part of his culture.

Sunday was seduced by materialism, equating prosperity with the rewards due the righteous. He succumbed to the chauvinism of early-twentieth-century America, believing without question in the superiority of his nation. While willing to extend the message of the gospel to all people and condemning racial or ethnic violence, he accepted the stereotypes of his day. He was wary of the new immigrant and lacked much tolerance for political or cultural diversity. While sometimes showing compassion for those whose frailties had brought them to unfortunate ends, he often oversimplified the complexities of human nature and of economic and social relationships.

The evangelist's concept of sin was almost exclusively individualistic, reflecting only a minimal grasp of the reality of collective or institutionalized evil. While he condemned the exploitation and mistreatment of women and recognized that they had an important role to play in family, church, and society, he did not challenge contemporary gender roles, even though the potential for disrespect, mistreatment, and exploitation was inherent in them. Although his ideas about manliness contained significant religious and moral dimensions, his own aura of masculinity was largely informed by notions of toughness, self-reliance, and aggressiveness that were a legacy of the frontier ethos.

It is easy to condemn Sunday for attitudes and actions that, to many contemporary Americans, seem misguided, intolerant, or lacking in Christian compassion. To be sure, he might be a more widely appealing figure today had he been able to transcend his times, but that is a feat more easily demanded of others than accomplished by ourselves. It is a daunting task to extricate oneself from the web of intellectual, emotional, and cultural relationships that constitute his or her heritage. Sunday, despite the persona of strength and courage he projected, had a psyche that was too fragile to rise to this challenge. He found peace and security through an acceptance of the evangelical gospel of nineteenth-century America and achieved success by championing his nation's prevailing social and economic norms. To question either the religious or cultural tenets he had embraced as he matured as a man and a Christian would have involved not only professional risks but a threat to his personal equilibrium. There is little evidence that Sunday ever acknowledged publicly or privately those moments that come to most, even the devout, when all gods are dead, all angels fallen, when there is no Lucifer, only the void.

In 1935, a journalist reflecting upon the revivalist's 40-year career observed that there was "something sublimely simple about Billy Sunday's faith." His God was personal and familiar, an ever-present ally, comforter, and protector. Good and evil were clearly distinguishable, and doing right as opposed to wrong was a matter of simple choice. The reward for a life of faith and obedience was eternity in a heaven as tangible as a midwestern village with a family and community life that resembled that of small-town America. Sunday once observed that when he arrived in heaven the first thing he would do would be to shake Jesus' hand and thank him for salvation and the privilege of preaching the gospel. Then, he explained,

> I'll walk all over God's heaven and think of the people I'll meet there. Think of sitting down on the bank of the river with Peter, James, John, Andrew, Philip and the others.
>
> And then I'll ask Jesus if he'll let me hang around the gate and be the first to welcome the wife and babies when they come in. And He'll say, "You can sit right there, Bill, if you want to; it's all right." And as they come one after another I will be there to welcome them.
>
> "Hello, Helen! Hey, George! Hey, Will! Hey, little Paul! Come on." And they'd ask where I live and I'd take them over to our mansion. And oh, what a good time we'll have in heaven.[4]

For some, such simplicity was the object of condescension or ridicule. For others, it was a quality to be admired and emulated. Whatever its merits, his childlike faith was the force that energized the revivalist's extraordinary life and work.

Billy Sunday was not a "man for all seasons," but he was in many respects a quintessential American of his day. Scarred by war, he struggled against poverty, left rural America for the city, made the most of his talents, took advantage of his opportunities, and achieved success. He lived the American dream of upward social mobility, material accomplishment, and popular acclaim. His life story was, therefore, one with which many of his contemporaries could identify. He embodied their loss, their grief, their pain, their poverty, their hopes, their fears, and their dreams. He understood them and they him. He was one of them, but he was bigger than life. He was Teddy Roosevelt, P. T. Barnum, Abraham Lincoln, Frank Merriwell, and John D. Rockefeller rolled into one. In his sincerity and unique embodiment of so much that was a part of his nation's past and present, he represented for millions of Americans a figure of heroic proportions.

NOTES

INTRODUCTION

1. Carl Sandburg, *Billy Sunday and Other Poems* (San Diego: Harcourt Brace & Company, 1993), 3–7; Ogden Nash, *I Wouldn't Have Missed It* (Boston: Little, Brown and Company, 1975), 69; Fred Fisher, "Chicago, That Toddling Town" [sheet music on-line] (New York: Fisher Music Corp., 1922, accessed July 18, 2001), available from http://www.chipublib.org/008subject/001artmusic/chgosongs/Chgofisher.

2. William T. Ellis, *Billy Sunday: The Man and His Message* (Chicago: Moody Press, 1936), vi.

3. Dixon Wecter, *The Hero in America: A Chronicle of Hero-Worship* (Ann Arbor: University of Michigan Press, 1966), 488.

1. A SON OF THE MIDDLE WEST

1. Iowa Census Board, *Census of Iowa [1836–1880]* (Des Moines: Iowa Executive Council, 1875–1925), 198–199.

2. *Biographical and Historical Memoirs of Story County, Iowa* (Chicago: The Goodspeed Publishing Company, 1890), 118–119.

3. Iowa Census Board, *Census of Iowa [1836–1880]*, 252–364.

4. Lyle W. Dorsett, *Billy Sunday and the Redemption of Urban America* (Grand Rapids, Mich.: William B. Eerdmans Publishing Company, 1991), 6; United States Census Office, *Population Schedules of the Eighth Census of the United States. Iowa: Story County*, Record Group (hereafter RG) M653, Microform Reel 339, National Archives and Records Administration (hereafter NARA), Washington, D.C.

5. Rev. William A. (Billy) Sunday, "The Sawdust Trail," *Ladies' Home Journal*, September 1932, 4; Pension File, Mary Jane Stowell Family, Cert. No. 653177, Records of the Veterans Administration, Civil War Pension File, RG 15, NARA, Washington, D.C. (hereafter Stowell Pension File).

6. Roger A. Bruns, *Preacher: Billy Sunday and Big-Time American Evangelism* (New York: W. W. Norton and Company, 1992), 22–24; Dorsett, *Billy Sunday*, 5; Stowell Pension File; United States Census Office, *Population Schedules of the Eighth Census. Iowa: Story County.*

7. Dorsett, *Billy Sunday*, 7; Sunday, "The Sawdust Trail," *Ladies' Home Journal*, September 1932, 4; Stowell Pension File; Bruns, *Preacher*, 22.

8. Story County Marriage Record I, 1854–1866, 111–112, Recorder's Office, Story County, Nevada, Iowa; United States Census Office, *Population Schedules of the Ninth Census of the United States Iowa: Story County*, RG M593, Microform Reel 420, NARA, Washington, D.C.; Bruns, *Preacher*, 25; Stowell Pension File; Record of Divorces, Story County [Index], 151–152, Recorder's Office, Story County, Nevada, Iowa.

9. L. O. Cheever, "Iowa Annie Wittenmyer Home," *Palimpsest* 48, no. 6 (June 1967): 253–254.

10. Stowell Pension File; Theodore T. Frankenberg, *Spectacular Career of Rev. Billy Sunday: Famous Baseball Evangelist* (Columbus, Ohio: McClelland and Company, 1913), 29–31; Sunday, "The Sawdust Trail," *Ladies' Home Journal*, September 1932, 84.

11. Billy Sunday, "The Sawdust Trail," *Ladies' Home Journal*, October 1932, 12; Cheever, "Iowa Annie Wittenmyer Home," 257.

12. Sunday, "The Sawdust Trail," *Ladies' Home Journal*, October 1932, 12.

13. Ibid., 12–13.

14. Ibid.

15. Ibid.

16. Billy Sunday, "The Sawdust Trail," *Ladies' Home Journal*, November 1932, 17; Stowell Pension File; Petition in the Circuit Court of the State of Iowa in and for Story County, In the matter of Alfred [sic] M. Sunday, J. A. Fitchpatrick, guardian, April Term 1885, filed May 2, 1885, Recorder's Office, Story County, Nevada, Iowa.

17. Sunday, "The Sawdust Trail," *Ladies' Home Journal*, November 1932, 17.

18. Sunday, "The Sawdust Trail," *Ladies' Home Journal*, October 1932, 99; "The Sawdust Trail," *Ladies' Home Journal*, November 1932, 17.

19. Sunday, "The Sawdust Trail," *Ladies' Home Journal*, October 1932, 99; "The Sawdust Trail," *Ladies' Home Journal*, November 1932, 17.

20. Billy Sunday, Marshalltown, Iowa, to Helen Thompson, February 4, 1887, Papers of William Ashley and Helen Amelia Thompson Sunday, The Billy Graham Center, Wheaton College, Wheaton, Ill. (hereafter Sunday papers), microfilm reel 5; Sunday, "The Sawdust Trail," *Ladies' Home Journal*, November 1932, 17.

21. Sunday, "The Sawdust Trail," *Ladies' Home Journal*, November 1932, 17, 110; Billy Sunday, Evening Sermon, New York City, April 14, 1917, 24, Sunday Papers, microfilm reel 10; Adrian C. Anson, *A Ball Player's Career* (Chicago: Era Publishing, 1900), 133–134.

22. Clarence Ray Aurner, *History of Education in Iowa* (Iowa City: State Historical Society of Iowa, 1914), 345.

23. Lewis Atherton, *Main Street on the Middle Border* (Bloomington: Indiana University Press, 1954), 69.

24. Ibid., 78–79, 83–84, 88–92.

25. Ibid., 106–108.

26. Sunday, "The Sawdust Trail," *Ladies' Home Journal*, September 1932, 4–5.

27. Ibid.

28. Ibid.

29. *Census of Iowa [1836–1880]*, 584.

30. Sunday, "The Sawdust Trail," *Ladies' Home Journal*, September 1932, 4; Deed-Book F (Story County), May 12, 1860, 473, Auditor's Office, Story County, Nevada, Iowa.

31. H. Summerfield Day, *The Iowa State University Campus and Its Buildings 1859–1979* (Ames: Iowa State University Press, 1980), 34.

32. Elijah P. Brown, *The Real Billy Sunday: The Life and Work of Rev. William Ashley Sunday, D.D., The Baseball Evangelist* (New York: Fleming H. Revell Company, 1914), 30; Sunday, "The Sawdust Trail," *Ladies' Home Journal*, November 1932, 17.

33. Billy Sunday, Boston, to Helen Thompson, May 21, 1887, Sunday Papers, microfilm reel 5.

34. *Biographical and Historical Memoirs of Story County*, 131; Sunday, "The Sawdust Trail," *Ladies' Home Journal*, September 1932, 5.

35. *Biographical and Historical Memoirs of Story County*, 103; Sunday, "The Sawdust Trail," *Ladies' Home Journal*, September 1932, 5.

36. Sunday, "The Sawdust Trail," *Ladies' Home Journal*, September 1932, 82.

37. Ibid.

38. Brown, *The Real Billy Sunday*, 17.

39. Billy Sunday, Detroit, to Helen Thompson, May 31, 1887, Sunday Papers, microfilm reel 5.

40. Sunday, "The Sawdust Trail," *Ladies' Home Journal*, September 1932, 4.

41. Ibid., 5.

42. Billy Sunday, Allegheny, Pa., to Helen Thompson, May 15, 1888, Sunday Papers, microfilm reel 6.

43. State of Iowa, Story County, in the Circuit Court of said county, In the Matter of guardianship of Albert M. and Eddie H. and William A. Sunday, minor heirs of Wm. Sunday, deceased, 10 March 1873, Walter Evans, guardian, Recorder's Office, Story County, Nevada, Iowa; Final Report of L[ycurgus] Irwin, Guar[dian], April 25, 1881, Recorder's Office, Story County, Nevada, Iowa.

44. Sunday, "The Sawdust Trail," *Ladies' Home Journal*, September 1932, 5.

45. Ibid., 84.

46. Farwell T. Brown, *Ames the Early Years in Word and Picture: From Marsh to Modern City* (Ames, Iowa: Farwell T. Brown and Heuss Printing, 1993), 131; Petition of Jennie M. Stowell, On the Circuit Court of the State of Iowa in and for Story County, April term A.D. 1885, Filed April 2, 1885, In the Matter of the Estate of Wm. M. Sunday, Recorder's Office, Story County, Nevada, Iowa (hereafter Petition of Jennie M. Stowell); Will Sunday, Horace, Kansas, to Nell Thompson, December 8, 1887, Sunday Papers, microfilm reel 1, Box 3, Folder 37 in Sunday Family Correspondence (misfiled in December 1888).

47. Petition of Jennie M. Stowell; Annual Report of Guardian, J. A. Fitchpatrick, State of Iowa, Story County, No. 224, in the Guardianship of Albert M. Sunday, Minor Heir of Wm. Sunday, Deceased, Filed May 2, 1885; Petition, In the Circuit Court of the State of Iowa in and for Story County, In the matter of the Estate of Alfred [sic] M. Sunday, by J. A. Fitchpatrick, guardian, Filed May 2, 1885, April Term 1885. All in Recorder's Office, Story County, Nevada, Iowa.

48. Sunday, "The Sawdust Trail," *Ladies' Home Journal*, September 1932, 84.

2. The Diamond and the Cross

1. Sunday, "The Sawdust Trail," *Ladies' Home Journal*, November 1932, 110; Carl Sandburg, "Chicago," in *The Complete Poems of Carl Sandburg* (New York: Harcourt Brace Jovanovich, 1970), 3; United States Census Office, *Report on Population of the United States at the Eleventh Census, 1890. Part I* (Washington, D.C.: GPO, 1895; reprint, New York: Norman Ross Publishing, 1993); United States Census Office, *Statistics of the Population of the United States at the Ninth Census: Embracing the Tables of Race, Nationality, Sex, Selected Ages, and Occupations . . . Compiled from the Original Returns of the Ninth Census* (Washington, D.C.: GPO, 1872; reprint, New York: Norman Ross Publishing, 1990); United States Census Office, *Statistics of the Population of the United States at the Tenth Census (June 1, 1880): Embracing the Tables of the Population of States, Counties, and Minor Civil Divisions, with Distinction of Race, Sex, Age, Nativity, and Occupations* (Washington, D.C.: GPO, 1883; reprint, New York: Norman Ross Publishing, 1991); William Cronon, *Nature's Metropolis: Chicago and the Great West* (New York: W. W. Norton, 1991), 99.

2. John A. Lucas and Ronald A. Smith, *Saga of American Sport* (Philadelphia: Lea and Febiger, 1978), 176.

3. Sunday, "The Sawdust Trail," *Ladies' Home Journal*, October 1932, 13; November 1932, 17.

4. Robert F. Burk, *Never Just a Game: Players, Owners, and American Baseball to 1920* (Chapel Hill: University of North Carolina Press, 1994), 29, 41, 54.

5. Benjamin G. Rader, *Baseball: A History of America's Game* (Urbana and Chicago: University of Illinois Press, 1992), 40.

6. Ibid., 38, 40–41, 43, 45–46.

7. Ibid., 36–37, 40–41.

8. Ibid., 41–42.

9. Burk, *Never Just a Game*, 60, 65–66.

10. Rader, *Baseball*, 42–44.

11. Ibid., 45, 47–51.

12. Sunday, "The Sawdust Trail," *Ladies' Home Journal*, November 1932, 110.

13. Ibid.

14. Ibid., 112.

15. Dorsett, *Billy Sunday*, 23; Joseph L. Reichler, ed., *The Baseball Encyclopedia: The Complete and Official Record of Major League Baseball* (New York: Collier Macmillan, 1985), 129, 136, 145, 150, 154, 159, 1441.

16. Anson, *A Ball Player's Career*, 133.

17. William T. Ellis, *Billy Sunday: The Man and His Message* (Chicago: Moody Press, 1936), 479.

18. Wendy Knickerbocker, *Sunday at the Ballpark: Billy Sunday's Professional Baseball Career, 1883–1890* (Lanham, Md.: The Scarecrow Press, 2000), 77, 124–125, 133.

19. Sunday, "The Sawdust Trail," *Ladies' Home Journal*, November 1932, 112.

20. Bessie Louise Pierce, *A History of Chicago: The Rise of a Modern City, 1871–1893* (New York: Alfred A. Knopf, 1957), 441–443.

21. Pierce, *A History of Chicago*, 442–445.

22. Carl F. H. Henry, *The Pacific Garden Mission: A Doorway to Heaven* (Grand Rapids, Mich.: Zondervan Publishing House, 1942), 25–29; Pierce, *A History of Chicago*, 432.

23. Sunday, "The Sawdust Trail," *Ladies' Home Journal*, December 1932, 16.

24. Story County Death Record I, 1880–1897, Recorder's Office, Story County, Nevada, Iowa; "First Sunday Sermon in Sodhouse," undated and unidentified newspaper article, Sunday Papers, microfilm reel 19.

25. Billy Sunday, Detroit, to Helen Thompson, June 4, 1887, Sunday Papers, microfilm reel 5.

26. Sunday, "The Sawdust Trail," *Ladies' Home Journal*, December 1932, 16.

27. "Mrs. Sunday Pays Tribute to 'Billy,'" March 16, 1938; "Ma Sunday Tells of Life with 'Billy,'" June 2, 1950, unidentified newspaper articles, Sunday Papers, microfilm reel 20.

28. Sunday, "The Sawdust Trail," *Ladies' Home Journal*, February 1933, 87.

29. Billy Sunday, Belle Plaine, Iowa, to Helen Thompson, November 25, 1887, Sunday Papers, microfilm reel 5.

30. Billy Sunday, Philadelphia, to Helen Thompson, May 21, 1887; Billy Sunday to "Mama" (Mrs. William Thompson), November 12, 1886; Billy Sunday to Helen Thompson, November 18, 1886; all in Sunday Papers, microfilm reel 5.

31. Billy Sunday to Helen Thompson, November 18, 1886; Billy Sunday to Helen Thompson, November 20, 1886; Billy Sunday to "Mama" (Mrs. William Thompson), November 23, 1886; Billy Sunday to Helen Thompson, February 9, 1887; all in Sunday Papers, microfilm reel 5.

32. In the late nineteenth century, Pittsburgh was spelled "Pittsburg." For consistency in the text, I have used the modern version of the city's name.

33. Burk, *Never Just a Game*, 65–68, 76–77.

34. Ibid., 90–91.

35. Rader, *Baseball*, 46–47, 57.

36. *The Pittsburg Press*, 16 April 1888, 5; Dorsett, *Billy Sunday*, 37, 39–40.

37. *The Pittsburg Press*, 19 April 1888, 5.

38. *The Pittsburg Press*, 25 April 1888, 5.

39. *The Pittsburg Press*, 9 May 1888, 5.

40. *The Pittsburg Press*, 8 August 1889, 5; 19 May 1888, 1; 24 June 1890, 3.

41. Ellis, *Billy Sunday: The Man and His Message*, 501; Dorsett, *Billy Sunday*, 40.

42. William G. McLoughlin, Jr., *Billy Sunday Was His Real Name* (Chicago: University of Chicago Press, 1955), 7.

43. Billy Sunday, New York City, to Helen Thompson, August 27, 1887, Sunday Papers, microfilm reel 5.

44. Knickerbocker, *Sunday at the Ballpark*, 133; *The Pittsburg Press*, 25 August 1890, 3; *The Philadelphia Inquirer*, 27 August 1890, 3.

45. Dorsett, *Billy Sunday*, 40–42; Sunday, "The Sawdust Trail," *Ladies' Home Journal*, February 1933, 89.

46. Rader, *Baseball*, 46; Ellis, *Billy Sunday: The Man and His Message*, 498; *The Pittsburg Press*, 6 September 1888, 5.

47. Steven A. Riess, "Professional Baseball and Social Mobility," *Journal of Interdisciplinary History* XI, no. 2 (Autumn 1980): 249.

3. Entrepreneurial Evangelism

1. McLoughlin, *Billy Sunday Was His Real Name*, 8.

2. Ibid., 8.

3. Billy Sunday, Afternoon Sermon, New York City, April 12, 1917, 19–20, Sunday Papers, microfilm reel 10.

4. McLoughlin, *Billy Sunday Was His Real Name*, 8–9; Sunday, "The Sawdust Trail," *Ladies' Home Journal*, February 1933, 89.

5. Ibid., 89–90.

6. McLoughlin, *Billy Sunday Was His Real Name*, 9; Sunday, "The Sawdust Trail," *Ladies' Home Journal*, December 1932, 94.

7. Sunday, "The Sawdust Trail," *Ladies' Home Journal*, February 1933, 90.

8. Brown, *The Real Billy Sunday*, 85–86; Lindsay Denison, "The Rev. Billy Sunday and His War on the Devil," *American Magazine* 64, no. 5 (September 1907): 459–460.

9. Theodore T. Frankenberg, *Billy Sunday, His Tabernacles and Sawdust Trails* (Columbus, Ohio: The F. J. Heer Printing Company, 1917), 42; McLoughlin, *Billy Sunday Was His Real Name*, 46–47.

10. *New York World*, June 14, 1917, Sunday Papers, microfilm reel 20.

11. Homer Rodeheaver, *Twenty Years with Billy Sunday* (Nashville: Cokesbury Press, 1936), 111–112; Denison, "The Rev. Billy Sunday," 456–457.

12. Rodeheaver, *Twenty Years with Billy Sunday*, 73.

13. "How a Baseball Idol 'Hit the Trail,'" *Literary Digest*, 8 July 1916, 92–95; Denison, "The Rev. Billy Sunday"; "Poll of the Religious Press on Billy Sunday," *Literary Digest*, 12 June 1915, 1404–1405; "Billy Sunday under Fire," *Literary Digest*, 18 April 1914, 907.

14. McLoughlin, *Billy Sunday Was His Real Name*, 16, 45.

15. Ibid., 271; Rodeheaver, *Twenty Years with Billy Sunday*, 141.

16. McLoughlin, *Billy Sunday Was His Real Name*, 18, 24; Frankenberg, *Spectacular Career*, 198; Brown, *The Real Billy Sunday*, 88.

17. Brown, *The Real Billy Sunday*, 111.

18. McLoughlin, *Billy Sunday Was His Real Name*, 58.

19. Rodeheaver, *Twenty Years with Billy Sunday*, 13; McLoughlin, *Billy Sunday Was His Real Name*, 73.

20. McLoughlin, *Billy Sunday Was His Real Name*, 116; Rodeheaver, *Twenty Years with Billy Sunday*, 119.

21. "Billy's Rubicon," *Literary Digest*, 21 April 1917, 1168.

22. Dorsett, *Billy Sunday*, 91–92; McLoughlin, *Billy Sunday Was His Real Name*, 103–104; Robert Laurence Moore, *Selling God: American Religion in the Marketplace of Culture* (New York: Oxford University Press, 1994), 186.

23. Dorsett, *Billy Sunday*, 91; Rodeheaver, *Twenty Years with Billy Sunday*, 117–118.

24. Dorsett, *Billy Sunday*, 132.

25. Ibid., 117; Homer Rodeheaver to Billy Sunday, October 20, 1929, Sunday Papers, microfilm reel 2.

26. George Creel, "Salvation Circus," *Harper's Weekly*, 19 June 1915, 582.

4. Playing the Game for God

1. Charles C. Alexander, *Our Game* (New York: Henry Holt and Company), 53; Steven A. Riess, *City Games: The Evolution of American Urban Society and the Rise of Sports* (Urbana and Chicago: University of Illinois Press, 1989), 4.

2. Riess, *City Games*, 5; Alexander, *Our Game*, 52.

3. Robert J. Higgs, *God in the Stadium: Sports and Religion in America* (Lexington: University Press of Kentucky, 1995), 22–27.

4. Higgs, *God in the Stadium*, 203–204; Dominick Cavallo, *Muscles and Morals: Organized Playgrounds and Urban Reform, 1880–1920* (Philadelphia: University of Pennsylvania Press, 1981), 33–34, 75.

5. Brown, *The Real Billy Sunday*, 48, 58.

6. Ibid., 86; Billy Sunday, "The Sawdust Trail," *Ladies' Home Journal*, April 1933, 60; Billy Sunday, "My All-Star Nine," *Collier's*, 18 October 1913, 19, 30; "Billy Arrives With Old Fire But Minus Gymnastic Pep," *News-Sentinel*, 10 April 1935, newspaper article, Sunday Papers, microfilm reel 20.

7. Brown, *The Real Billy Sunday*, 32, 58; Ellis, *Billy Sunday: The Man and His Message*, 28.

8. "Billy Sunday Favors the Continuance of Sports during the War," 10 April 1917, unidentified newspaper article, Sunday Papers, microfilm reel 19.

9. "Calls Baseball Cleanest Sport," 5 January 1909, unidentified newspaper article, Billy Sunday biographical file, National Baseball Hall of Fame Library Archives, Cooperstown, New York.

10. Ibid.

11. Sunday, "My All-Star Nine," 19.

12. Ibid.

13. "Sunday Favors the Continuance of Sports."

14. Rodeheaver, *Twenty Years with Billy Sunday*, 133–134.

15. "Sunday Favors the Continuance of Sports."

16. Sunday, "The Sawdust Trail," *Ladies' Home Journal*, December 1932, 16.

17. Sunday, "The Sawdust Trail," *Ladies' Home Journal*, November 1932, 112–113.

18. Knickerbocker, *Sunday at the Ballpark*, 80–83.

19. William Sunday to Helen Thompson, April 13, 1888, Sunday Papers, microfilm reel 1.

20. Joseph Pallen, *Burning Truths from Billy's Bat: A Graphic Description of the Remarkable Conversion of Rev. "Billy" Sunday* (Philadelphia: Diamond Publishing Company, 1914), 10.

21. Ibid., 11.

22. Ibid., 13–16.

23. Ibid., 16.

24. Susan Curtis, *A Consuming Faith: The Social Gospel and Modern American Culture* (Baltimore: Johns Hopkins University Press, 1991), 46–47.

25. Ibid., 24–25.

26. Sunday, "The Sawdust Trail," *Ladies' Home Journal*, November 1932, 113.

5. MAN ENOUGH TO BE A CHRISTIAN

1. Rodeheaver, *Twenty Years with Billy Sunday*, 97; Bruns, *Preacher*, 137–139; Douglas Frank, *Less Than Conquerors* (Grand Rapids, Mich.: William B. Eerdmans Publishing Company, 1986), 188–193.

2. E. Anthony Rotundo, "Learning about Manhood: Gender Ideals and the Middle-Class Family in Nineteenth-Century America," in *Manliness and Morality*, edited by J. A. Mangan and James Walvin (New York: St. Martin's Press, 1987), 35–51. See also Rotundo's *American Manhood: Transformations in Masculinity from the Revolution to the Modern Era* (New York: Basic Books, 1993).

3. Lucas and Smith, *Saga of American Sport*, 289–290.

4. Mark C. Carnes, "Middle-Class Men and the Solace of Fraternal Ritual," in *Meanings for Manhood: Constructions of Masculinity in Victorian America*, edited by Mark C. Carnes and Clyde Griffen (Chicago: University of Chicago Press, 1990), 37–66; Joe L. Dubbert, *A Man's Place: Masculinity in Transition* (Englewood Cliffs, N.J.: Prentice Hall, 1979), 148–149; David I. Macleod, *Building Character in the American*

Boy: The Boy Scouts, YMCA, and Their Forerunners, 1870–1920 (Madison: University of Wisconsin Press, 1983), 83–93, 130–145.

5. Tony Ladd and James A. Mathisen, *Muscular Christianity: Evangelical Protestants and the Development of American Sport* (Grand Rapids, Mich.: Baker Books, 1999), 14, 20; Clifford Putney, "Character Building in the YMCA, 1880–1930," *Mid-America: An Historical Review* 73, no. 1 (January 1991): 49–69; Gail Bederman, "'The Women Have Had Charge of the Church Work Long Enough': The Men and Religion Forward Movement of 1911–1912 and the Masculinization of Middle-Class Protestantism," *American Quarterly* 41, no. 3 (1989): 432–465; Barbara Welter, "The Feminization of American Religion: 1800–1860," in *Clio's Consciousness Raised: New Perspectives on the History of Women*, edited by Mary S. Hartman and Lois Banner (New York: Harper & Row, 1974), 137–157.

6. Billy Sunday, Afternoon Sermon, New York, April 28, 1917, 7–8, Sunday Papers, microfilm reel 10; McLoughlin, *Billy Sunday Was His Real Name*, 226–227.

7. Barbara Welter, "The Cult of True Womanhood: 1820–1860," *American Quarterly* 18, no. 2, pt. 1 (1966): 151–174; Billy Sunday, "Banish Blue Monday," *The Country Gentleman*, 31 July 1921, Sunday Papers, microfilm reel 20; Karen Gullen, ed., *Billy Sunday Speaks* (New York: Chelsea House Publishers, 1970), 110–111.

8. Gullen, *Billy Sunday Speaks*, 107, 110–111; "Dirty Tobacco Habit," undated and unidentified newspaper article, Sunday Papers, microfilm reel 25; William G. McLoughlin, "Billy Sunday and the Working Girls, 1915," *Journal of Presbyterian History* 54, no. 3 (1976): 376–384.

9. Gullen, *Billy Sunday Speaks*, 107, 109–110.

10. "Time to Lay Aside Mock Modesty Sunday Asserts," *The Richmond Item* (Indiana), 21 May 1922, Sunday Papers, microfilm reel 20; Gullen, *Billy Sunday Speaks*, 109.

11. Gullen, *Billy Sunday Speaks*, 109, 111.

12. Ibid., 109, 111, 112.

13. Sunday, "Banish Blue Monday."

14. Billy Sunday, Sermon, "Chickens Come Home to Roost," (hereafter "Chickens Sermon"), New York City, April 29, 1917, 14–15, Sunday Papers, microfilm reel 10.

15. Billy Sunday, Sermon, "The Devil's Boomerang, or Hot Cakes Right Off the Griddle," (hereafter "Griddle Sermon"), New York City, May 6, 1917 (Sunday afternoon), 19–20, 22, Sunday Papers, microfilm reel 10.

16. "Griddle Sermon," 18, 22.

17. *Waterloo Evening Courier and Reporter*, 27 January 1915, 7; Rodeheaver, *Twenty Years with Billy Sunday*, 32.

18. Frank, *Less Than Conquerors*, 189.

19. Billy Sunday, Evening Sermon, New York City, April 8, 1917, 3, 13–14, Sunday Papers, microfilm reel 9; McLoughlin, *Billy Sunday Was His Real Name*, 175; "Enthusiasm High as Sunday Opens Great Campaign," *Des Moines Register and Leader*, 2 November 1914, 3; Gullen, *Billy Sunday Speaks*, 90; Bruns, *Preacher*, 138.

20. "Forces That Win," *Des Moines Register and Leader*, 7 November 1914, 12; McLoughlin, *Billy Sunday Was His Real Name*, 135; Billy Sunday, Evening Sermon, New York City, April 15, 1917, 32, Sunday Papers, microfilm reel 9; Billy Sunday, Evening Sermon, New York City, April 28, 1917, 16–17, Sunday Papers, microfilm reel 10; Gullen, *Billy Sunday Speaks*, 72–73, 204.

21. Frank, *Less Than Conquerors*, 189.

22. Billy Sunday, Evening Sermon, New York City, May 1, 1917, 18, 21, Sunday Papers, microfilm reel 10; Michael S. Kimmel, "Baseball and the Reconstitution of American Masculinity, 1880–1920," in *Baseball History 3: An Annual of Original Baseball Research*, edited by Peter Levine (Westport, Conn.: Meckler, 1990), 101.

23. Billy Sunday, Evening Sermon, New York City, May 1, 1917, 17, Sunday Papers, microfilm reel 10; Gullen, *Billy Sunday Speaks*, 90; "Revival Season On," 1895, unidentified newspaper article, Sunday Papers, microfilm reel 19.

24. Rodeheaver, *Twenty Years with Billy Sunday*, 98.

25. Billy Sunday, Evening Sermon, New York City, May 1, 1917, 21, Sunday Papers, microfilm reel 10.

26. Rodeheaver, *Twenty Years with Billy Sunday*, 12.

27. Billy Sunday, Evening Sermon, New York City, April 15, 1917, 19, Sunday Papers, microfilm reel 9.

28. Sunday, "The Sawdust Trail," *Ladies' Home Journal*, February 1933, 90, 92.

29. Gullen, *Billy Sunday Speaks*, 91.

30. "Enthusiasm High as Sunday Opens Great Campaign," *Des Moines Register and Leader*, 2 November 1914, 3.

31. Rodeheaver, *Twenty Years with Billy Sunday*, 92.

32. Ibid., 92–94.

33. Ibid., 94–95; "How Evangelist Maintains His Fighting Trim," 2 September 1917, unidentified newspaper article, Sunday Papers, microfilm reel 25.

34. Dorsett, *Billy Sunday*, 93–94.

35. Jim Holston, "Billy Sunday, The Calliope of Zion," *The Iowan* 33 (Spring 1985), 19; Bruns, *Preacher*, 112.

36. Ellis, *Billy Sunday: The Man and His Message*, 22.

37. Kimmel, *Baseball*, 102.

38. Ibid., 288.

39. Gail Bederman, *Manliness and Civilization: A Cultural History of Gender and Race in the United States, 1880–1917* (Chicago: University of Chicago Press, 1995), 18.

40. Bruns, *Preacher*, 137.

41. "Revival Life Enjoyed by Ma," *Boston Herald*, 18 February 1931, Sunday Papers, microfilm reel 20; "'Ma' Sunday Says She Has No Time For Career Stuff," *Los Angeles Evening Express*, undated newspaper article, Sunday Papers, microfilm reel 20.

42. Billy Sunday to Helen Sunday, 1897, Sunday Papers, microfilm reel 7.

43. Billy Sunday, Coffeyville, Kans., to Helen Sunday, September 15–October 27, 1929, Sunday Papers, microfilm reel 7; Billy Sunday to Helen Sunday, undated letter, Sunday Papers, microfilm reel 5.

44. Helen Haines, Sturgis, Mich., to Billy Sunday, January 26, 1925, Sunday Papers, microfilm reel 7; Helen Haines, Sturgis, Mich., to Helen Sunday, December 22, 1929, Sunday Papers, microfilm reel 7.

45. Helen Haines, Sturgis, Mich., to Helen and Billy Sunday, December 4, 1923, Sunday Papers, microfilm reel 7.

46. George Sunday to William A. Sunday, Sr., undated, Sunday Papers, microfilm reel 5.

47. Ibid.

6. PROGRESSIVE ORTHODOXY

1. A. F. Ernst, Macomb, Ill., to Bro. Hosmer, August 26, 1905 ("Study of First Presbyterian Church"), Sunday Papers, microfilm reel 1; William G. McLoughlin, Jr., *Revivals, Awakenings, and Reform: An Essay on Religion and Social Change in America, 1607–1977* (Chicago: University of Chicago Press, 1978), 147; McLoughlin, *Billy Sunday Was His Real Name*, 223–224.

2. McLoughlin, *Revivals, Awakenings, and Reform*, 173–174; Creel, "Salvation Circus," 582.

3. McLoughlin, *Billy Sunday Was His Real Name*, 225.

4. David T. Morgan, "The Revivalist as Patriot: Billy Sunday and World War I," *Journal of Presbyterian History* 51 (Summer 1973): 203; Billy Sunday, Evening Sermon, New York City, April 11, 1917, 25, Sunday Papers, microfilm reel 9.

5. Frank, *Less Than Conquerors*, 193–194.

6. Gullen, *Billy Sunday Speaks*, 11.

7. Bruce Barton, "Billy Sunday—Baseball Evangelist," *Collier's: The National Weekly*, 26 July 1913, 7; Ellis, *Billy Sunday: The Man and His Message*, 504; Denison, "The Rev. Billy Sunday," 452.

8. McLoughlin, *Billy Sunday Was His Real Name*, 226; Maynard D. Hilgendorf, "Billy Sunday: 'I Am Glad I Came To Detroit'—A Study of Rhetorical Strategies in the 1916 Campaign" (Ph.D. diss., University of Michigan, 1985), 166–167.

9. Billy Sunday, Evening Sermon, New York City, April 11, 1917, 29, Sunday Papers, microfilm reel 9.

10. Sunday, "Griddle Sermon," 2.

11. Ibid., 1.

12. Sunday, "Chickens Sermon," 8, 10.

13. Ibid., 8.

14. Sunday, "Griddle Sermon," 39.

15. Billy Sunday, Evening Sermon, April 15, 1917, 3, Sunday Papers, microfilm reel 9.

16. Rev. "Billy" Sunday, "Has the Working Girl a Better Chance of Salvation Than Her Idle Sister?" April 15, 1917, unidentified newspaper article, Sunday Papers, microfilm reel 25.

17. Sunday, "Griddle Sermon," 9, 10.

18. Paul Boyer, *Urban Masses and Moral Order in America, 1820–1920* (Cambridge, Mass.: Harvard University, 1963), 196; Herbert Croly, *The Promise of American Life* (New York: Macmillan, 1965), 150.

19. Boyer, *Urban Masses*, 195–196.

20. James Timberlake, *Prohibition and the Progressive Movement, 1900–1920* (Cambridge, Mass.: Harvard University Press, 1963), 1–3; Boyer, *Urban Masses*, 196–197; Norman Clark, *Deliver Us from Evil: An Interpretation of American Prohibition* (New York: Norton, 1976), 1–13.

21. Boyer, *Urban Masses*, 196–197.

22. Gullen, *Billy Sunday Speaks*, 51, 203; Sunday, "Griddle Sermon," 40.

23. Sunday, "Griddle Sermon," 24, 33–37.

24. Gullen, *Billy Sunday Speaks*, 53, 55, 58.

25. Ibid., 59.

26. Ibid., 57–58.

27. Ibid., 52, 60, 61.

28. Sunday, "Griddle Sermon," 39–40; Gullen, *Billy Sunday Speaks*, 64.

29. Gullen, *Billy Sunday Speaks*, 202, 204.

30. Sunday, "Chickens Sermon," 9; Gullen, *Billy Sunday Speaks*, 73.

31. Boyer, *Urban Masses*, 208.

32. Gullen, *Billy Sunday Speaks*, 56.

33. Billy Sunday, Evening Sermon, New York City, April 11, 1917, 30, Sunday Papers, microfilm reel 9; Dr. J. B. Herbert, ed., *The Live Wire: Collection of Prohibition Songs* (Chicago: The Rodeheaver Company, c. 1916, no. 25); Dorsett, *Billy Sunday*, 152–154; "Billy Sunday Here, Sees Country in Grip of Lawless," *Inquirer*, 11 April 1922, unidentified newspaper article, Sunday Papers, microfilm reel 20.

34. Billy Sunday, Evening Sermon, April 11, 1917, 1–2, Sunday Papers, microfilm reel 9.

35. "Sunday Opposes Smith Only As Wet," September 11, 1928, unidentified newspaper article, Sunday Papers, microfilm reel 20; Sunday, "Griddle Sermon," 42.

36. Billy Sunday, Evening Sermon, April 15, 1917, 6–7, Sunday Papers, microfilm reel 9.

7. Hero of the Heartland

1. Rodeheaver, *Twenty Years with Billy Sunday*, 141–142; McLoughlin, *Billy Sunday Was His Real Name*, 270; Dorsett, *Billy Sunday*, 135–136.

2. H. U. Bailey, "Mrs. Billy Sunday Talk Heard by Large Crowd at Forum in Princeton," *Bureau Co. Republican*, 1942 newspaper article, Sunday Papers, microfilm reel 19.

3. Billy Sunday, Dodge City, Kans., to Helen Sunday, November 3–December 15, 1929 (Dodge City Campaign), Sunday Papers, microfilm reel 7.

4. Billy Sunday, Cincinnati, Ohio, to Helen Sunday, April–May 1921 (Cincinnati Campaign), Sunday Papers, microfilm reel 7.

5. Billy Sunday to Helen Sunday, November 12, 1929, Sunday Papers, microfilm reel 7.

6. Dorsett, *Billy Sunday*, 127, 129.

7. Ibid., 131–132; William C. Martin, *A Prophet with Honor: The Billy Graham Story* (New York: W. Morrow and Company, 1991), 599.

8. Dorsett, *Billy Sunday*, 130–131.

9. John Bodner, *Remaking America: Public Memory, Commemoration, and Patriotism in the Twentieth Century* (Princeton: Princeton University Press, 1992), 28–35; Michael Kammen, *Mystic Chords of Memory: The Transformation of Tradition in American Culture* (New York: Knopf, 1991), 179.

10. Kammen, *Mystic Chords of Memory*, 128.

11. James R. Shortridge, "The Emergence of 'Middle West' as an American Regional Label," *Annals of the Association of American Geographers* 74, no. 2 (June 1984): 213, 216–217.

12. Andrew R. L. Cayton and Peter S. Onuf, *The Midwest and the Nation* (Bloomington: Indiana University Press, 1990), 112.

13. James R. Shortridge, *The Middle West: Its Meaning in American Culture* (Lawrence: University Press of Kansas, 1989), 30–33; Cullom Davis, "Illinois: Crossroads and Cross Section," in *Heartland: Comparative Histories of the Midwestern States*, edited by James H. Madison (Bloomington: Indiana University Press, 1988), 127–157.

14. Shortridge, *The Middle West*, 39–40; McLoughlin, *Billy Sunday Was His Real Name*, 260.

15. Brown, *The Real Billy Sunday*, 220–221.

16. Billy Sunday, Sermon, New York City, May 4, 1917, 17, Sunday Papers, microfilm reel 10.

17. Sunday, "Griddle Sermon," 42.

18. "How A Baseball Idol 'Hit The Trail,'" *The Literary Digest*, 8 July 1916, 95.

19. Brown, *The Real Billy Sunday*, 86.

20. Ellis, *Billy Sunday: The Man and His Message*, 504.

21. Denison, "The Rev. Billy Sunday," 452.

22. Barton, "Billy Sunday—Baseball Evangelist," 7.

23. "Rise from Log Cabin to Great Preacher by 'Billy' Sunday," *Philadelphia Evening Ledger*, 22 December 1914, Sunday Papers, microfilm reel 19; Billy Sunday, Afternoon Sermon, New York, May 6, 1917, microfilm reel 9.

24. Billy Sunday, Evening Sermon, New York, April 13, 1917, Sunday Papers, microfilm reel 9.

25. Billy Sunday, Cincinnati, Ohio, to Helen Sunday, 1921, Sunday Papers, microfilm reel 7; McLoughlin, *Billy Sunday Was His Real Name*, 276–277.

26. Lynn Dumenil, *The Modern Temper: American Culture and Society in the 1920s* (New York: Hill and Wang, 1995), 275.

27. "Sunday Urges Stiffer Spine," *News Sentinel*, 11 April 1935, newspaper article, Sunday Papers, microfilm reel 20.

28. "Billy Sunday Here," Sunday Papers, microfilm reel 20; "Billy Threatens To Run For President," February 1931, unidentified newspaper article, Sunday Papers, microfilm reel 20; "Billy Sunday Spurns 'Monkey Descent,'" 1 February 1931, unidentified newspaper article, Sunday Papers, microfilm reel 20.

29. "Billy Sunday Makes Attack on Modernists," 1931 newspaper article, Sunday Papers, microfilm reel 20.

30. "Church Drunk with Infidel Modernism, Sunday Charges," *The Buffalo Evening News*, 4 January 1930, Sunday Papers, microfilm reel 20.

31. "Sunday Warns Wets He May Run for President," *Evening Post*, 6 January 1928; "Billy Sunday, Evangelist Extraordinary, Talks about Religion, Baseball, Sinclair, Prohibition," *The Houston Press*, 9 April 1929; John T. Brady, "'Hang the Rascal' Yelled Old

Rebel Soldier When the Rev. Billy Sunday Socked Unpatriotic Heckler," *Boston Sun Post*, 8 February 1931, all newspaper articles in Sunday Papers, microfilm reel 20.

32. Brady, "Hang the Rascal," Sunday Papers, microfilm reel 20.

33. "Billy Sunday Here," Sunday Papers, microfilm reel 20.

34. Ibid.; "Too Much Prosperity in America for Country's Good, Says Sunday," *The Hutchinson News*, 21 November 1930, Sunday Papers, microfilm reel 20.

35. "Billy Sunday Raps Administration for Meddling in People's Affairs," *The Knoxville Journal*, 10 April 1935, Sunday Papers, microfilm reel 20.

EPILOGUE

1. "Billy Sunday Dies; Evangelist Was 71," *New York Times*, 7 November 1935.

2. "President Tells Grief at Death of Billy Sunday," *Chicago Herald Tribune*, 8 November 1935.

3. "Comes to End of 'Sawdust Trail' at 72," *Des Moines Register*, 7 November 1935.

4. Walter W. Van Kirk, "Religion in the News," Presentation of the National Broadcasting Company, November 16 1935, Sunday Papers, microfilm reel 20.

BIBLIOGRAPHY

PRIMARY SOURCES

Archives and Manuscript Collections

Baseball Hall of Fame Archives, Cooperstown, New York.

Sunday, William Ashley, and Helen Amelia Thompson. Papers. The Billy Graham Center at Wheaton College, Wheaton, Illinois. Microfilm edition.

Other Unpublished Materials

Boone County Marriage Records. Recorder's Office, Boone County, Boone, Indiana.

Deed-Book F (Story County), May 12, 1860. Auditor's Office, Story County, Nevada, Iowa.

Final report of L[ycurgus] Irwin, Guard[ian], In the matter of the Estate of the minor heirs Wm. Sunday (deceased), In Probate, 25 April 1881. Recorder's Office, Story County, Nevada, Iowa.

Hilgendorf, Maynard D. "Billy Sunday: 'I Am Glad I Came to Detroit'—A Study of Rhetorical Strategies in the 1916 Campaign." Ph.D. diss., University of Michigan, 1985.

Petitions, April term A.D. 1885. Circuit Court of the State of Iowa in and for Story County, In the matter of the estate of William M. Sunday, deceased. Recorder's Office, Story County, Nevada, Iowa.

Record of Divorces Story County [Index]. Recorder's Office, Story County, Nevada, Iowa.

Records of the Veterans Administration, Civil War Pension File, Mary Jane Stowell Family, RG 15, National Archives and Records Administration, Washington, D.C..

Sass, Frances E. "Marriage Records—Story Co., Iowa, 1854–July 1907." Typescript produced April 1962. State Historical Society of Iowa, Iowa City, Iowa.

State of Iowa, Story County, in the Circuit Court of said county, In the Matter of guardianship of Albert M. and Eddie H. and William A. Sunday, minor heirs of Wm. Sunday, deceased, 10 March 1873, Walter Evans, guardian. Recorder's Office, Story County, Nevada, Iowa.

Story County Death Record I, 1880–1897. Recorder's Office, Story County, Nevada, Iowa.

Story County Marriage Record I, 1854–1866. Recorder's Office, Story County, Nevada, Iowa.

Story County Marriage Record I, 1854–1866.

United States Census Office. *Population Schedules of the Eighth Census of the United States [1860]. Iowa: Poweshiek, Ringgold, Sac, Shelby, Sioux, Story, and Tama Counties.* NARA, RG M653. Microform roll 339.

———. *Population Schedules of the Ninth Census of the United States [1870]. Iowa: Shelby, Sioux, Story, and Tama Counties.* NARA, RG M593. Microform roll 420.

———. *Population Schedules of the Tenth Census of the United States [1880]. Iowa: Scott, Shelby, Sioux, Story, and Tama Counties.* NARA, RG T9. Microform rolls 364 and 365.

————. *Report on Population of the United States at the Eleventh Census, 1890. Part I.* Washington, D.C.: GPO, 1895. Reprint, New York: Norman Ross Publishing, 1993.

————. *Statistics of the Population of the United States at the Ninth Census: Embracing the Tables of Race, Nationality, Sex, Selected Ages, and Occupations . . . Compiled from the Original Returns of the Ninth Census.* Washington, D.C.: GPO, 1872. Reprint, New York: Norman Ross Publishing, 1990.

————. *Statistics of the Population of the United States at the Tenth Census (June 1, 1880): Embracing the Tables of the Population of States, Counties, and Minor Civil Divisions, with Distinction of Race, Sex, Age, Nativity, and Occupations.* Washington, D.C.: GPO, 1883. Reprint, New York: Norman Ross Publishing, 1991.

Newspapers

Ames Evening Times
Boston Herald
Boston Sun Post
Buffalo Evening News
Chicago Herald Tribune
Des Moines Register and Leader
Houston Press
Hutchinson News
Knoxville Journal
Los Angeles Evening Express
New York Times
New York World
Philadelphia Evening Ledger
Philadelphia Inquirer
Pittsburg Press
Waterloo Evening Courier and Reporter

SECONDARY SOURCES

Books

Alexander, Charles C. *Our Game: An American Baseball History.* New York: Henry Holt and Company, 1991.

Allen, William G. *A History of Story County, Iowa.* Des Moines: Iowa Printing Company, 1887.

Anson, Adrian C. *A Ball Player's Career.* Chicago: Era Publishing, 1900.

Atherton, Lewis. *Main Street on the Middle Border.* Bloomington: Indiana University Press, 1954.

Aurner, Clarence Ray. *History of Education in Iowa.* Iowa City: State Historical Society of Iowa, 1914.

Bederman, Gail. *Manliness and Civilization: A Cultural History of Gender and Race in the United States, 1880–1917.* Chicago: University of Chicago Press, 1995.

Biographical and Historical Memoirs of Story County, Iowa. Chicago: The Goodspeed Publishing Company, 1890.

Bodner, John. *Remaking America: Public Memory, Commemoration, and Patriotism in the Twentieth Century.* Princeton, N.J.: Princeton University Press, 1992.

Boyer, Paul. *Urban Masses and Moral Order in America, 1820–1920.* Cambridge, Mass.: Harvard University Press, 1978.

Brown, Elijah P. *The Real Billy Sunday: The Life and Work of Rev. William Ashley Sunday, D.D., The Baseball Evangelist.* New York: Fleming H. Revell Company, 1914.

Brown, Farwell T. *Ames the Early Years in Word and Picture: From Marsh to Modern City.* Ames, Iowa: Farwell T. Brown and Heuss Printing, 1993.

Bruns, Roger A. *Preacher: Billy Sunday and Big-Time American Evangelism.* New York: W. W. Norton and Company, 1992.

Burk, Robert F. *Never Just a Game: Players, Owners, and American Baseball to 1920.* Chapel Hill: University of North Carolina Press, 1994.

Cavallo, Dominick. *Muscles and Morals: Organized Playgrounds and Urban Reform, 1880–1920.* Philadelphia: University of Pennsylvania Press, 1981.

Cayton, Andrew R. L., and Peter S. Onuf. *The Midwest and the Nation.* Bloomington: Indiana University Press, 1990.

Clark, Norman. *Deliver Us from Evil: An Interpretation of American Prohibition.* New York: Norton, 1976.

Croly, Herbert. *The Promise of American Life.* New York: Macmillan, 1965.

Cronon, William. *Nature's Metropolis: Chicago and the Great West.* New York: W. W. Norton, 1991.

Curtis, Susan. *A Consuming Faith: The Social Gospel and Modern American Culture.* Baltimore: Johns Hopkins University Press, 1991.

Day, H. Summerfield. *The Iowa State University Campus and Its Buildings 1859–1979.* Ames: Iowa State University Press, 1980.

Dorsett, Lyle W. *Billy Sunday and the Redemption of Urban America.* Grand Rapids, Mich.: William B. Eerdmans Publishing Company, 1991.

Dubbert, Joe L. *A Man's Place: Masculinity in Transition.* Englewood Cliffs, N.J.: Prentice Hall, 1979.

Dumenil, Lynn. *The Modern Temper: American Culture and Society in the 1920s.* New York: Hill and Wang, 1995.

Ellis, William T. *Billy Sunday: The Man and His Message.* Chicago: Moody Press, 1936.

Frank, Douglas. *Less Than Conquerors.* Grand Rapids, Mich.: William B. Eerdmans Publishing Company, 1986.

Frankenberg, Theodore T. *Spectacular Career of Rev. Billy Sunday: Famous Baseball Evangelist.* Columbus, Ohio: McClelland and Company, 1913.

———. *Billy Sunday, His Tabernacles and Sawdust Trails.* Columbus, Ohio: The F. J. Heer Printing Company, 1917.

Gullen, Karen, ed. *Billy Sunday Speaks.* New York: Chelsea House Publishers, 1970.

Henry, Carl F. H. *The Pacific Garden Mission: A Doorway to Heaven.* Grand Rapids, Mich.: Zondervan Publishing House, 1942.

Herbert, Dr. J. B. *The Live Wire: Collection of Prohibition Songs.* Chicago: The Rodeheaver Company, c. 1916.

Higgs, Robert J. *God in the Stadium: Sports and Religion in America.* Lexington: University Press of Kentucky, 1995.

Iowa Census Board. *Census of Iowa [1836–1880].* Des Moines: Iowa Executive Council, 1875–1925.

Kammen, Michael. *Mystic Chords of Memory: The Transformation of Tradition in American Culture.* New York: Knopf, 1991.

Kimmel, Michael S. *Manhood in America: A Cultural History.* New York: Free Press, 1996.

Knickerbocker, Wendy. *Sunday at the Ballpark: Billy Sunday's Professional Baseball Career, 1883–1890.* Lanham, Md.: The Scarecrow Press, Inc., 2000.

Ladd, Tony, and James A. Mathisen. *Muscular Christianity: Evangelical Protestants and the Development of American Sport.* Grand Rapids, Mich.: Baker Books, 1999.

Lucas, John A., and Ronald A. Smith. *Saga of American Sport.* Philadelphia: Lea and Febiger, 1978.

Macleod, David I. *Building Character in the American Boy: The Boy Scouts, YMCA, and Their Forerunners, 1870–1920.* Madison: University of Wisconsin Press, 1983.

Martin, William C. *A Prophet with Honor: The Billy Graham Story.* New York: W. Morrow and Company, 1991.

McLoughlin, William G., Jr. *Billy Sunday Was His Real Name.* Chicago: University of Chicago Press, 1955.

————. *Revivals, Awakenings, and Reform: An Essay on Religion and Social Change in America, 1607–1977.* Chicago: University of Chicago Press, 1978.

Moore, Robert Laurence. *Selling God: American Religion in the Marketplace of Culture.* New York: Oxford University Press, 1994.

Pallen, Joseph. *Burning Truths from Billy's Bat: A Graphic Description of the Remarkable Conversion of Rev. "Billy" Sunday.* Philadelphia: Diamond Publishing Company, 1914.

Pierce, Bessie Louise. *A History of Chicago: The Rise of a Modern City, 1871–1893.* New York: Alfred A. Knopf, 1957.

Rader, Benjamin G. *Baseball: A History of America's Game.* Urbana and Chicago: University of Illinois Press, 1992.

Reichler, Joseph L., ed. *The Baseball Encyclopedia: The Complete and Official Record of Major League Baseball.* New York: Macmillan, 1985.

Riess, Steven A. *City Games: The Evolution of American Urban Society and Rise of Sports.* Urbana and Chicago: University of Illinois Press, 1989.

Rodeheaver, Homer. *Twenty Years with Billy Sunday.* Nashville: Cokesbury Press, 1936.

Sandburg, Carl. *Billy Sunday and Other Poems.* San Diego: Harcourt Brace & Company, 1993.

Shortridge, James R. *The Middle West: Its Meaning in American Culture.* Lawrence: University Press of Kansas, 1989.

Timberlake, James. *Prohibition and the Progressive Movement, 1900–1920.* Cambridge, Mass.: Harvard University Press, 1963.

Wecter, Dixon. *The Hero in America: A Chronicle of Hero-Worship.* Ann Arbor: University of Michigan Press, 1966.

Articles

Barton, Bruce. "Billy Sunday—Baseball Evangelist." *Collier's: The National Weekly,* 26 July 1913, 7.

Bederman, Gail. "'The Women Have Had Charge of the Church Work Long Enough': The Men and Religion Forward Movement of 1911–1912 and the Masculinization of Middle-Class Protestantism." *American Quarterly* (1989): 432–465.

"Billy Sunday under Fire." *Literary Digest,* 18 April 1914, 907.

"Billy's Rubicon." *Literary Digest,* 21 April 1917, 1168.

Carnes, Mark C. "Middle Class Men and the Solace of Fraternal Ritual." In *Meanings for Manhood: Constructions of Masculinity in Victorian America,* edited by Mark C. Carnes and Clyde Griffen, 37–66. Chicago: University of Chicago Press, 1990.

Cheever, L. O. "Iowa Annie Wittenmyer Home." *Palimpsest,* June 1967, 253–254.

Creel, George. "Salvation Circus." *Harper's Weekly,* 19 June 1915, 582.

Davis, Cullom. "Illinois: Crossroads and Cross Section." In *Heartland: Comparative Histories of the Midwestern States,* edited by James H. Madison, 127–157. Bloomington: Indiana University Press, 1988.

Denison, Lindsay. "The Rev. Billy Sunday and His War on the Devil." *American Magazine,* September 1907, 452, 459–460.

Holston, Jim. "Billy Sunday, The Calliope of Zion." *The Iowan* 33 (Spring 1985): 19.

"How a Baseball Idol 'Hit the Trail.'" *Literary Digest,* 8 July 1916, 92–95.

Kimmel, Michael S. "Baseball and the Reconstitution of American Masculinity, 1880–1920." In *Baseball History 3: An Annual of Original Baseball Research,* edited by Peter Levine, 101. Westport, Conn.: Meckler, 1990.

Martin, Robert F. "Billy Sunday and Christian Manliness." *The Historian* 58 (1996): 811–823.

————. "Billy Sunday and the Mystique of the Middle West." *The Annals of Iowa* 55, no. 4 (Fall 1996): 345–360.

McLoughlin, William G., Jr. "Billy Sunday and the Working Girls, 1915." *Journal of Presbyterian History* (1976): 376–384.

Morgan, David T. "The Revivalist as Patriot: Billy Sunday and World War I." *Journal of Presbyterian History* 51 (Summer 1973): 203.

"Poll of the Religious Press on Billy Sunday." *Literary Digest*, 12 June 1915, 1404–1405.

Putney, Clifford. "Character Building in the YMCA, 1880–1930." *Mid-America: An Historical Review* (January 1991): 49–69.

Riess, Steven A. "Professional Baseball and Social Mobility." *Journal of Interdisciplinary History* XI (Autumn 1980): 249.

Rotundo, E. Anthony. "Learning about Manhood: Gender Ideals and the Middle-Class Family in Nineteenth-Century America." In *Manliness and Morality*, edited by J. A. Mangan and James Walvin, 35–51. New York: St. Martin's Press, 1987.

Sandburg, Carl. "Chicago." In *The Complete Poems of Carl Sandburg*, 3. New York: Harcourt Brace Jovanovich, 1970.

Shortridge, James R. "The Emergence of 'Middle West' as an American Regional Label." *Annals of the Association of American Geographers* 74, no. 2 (June 1984): 213, 216–217.

Sunday, Billy. "Banish Blue Monday." *The Country Gentleman*, 31 July 1921.

———. "My All-Star Nine." *Collier's*, 18 October 1913, 19, 30.

Sunday, Rev. William A. (Billy) "The Sawdust Trail," *Ladies' Home Journal*, September 1932, 4; October 1932, 12; November 1932, 17; December 1932, 16; February 1933, 87; April 1933, 60.

Welter, Barbara. "The Cult of True Womanhood: 1820–1860." *American Quarterly* 18, no. 2, pt. 1 (1966): 151–174.

———. "The Feminization of American Religion: 1800–1860." In *Clio's Consciousness Raised: New Perspectives on the History of Women*, edited by Mary S. Hartman and Lois Banner, 137–157. New York: Harper and Row, 1974.

INDEX

ROBERT F. MARTIN is Professor of History
at the University of Northern Iowa and
author of *Howard Kester and the Struggle for
Social Justice in the South, 1904–77.*